Y

Choosing to Feel

Virtue, Friendship, and Compassion for Friends

DIANA FRITZ CATES

The University of Notre Dame Press

Copyright © 1997 by
University of Notre Dame Press
Notre Dame, Indiana 46556
All rights reserved

Manufactured in the United States of America

Book Design by Wendy McMillen
Set in 10.5/13 Berkeley by Books International
Printed and bound by Braun-Brumfield

Library of Congress Cataloging-in-Publication Data
Cates, Diana Fritz.
    Choosing to feel : virtue, friendship, and compassion for friends
/ Diana Fritz Cates.
        p.   cm.
    Includes bibliographical references and index.
    ISBN 0-268-00814-0 (alk. paper)
    1. Ethics.   2. Aristotle—Ethics.   3. Thomas, Aquinas, Saint,
1225?–1274—Ethics.   4. Caring.   5. Friendship—Moral and
ethical aspects.   I. Title.
BJ1012.C36   1996
177—dc20   95-50517
                                                                     CIP

∞ The paper used in this publication meets the minimum
requirements of the American National Standard for Information
Sciences—Permanence of Paper for Printed Library Materials,
ANSI Z 36.48-1984

To Bryan

Contents

Preface

The voice that emerges in the following pages as "mine" is an echo of everyday conversations, silent encounters, and focused academic discussions with friends, family members, teachers, colleagues, and students. I wish to express my gratitude to those who are most likely, in reading this book, to hear resonances of past exchanges with me. Thanks to my husband, Bryan Cates, my friend, Lori Baldwin, and my mother, Donna Fritz, for being exemplars of virtuous compassion in my life. Thanks to my children, Ben and Hannah, for sharing with me so generously the painful, yet delightful experiences of growing up. Thanks to my teacher and mentor, J. Giles Milhaven, for teaching me that the most valuable ethical insights can be gleaned by reflecting on ordinary human experience. Thanks also to John P. Reeder, Jr., Martha C. Nussbaum, Sumner B. Twiss, George W. E. Nickelsburg, G. Simon Harak, S.J., J. Keith Green, and Don L. Davis.

For generous financial assistance, I am grateful to Brown University (for a Brown University Dissertation Fellowship), The Woodrow Wilson National Fellowship Foundation (for a Charlotte W. Newcombe Doctoral Dissertation Fellowship), and The University of Iowa (for an Old Gold Summer Fellowship, a College of Liberal Arts Research Grant, and a Semester Assignment Award).

Introduction

Countless people are suffering in our midst. Women are being beaten and raped. Children are being neglected and abused. The homeless are dying of exposure and malnutrition. Political prisoners are being tortured. The urban poor are being crushed under the weight of social and economic oppression. How ought we to live in the presence of so much suffering?

All of us suffer. We suffer loss, abandonment, loneliness, and despair. We suffer weakness and disease, debilitation and death. How ought we to receive and respond to each other in our pain? How ought we to be and what ought we to do as moral agents who wish to live decent lives?

Many of us would agree that among other things, we ought to be compassionate. But what is it to be compassionate, and what makes compassion a good response to human suffering? This question is of academic interest to moral psychologists, moral philosophers, and religious ethicists who seek to grasp from a moral and/or religious point of view the sorts of beings that human beings are and the features of a life that make it worth living. The question may be of special interest to persons who are sympathetic to the feminist ethical enterprise, i.e., those who believe that analyzing the moral experiences of women (and of men who love and share their lives deeply with women) is likely to yield penetrating insights into the human condition and the constituents of human flourishing. *Choosing to Feel* is partly an effort to uncover, elucidate, and celebrate a moral excellence that is all too frequently dismissed as a mark of weakness. Of course, the question of compassion is of more than academic interest. *Choosing to Feel* seeks to encourage in all readers the deliberate cultivation of compassion.[1]

The thesis of this book is three-fold: First, compassion is not, strictly speaking, a passion, although it has a great deal to do with passion. It is, instead, a virtue, i.e., a habitual disposition concerned with choosing both to act and to feel in accordance with a certain rule. Second, compassion is a virtue that human beings can, do, and should learn to exercise within the context of certain relationships, most notably relationships in which friends are attracted and attached to each other on the basis of each other's moral character. Third, compassion is a virtue that human beings can, do, and should learn, within the context of character-friendships, to extend toward those whom we would not ordinarily regard as friends. Christian ethicists tend to begin ethical analyses with accounts of universal neighbor-love; then they attempt to find a place for "special relations" in the good Christian life.[2] I begin with the compassion that friends exhibit toward their friends, and I go on to show that the cultivation of compassion for friends can promote habits of desiring, perceiving, imagining, deliberating, and choosing that contribute to the exercise of a particularized compassion for the stranger and even the enemy.

The structure of this project is architectonic, which means that each chapter provides something basic for understanding the chapters that follow. Each chapter develops one or more aspects of a line of argumentation that extends from the beginning of the project to the end. The argument proceeds in three major stages. In Part I, I detail the nature of virtue and some of the ways in which Christian faith can condition the desires, beliefs, and perceptions that combine to constitute the exercise of virtue. I begin with Aristotle and Thomas Aquinas, in particular, because my own understanding of virtue is closest to Thomas's Christian Aristotelian understanding and has been formed in conversation with it.[3] I extend these accounts, attending to issues that bear directly on an analysis of compassion: What is passion? How can passion contribute to the self's knowledge of other selves and thus to its ability to exercise virtue in their regard? In what way and to what extent can one self *choose* to feel passion relative to other selves? How can Christian faith influence the self's choices to feel or not to feel?

In Part II, I explore the nature of friendship and some of the impact that Christian faith can have on the way in which the self stands in relation to itself and to its friends. Again, I begin with Aristotle and Thomas,

critiquing and extending their classic accounts of friendship with attention to issues that are central to an analysis of compassion: What does it
mean to say, as both Aristotle and Thomas do, that my friend is "another
myself?" In what sense is the self one and the same relative to its "other
selves," and in what sense does it remain separate and different? In what
sense can God be referred to as Friend, and what impact can a friendship with God have on the self's relation to itself and to its "other selves?"

In Part III, I integrate and expand upon the first two parts in order
to provide a Christian ethical account of the virtue of compassion. Although I focus mainly on the compassion that the self exercises in relation
to its most intimate "other selves," I seek to reveal the way in which all
compassion—even compassion for the complete stranger—resembles the
compassion that the self feels toward its closest friends. Orienting my
constructive efforts vis-à-vis some modern work on caring and compassion,[4] I attend to several issues: In what sense, and to what extent, can the
self choose in compassion to feel the same pain as its "other selves?" In
what sense, and to what extent, does the pain of "other selves" remain
other than the self's own? What is it, and how is it possible, to *choose*
to feel compassion? What impact can Christian faith have on the way
in which the self chooses to receive and respond to its "other selves" in
their pain?

I began this project, of necessity, with a definition of compassion in
mind. I had to have some definition in mind if I was to look for, locate,
and then say about some characteristic that "*this* is compassion" and "it is
this characteristic that I wish to analyze." The definition with which I
began is general and open-ended and reflects what I take to be a common
(albeit largely implicit) western understanding of compassion as a kind
of suffering-with. Lawrence Blum articulates this understanding well:

> Compassion is . . . a complex emotional attitude toward another,
> characteristically involving imaginative dwelling on the [painful]
> condition of the other person, an active regard for his good, a view
> of him as a fellow human being, and emotional responses of a cer-
> tain degree of intensity. . . . Characteristically, . . . compassion [also]
> requires the disposition to perform beneficent actions, and to per-
> form them because the agent has had a certain sort of imaginative
> reconstruction of someone's condition and has a concern for his
> good.[5]

I began with such a definition in mind, but also with a certain dissatis-faction—a sense that this and other definitions that I had encountered in the available philosophical literature fail to capture what is most profound, puzzling, and precious about compassion. My dissatisfaction stemmed partly from sustained reflection upon experiences with com-passionate friends in my life. I had observed in these friends a disposition whose dimensions did not appear to be fully articulated in definitions like Blum's.

I began, then, by walking some common definitional ground, but with the expectation that this ground would shift as relevant phenomena were subjected to philosophical analysis. I also began with an intention to offer more than a description of a certain range of phenomena. I in-tended to provide a description of an ideal, i.e., a prescription of a good way of being human in the face of ubiquitous suffering. The purpose of this project is to offer an account of compassion that identifies, further specifies, and seeks to sanction a moral orientation that I take to be partly constitutive of doing humanly well in the presence of people in pain.

In short, I am not concerned with arguing for an account of com-passion that corresponds as closely as possible to the way in which the majority of persons would define the term if they were asked to do so. Nor am I concerned with arguing for an account of compassion that cor-responds as closely as possible to some classical definition, for even the best of these definitions fail to capture the compassion that I have in mind. I am concerned, instead, with arguing for a way of construing the disposition to suffer-with that is adequate to the experiences of people whom I regard as deeply and richly human. The burden of my analysis is to show that this construal is truest, not necessarily to our preconceived notions of what compassion *is*, but to the way that many of us would wish, upon reflection, to live our lives. In the end, the relative merit of a competing description of moral experience rests on the extent to which that description promotes greater conceptual clarity, a more nuanced self-understanding, and a stronger desire to be good.

One

Aristotle on Character Virtue

Compassion is more than a passion. It is more than a feeling of being pained at the sight of another's suffering. It is more than a feeling of being moved to alleviate the suffering that we see. Compassion is an abiding state of character. It is an intricate pattern of desires, beliefs, and perceptions—a pattern that disposes us, time and again, to receive and respond in a characteristic way to persons in pain. The lines of this pattern are revealed most clearly when compassion is construed as a virtue. Of course, such a construal is unhelpful apart from an adequate understanding of virtue. In this and the following two chapters, we will prepare the way for a contemporary Christian ethical account of compassion by analyzing selected elements of Aristotle and Thomas Aquinas's theories of virtue. Aristotle and Thomas continue to stand out as the classic theorists of virtue to whom contemporary theorists are ineluctably indebted, and we cannot do better than to begin with their accounts. Anticipating a subsequent discussion of the virtue of compassion, in particular, we will pay special attention to what Aristotle and Thomas had to say about passion's role in the exercise of virtue. Although compassion is more than a passion, it obviously has a lot to do with passion.

In the *Nicomachean Ethics*, Aristotle contends that the best sort of life for a human being to live is one characterized by *eudaimonia*, which is "a sort of living well and doing well in action" (1098b21–23).[1] Although *eudaimonia* is often rendered in English as "happiness," it is not the feeling of pleasure that attends our living well and doing well; rather, it is the activity of living well and doing well itself. *Eudaimonia* "is an activity of soul in accordance with perfect virtue" (1102a5).[2] According to Aristotle, human beings flourish when they perform well the function (*ergon*) or characteristic activity that human beings are uniquely suited to perform. They flourish when reason guides them consistently in the integrated exercise of all the human virtues or excellences (1098a5–20).[3]

Aristotle recognizes two kinds of virtue (*aretē*), namely, virtues of thought and virtues of character (1138b35).[4] Virtues of thought or intellectual virtues are states of the rational element of the soul, which contribute to thinking well. Character virtues are states of the nonrational element of the soul. The nonrational element of the soul includes a nutritive part, which "shares in reason not at all," and an appetitive part, which "shares in reason in a way, in so far as it both listens to reason and obeys it" (1102b30). Character virtues are states of the appetitive part of the nonrational element of the soul, which contribute to acting and undergoing passion well. Our focus in this chapter and throughout this project will be on character virtue, but we cannot grasp the nature of character virtue without some reference to intellectual virtue, most notably the intellectual virtue of practical wisdom (*phronēsis*). This is not surprising given that acting, feeling, *and* thinking well are all constitutive of doing humanly well.

In Book II of the *Nicomachean Ethics*, Aristotle defines character virtue as "a character state concerned with choice, lying in the mean relative to us, being determined by reason and the way the person of practical wisdom would determine it" (1107a1).[5] Character virtue is a *hexis*— a habituated state on account of which we are well or ill disposed with respect to action and passion (1106b15–36).[6] In sum, character virtue is a habitual disposition concerned with choosing both to act and to feel in accordance with the mean, where the mean relative to us is determined with reference to what a person of practical wisdom would choose. This working definition warrants careful scrutiny. Let us consider each of its component parts in turn.

A HABITUAL DISPOSITION . . .

First, character virtue is a habitual disposition. It is a *disposition* in that it is a liability "to undergo a particular change, when a particular condition is realized."[7] It is an inclination to be delighted and repulsed by the right things—to love what is good for us and to despise what is evil (1104b10–16). It is a readiness to respond to what is pleasurable and painful by "enjoying and hating finely" (1179b25). Character virtue is a *habitual* disposition in that it is a disposition acquired by means of a slow process of habituation and moral education. Aristotle argues that, "A state [of character] arises from [the repetition of] similar activities. Hence we must display the right activities, since differences in these imply corresponding differences in the states" (1103b21). Virtue is acquired by practicing the right activities, but in conjunction with the right enjoyment of these activities: "Hence we need to have had the appropriate upbringing—right from early youth, as Plato says—to make us find enjoyment or pain in the right things; for this is the correct education" (1104b11).[8]

Character virtue is a habitual disposition that is deeply and stably embedded in those who acquire it. It is deeply embedded in that it sets us up to receive and respond to the world in a particular way. It disposes us to perceive consistently from this angle rather than that, noticing these features of a situation instead of those, marking certain of these features as more worthy of attention than others (1114b1–25). It disposes us to be moved by some particulars in place of others, in accordance with feelings of pleasure and pain that have been, "dyed into our lives," from infancy on, so that the actions and passions that arise in response to pleasant or painful particulars acquire one form rather than another (1105a2–7). It is undoubtedly because virtue is so deeply embedded that it is so stable. Although it is manipulable through moral education and vulnerable to the vicissitudes of luck, virtue resists change over time (1100a6, 1100b18–22).[9]

. . . CONCERNED WITH CHOOSING

Second, virtue is a habitual disposition concerned with choosing. Aristotle indicates that choice (*prohairesis*) can be characterized as either desiderative deliberation or deliberative desire (1139b4). He says in the *Eudemian Ethics* that choice is neither belief nor desire per se, but rather a composite of both: "choice is neither simply wish nor opinion, but opinion *together with* wish, whenever as a result of deliberation they are brought to a conclusion."[10] As Martha Nussbaum puts it, Aristotle describes choice as "an ability that is on the borderline between the intellectual and passional, partaking of both natures."[11] Aristotelian choice is the intention to act on the results of deliberation, where deliberation is construed as the process by which an agent discerns the best available way to realize a desired end.

The deliberative process that terminates in choice can be represented in the form of a practical syllogism, which is an argument composed of two premises and a conclusion.[12] The major premise of the practical syllogism is a *desire* for a given end. The minor premise is a *belief* or a *perception* regarding what in the present situation best contributes to the desired end. The conclusion combines desire, belief and perception. It is an *action* or the *intention to act* (when the time is appropriate) in a way that best contributes to the desired end.[13]

Within the context of a particular deliberative process, the relationship between desire, represented by the major premise, and belief and perception, represented by the minor premise, is actually more complex than the practical syllogism might suggest. To begin with, belief and perception play a significant role in the formation of a given major premise. First, the desire represented by the major premise is an intentional desire.[14] It is a desire for an end that is conceived of or imaged in a certain way. It is a desire that is partly constituted by certain beliefs and perceptions. Whether and in what way we desire certain ends depends on how we perceive or conceive of them—which, in turn, depends upon the state of our character: "by having the sort of character we have we lay down the sort of end we do" (1114b24).

Because a desired end can be open to different specifications or interpretations, it can be an object of deliberation. Aristotle might seem to deny this when he says that "we deliberate not about the end, but about what pertains to the end" (1112b12).[15] However, a careful reading of the text suggests otherwise. When Aristotle says that we deliberate about "what pertains to the end," he is not saying that we deliberate only about means to the end. We do, indeed, deliberate about what causal conditions are necessary, sufficient, and most efficient in the situation at hand for bringing about a desired end. We also deliberate, however, about what, by definition, constitutes the end in question and what course of action here and now would count as realizing that end. We deliberate about how the end in question fits into the larger scheme of ends that gives unity to our lives. We deliberate about whether and how the end contributes to *eudaimonia*.[16] When Aristotle says we deliberate "not about ends," he is pointing to the fact that we begin a given piece of deliberation by setting certain ends as fixed. The fixed ends give point and direction to the deliberations. The ends fixed for one piece of deliberation, however, might be the products of another piece of deliberation: "Thus what is an end for one piece of deliberation may be a means to another deliberation hierarchically prior."[17]

There is a second way in which belief and perception contribute to the formation of a major premise. Belief and perception partly determine whether and in what way we are disposed to desire certain ends in certain sorts of circumstances. What we believe and perceive to be the case about the good life, for example, is partly determinative of whether or not we are disposed to desire this or that good *qua* constitutive of the good life. In addition, belief and perception partly determine whether and in what way desires that we have dispositionally become occurrent or activated at the right times. What we believe and perceive to be the case in a given situation is partly determinative of whether or not we recognize "that now is the time for introducing a particular major premiss, that there is an occasion at hand relevant to a specific end or universal."[18] In sum, certain beliefs and perceptions elicit and partly constitute certain intentional desires. These intentional desires then serve as the starting points for given deliberative processes.

Just as belief and perception, represented by the minor premise of the practical syllogism, contribute to the formation of the major premise, desire, represented by the major premise, contributes to the formation of the minor premise. First, the deliberative activity represented by the minor premise concerns, in large part, discernment of the morally relevant features of a given situation (e.g. that someone is in need, that the someone in need is my friend, that my friend is depending upon me to help meet her needs). Discernment is, in large part, a matter of perception (1109b13–24, 1126a33–1126b5, 1143b2–6). As Martha Nussbaum has argued, it is for Aristotle a matter of imaginative and passionate perception.[19]

Discernment is a matter of *imaginative* perception in that it involves "seeing" a situation in all of its complexity, while focusing at the same time on aspects of the situation that correspond to our well-deliberated desires for the good. It involves calling to mind similar situations from the past and construing the present predicament in light of these, while appreciating at the same time the unique demands of *this* predicament. It involves projecting on the basis of experience the outcomes that are likely to result from various courses of action committed here and now (e.g., will treating this friend in this way really meet her needs?).

Discernment is a matter of *passionate* perception in that it involves being receptive and responsive to the particulars of a given situation. It involves allowing the intentional desires that partly constitute our passions to play a role in determining which aspects of the situation warrant attention, how much, and to what end, such that we are motivated partly *in* passion to choose what is fine (*kalon*). Passionate perception is not perception following closely on the heels of passion. Rather, it is perception that has within itself an affective component, so that when the appropriate passion is missing from a given perception, the perceiver fails to "see" the situation for what it is (e.g. that my friend *to whom I have been deeply attached for years* is depending upon me to help meet her needs). One way in which desire enters into the formation of the minor premise, then, is by being partly constitutive of our perceptions regarding what is at issue in a given situation and how much it matters.

A second way in which desire enters into the formation of the minor premise is implied by the first. Desire partly determines whether or not we are disposed, as a matter of habit, to perceive situations of moral import with passion. That is to say, whether or not we are habitually disposed toward passionate perception depends on whether or not we want to be so disposed. Whether or not we want to be so disposed depends on whether or not we want to be the sorts of persons who are deeply, complexly, and sometimes painfully affected by others in our moral encounters with them. Out of fear or a sense of duty, for example, we may desire as a general policy to remain aloof, detached, disinterested, and invulnerable in these encounters.

As we move farther away from the practical syllogism as a representation of the deliberative process or more deeply into the implicit meanings of this representation, we see that choices of character are not dispassionate, scientific applications of unchanging universal rules to particular cases, as the representation might initially suggest. They are passionate, imaginative, and thoughtful discernments of moral relevance and significance—desiderative determinations that yield responsive commitments to action on the part of those who are relatively well-developed and well-integrated emotionally and intellectually. Choices are intricate interactions and interpenetrations of general and more particular beliefs, perceptions, and desires, where the elements of thought and desire are "so blended . . . that either one can guide [decision-making] and their guidance will be one and the same," at least in persons of well-formed character.[20]

A final comment on choice: all choices that exhibit virtue are deliberated, in Aristotle's scheme, but some may only be implicitly so. We are often required to make snap decisions in moral matters without the opportunity to weigh alternative courses of action, rank competing values and desires, gather relevant empirical data, calculate probabilities, experiment with various perspectives, and so on. Snap decisions can reveal our deepest habits of belief, perception, and desire, as Aristotle recognized (1117a17–23). Decisions of this kind are not explicitly deliberated, but if they are well-made, they are deliberated in the important sense that they are "backed by reasons which, when made explicit, constitute a deliberative argument in favor of the decision."[21] They are open to deliberation upon reflection. They are explainable and justifiable. More importantly, they proceed from a firm and stable character that is itself deliberately chosen over time (1117a18–23). Even though the virtuous person does not have the opportunity to deliberate carefully every decision she makes, she does, with frequency, think about what ends, ranked and coordinated in what manner, are worthy of promotion. She commits herself to becoming the sort of person who acts consistently to promote these ends. This commitment, strengthened through repeated application, gives force and direction to all of her decisions.

. . . BOTH TO ACT AND TO FEEL

To continue our discussion of Aristotle's definition of character virtue, recall that a virtue is a habitual disposition concerned with choosing both to act and to feel. As L. A. Kosman points out, it is not "that there are a number of virtues that are dispositions with respect to actions and a number of other virtues that are dispositions with respect to feelings, any given virtue being a disposition with respect to one or the other, but rather that a given virtue is a disposition with respect to a characteristic set of actions and feelings."[22] It is therefore misleading to talk about choosing right action apart from choosing right passion. Both sorts of choice are integral to the rational activity in and through which the practically wise person (*phronimos*) pursues what is fine. Still, it seems odd to say that we choose to feel in the same sense that we choose to act. Feelings seem to "happen" to us in a way that actions do not. Feelings seem less subject to self-command.

The ambiguity is present in Aristotle. On the one hand, Aristotle holds that actions are instances of self-controlled movement. Passions are instances of uncontrollably being moved. Actions are committed. Passions are suffered. Actions are chosen. Passions are not (1105b29–1106a6). When we examine Aristotle's larger theory of the passions, however, a different picture begins to emerge. In the *Rhetoric*, for example, Aristotle makes plain that passions are partly cognitive. They are constituted, in part, by beliefs and evaluative judgments. They are constituted by beliefs about what is the case in a given situation and evaluative judgments concerning the meaning and significance of what is the case. Anger, for example, is defined by Aristotle as "an impulse, accompanied by pain, to a conspicuous revenge for a conspicuous slight directed without justification towards what concerns oneself or towards what concerns one's friends."[23] Without the beliefs that so-and-so intentionally did such-and-such, and that such-and-such was indeed a slight; without the evaluative judgments that the slight was unjustified and that unjustified slights are bad; without the desire for revenge which is itself intentional or partly constituted by belief, there is no anger. Without reference to these and other cognitive components, what is experienced cannot be identified and differentiated as the passion of anger.[24]

If passions are simply pleasant or painful feelings that we suffer passively, then we have little choice concerning the shape, the timing, and the intensity of their occurrence. If, however, passions have a cognitive component, if they are composites of feeling *and* cognition, then it begins to look like we can exercise some choice in their regard. Sometimes we can choose, for example, to perceive a given situation in such a way that certain passions will likely be elicited with a certain intensity. We can, in conversation with friends and other moral educators, reflect and deliberate about how to describe a certain object, what to believe about it, what aspects of it to focus on, and for what reasons. We can deliberate about how to value the object that we see. We can reevaluate what we see and how we see it, on the basis of new information, a new perspective on old information, or a change in values and commitments. We can change how we feel about an object by re-imaging it with an altered focus on its pleasant or painful aspects.

We can do this and more, as members of a moral community, to give deliberate shape to our passions. We can alter occurrent perceptions, beliefs and desires by re-imaging and reevaluating what we see. More effectively, we can slowly alter our deeper patterns of belief, perception, and desire. We can choose to become, with attentiveness and disciplined practice, persons disposed to engage the world in one way rather than another, upholding certain values more than others. Precisely how such alterations can be made and with what degree of success is another matter, but the point here is simply that it makes sense for Aristotle to say that virtue is a habitual disposition concerned with choosing both to act and to feel, for it makes sense to say that we can choose (to some extent) both our actions and our passions.

Keep in mind the fullness of Aristotle's notion of choice. We can and do make choices to do and (less readily) to feel something here and now or to alter upon reflection what we are already doing and feeling here and now. Of more significance in Aristotle's scheme, however, is the way in which individual choices like these give rise to habitual patterns of reception and response that elicit certain actions and passions without benefit of explicit reflection and deliberation.[25] Aristotle seems to want to say that the virtuous person chooses how to act and to feel in a given situation most significantly in that she has chosen in the past and she continues in the present to choose to fall into and perpetuate a characteristic way of construing her world. She has chosen to construe her world in such a way that certain actions and passions are regularly elicited in response to certain particulars while others are not. She has chosen to construe her world in this way rather than some other way because she has been educated to regard this way as fine. She has also been educated to take pleasure in doing what is fine.

This is the direction in which Aristotle's reflections on choice seem to me to point. I go beyond his explicit reflections when I explore what it might mean to choose our passions. Aristotle works with a cognitive understanding of the passions. He says that passion "shares in reason in a way, in so far as it both listens to reason and obeys it" (1102b30–32). He insists that we have some control over and responsibility for how things appear to us as moral agents (e.g., 1114a3–11, 1114a32–1114b25). But he does not take the opportunity to discuss how we might deliberate

about and deliberately effect the perceptions, beliefs, evaluative judgments, and intentional desires that partly constitute our passions. What
I have said on these matters, however, is consistent with his broader ethic
of virtue.[26]

. . . IN ACCORDANCE WITH THE MEAN

Finally, for Aristotle, virtue is a habitual disposition concerned with
choosing both to act and to feel in accordance with the mean, where the
mean relative to us is determined with reference to what a person of practical wisdom would choose.[27] Achieving the mean of virtue is a matter of
steering an intermediate course between excess and deficiency. It is a
matter of acting and feeling "at the right times, with reference to the right
objects, towards the right people, with the right motive, and in the right
way" (1106b20). It is not a matter of observing moderation if this means
that the terms of excess and deficiency are defined ahead of time, such
that the same person will be expected to act and to feel the same way
under different circumstances or different persons will be expected to act
and to feel the same way under the same circumstances.[28] It is, instead, a
matter of observing the details of given situations, allowing relevant features of those situations to signal the terms of excess and deficiency and
thus to suggest what is intermediate and best for us (1126a33–1126b4;
1103b32–1104a11).

Nor is achieving the mean a matter of applying universal rules
to particular cases with the assumption that "universal rules are themselves the ultimate authorities against which the correctness of particular
decisions is to be assessed."[29] It is instead, for Aristotle, a matter of grant-
ing a kind of priority to the particular—approaching situations in such a
way that we are open to being surprised by the new, the unrepeatable, the
indeterminate. It is also a matter of allowing the unique and the idiosyncratic to challenge cherished assumptions and elicit reactive response. To
be sure, universal rules are helpful as summaries of decisions made by
wise persons to date. We need them to help organize our perceptions of
complex predicaments, focus our attention on important aspects of those
predicaments, and keep our settled commitments and values in view.
But such rules ought to be thought of as flexible and revisable "rules of
thumb." In Aristotle's judgment, "practical choices cannot, even in prin-

ciple, be adequately and completely captured in a system of universal rules."[30]

Achieving the mean means choosing well, which means choosing as a person of practical wisdom (*phronimos*) would choose. A person of practical wisdom is someone who is "able to deliberate finely about what is good and beneficial for himself, not about some restricted area—e.g. about what promotes health or strength—but about what promotes living well in general" (1140a26). With a well-considered conception of the good life in view, the person of practical wisdom is able to discern the most salient aspects of a situation and deliberate finely about what virtue requires of him with respect to those aspects (1141b15, 1143a25–35). Because practical wisdom has so much to do with the discernment of particulars, its cultivation requires a great deal of experience.

To choose as a person of practical wisdom would choose is to choose as the community's most experienced moral educators and exemplars have taught us to choose (1143b11). It is to choose as the distinctive persons we are, in light of a well-deliberated vision of the good, with practiced attention to our own and relevant others' needs, capabilities, commitments, and desired ends, with carefully-honed sensitivities and attunements to shifting particulars. There is no formula for computing what is intermediate and best in a given situation. There is no mathematical equation for solving moral problems or, more generally, for constituting humanly good living. Yet there is, in the virtuous person, a firm and abiding commitment to becoming "finely aware and richly responsible."[31] This commitment gives determinate shape to what she sees and how she responds to what she sees.

This should suffice for an account of the main elements of Aristotle's ethic of virtue relevant to this project. As we have seen, character virtue is a habitual disposition concerned with choosing both to act and to feel in accordance with the mean, where the mean relative to us is determined with reference to what a person of practical wisdom would choose. In other words, it is a deeply-rooted, stable disposition to act and to feel in light of rational deliberation—where rational deliberation is guided by desires for goods that we judge reasonably and with keen perception to be productive or constitutive of *eudaimonia*.

Two
Thomas Aquinas on Acquired Moral Virtue

We are now in a good position to con-
sider Thomas Aquinas's account of virtue. Thomas was heavily influenced by Aristotle, but he was also entrenched in Christian teaching and
tradition. He affirmed much that Aristotle had to say about virtue, but he
gave it a distinctively Christian spin. In the *Summa Theologica*,[1] Thomas
recognizes three, as opposed to two, kinds of virtue: intellectual, moral,
and theological. He also distinguishes between acquired virtue and infused virtue. In this chapter, I offer a selective reading of Thomas's theory
of acquired moral virtue. This reading will prepare us to consider, in
the following chapter, Thomas's understanding of the way in which
Christian beliefs, perceptions, and desires can condition the exercise of
acquired moral virtue.

Human happiness (*beatitudo*), for Thomas, consists in the actualization of our distinctively human potential (I–II 1.5, 1.7, 3.2). Our distinctively human potential is actualized in the consistent exercise of all
the virtues.[2] The virtues are habitual dispositions of the soul toward its
ordered operation (I–II 55.2 *ad* 1). The soul's operation is ordered with
reference to a two-fold rule (I–II 71.6). The first rule is the natural law,
which humans understand by the natural light of reason. The second
is the eternal law, the understanding of which "surpasses the natural
reason, and requires the supernatural light of a gift of the Holy Ghost"
(II–II 8.3 *ad* 3).

Operations of the soul that are carried out in accordance with the
natural light of reason actualize our distinctively human potential to the
extent possible by means of human effort alone. Choosing deliberately

to think, to feel, and to act in accordance with the dictates of reason is constitutive of a natural human happiness proportionate to human nature *qua* human. Operations of the soul that are carried out in accordance with the supernatural light of a gift of the Holy Spirit actualize our distinctively human potential to an extent possible only with the help of grace.[3] Choosing deliberately to think, to feel, and to act as participants in the very life of God is constitutive of a supernatural human happiness that surpasses human nature—a supernatural happiness proportionate to human nature, but only *qua* partaker of the divine nature (I–II 62.1 *ad* 1). The most perfect human happiness possible in this life is achieved by consistently conforming the operations of the soul to both the natural law and the eternal law, that is, by following the dictates of reason while, at the same time, being receptive to the gratuitous movement of the Holy Spirit in our hearts and in our minds.[4]

Habitual dispositions of the soul that orient the soul's operation in accordance with the dictates of right reason and thus make possible a reasonable thinking, feeling, and acting that is proportionate to human powers are characterized by Thomas as *acquired* virtues (I–II 63.4). Thomas's understanding of acquired *moral* virtue, with which we are concerned in this chapter, is deeply Aristotelian. Thomas quotes Aristotle's definition of moral (i.e., character) virtue with approval (I–II 59.1). He agrees that moral virtue is a habitual disposition concerned with choosing both to act and to feel in accordance with the mean, where the mean relative to us is defined with reference to the rule of human reason (I–II 59.1 passim and *ad* 3). Once again, let us consider the component parts of this definition, but now with reference to the *Summa*.

A HABITUAL DISPOSITION . . .

Thomas, following Aristotle, holds that acquired moral virtue is an "ordered disposition of the soul," an "operative habit" that functions as a principle of the soul's operation (I–II 55.2 passim and *ad* 1). It is a deep-seated, lasting, and stable tendency to be well disposed with respect to action and passion. It is a characteristic inclination to do and to feel what is suitable to our nature (I–II 49.2 *ad* 1 and 3). Virtuous dispositions are natural to human beings "in so far as in [human] reason are to be found instilled by nature certain naturally known principles of both knowledge and action, which are the nurseries of intellectual and moral virtues, and in so far as there is in the will a natural appetite for good in accordance with reason" (I–II 63.1). Dispositions toward right action and passion are not, however, natural in their perfected form. They are the sorts of things that have to be perfected deliberately through a long process of habituation (I–II 51.3). A person "does not acquire all at once a firm and difficultly changeable disposition" (I–II 54.4 *ad* 1).

. . . CONCERNED WITH CHOOSING

Acquired moral virtue is a habitual disposition concerned with choosing (I–II 58.4). Thomas, like Aristotle, indicates that choice can be characterized as either desiderative deliberation or deliberative desire, but he indicates his preference for the second characterization, as "choice is substantially not an act of the reason but of the will: for choice is accomplished in a certain movement of the soul towards the good which is chosen" (I–II 13.1). Choice, then, is a desire for what has already been deliberated or counselled (I–II 14.1).

For Thomas, as for Aristotle, the deliberative process that terminates in choice can be represented in syllogistic form. The major premise is a desire for some end. The minor premise is a belief or a perception regarding what, in the present situation, will best promote the end desired. The conclusion is an act or an intention to act (at the right time) in a way that will best promote the end desired (I–II 13.3, 15.3, 14.1 *ad* 1).

Of course, Thomas, like Aristotle, recognizes that interactions between desire, belief, and perception within the context of a given deliberative process are too complex to be captured fully by such a representation. To begin with, belief and perception, which are formally represented by the minor premise, have considerable impact on the formation of the major premise. First, the desire represented by the major premise is an intentional desire that is specified with reference to an object of perception or belief. What is wanted is *this* object, imaged in accordance with *this* description of the situation at hand (I–II 9.1). Second, the desire represented by the major premise is a movement of the intellective appetite or will.[5] What is wanted by the intellective appetite is wanted because it is believed or perceived to be good (I–II 1.5). Without the belief or perception that this object is productive of the humanly good, there is no movement of the will (I–II 8.1).

Deliberation is chiefly concerned with reaching decisions about what to do here and now in order to promote desired ends. The desire represented by the major premise is ordinarily a desire for some concrete good specific to a given circumstance. It is important to note, however, that desires for specific goods tend to assume their full intentional content relative to other desires, including desires for a good human life, generally, and for particular goods believed or perceived to be ingredient in such a life (I–II 1.7, 12.3). Beliefs and perceptions regarding the constituents of human well-being can thus exert a significant influence on the formation of context-specific desires.

Just as belief and perception contribute to the formation of the major premise, desire contributes to the formation of the minor premise. It is the intellective desire for something perceived to be good that drives the deliberative process (I–II 14.1 *ad* 1). That is to say, desire generates and sustains the impetus needed to entertain a variety of beliefs and perceptions concerning how best to promote a given end. In addition, desire focuses an inquiry by directing attention to certain beliefs and perceptions more than others, namely, those that seem to answer to the governing desire.

PASSION

Complicating this account of the interactions between intellective desire, belief, and perception during the decision-making process is the presence of *sense* desire (*actus appetitus sensitivi*).[6] Of particular interest to us are sense desires that Thomas characterizes as passions (*passiones*). Prerequisite to an understanding of passion's role in the deliberative process is an understanding of what sense desire is for Thomas, and how it is distinguished from intellective desire.

Intellective desire and sense desire both have as their intentional objects something that is apprehended as good, but objects can be apprehended as good by the intellect or by the senses. *Intellective apprehension* is apprehension wherein some universal is abstracted from particular conditions, such that a particular is grasped as "standing under the universal" (I 79.4, 80.2 *ad* 2). *Intellective desire*, accordingly, is desire for an object that is apprehended by the intellect under the formal aspect of its goodness, i.e., as productive of human happiness (I 80.2 *ad* 2). Thomas insists that movements of the intellective appetite take place apart from specific alterations in bodily states "because this appetite is not exercised by means of a corporeal organ" (I–II 22.3). Movements of the intellective appetite can and do, however, "redound" upon the body indirectly "because, to wit, when the higher part of the soul is intensely moved to anything the lower part also follows that movement" (I–II 24.3 *ad* 1).

Sense apprehension, by contrast, is apprehension in which particular conditions are grasped in their particularity (I 78.4). *Sense desire*, accordingly, is desire for an object that is apprehended by the senses as delectable in its singularity (I 81.2). It can also be desire for an object that is apprehended by the senses as advantageous, but where one object's advantageousness relative to another is "estimated" by means of a "coalition of ideas" or images that falls short of an appeal to a universal.[7] Unlike movements of the intellective appetite, movements of the sense appetite are "properly to be found where there is corporeal transmutation" and commotion (I–II 22.2). They have as their "material element" a "natural change" in the disposition of bodily organs (I–II 22.2 *ad* 3). The arousal of sense desire commonly involves a heating up or cooling down of the body.

Thomas maintains that passion is "more properly in the act of the sensitive appetite, than in that of the intellectual appetite" (I–II 22.3). To be sure, a passion like anger includes several complex beliefs and evaluative judgments regarding what is the case and how much it matters.[8] Anger includes a belief that one's excellence has been slighted unjustly—a belief that appears to require reference to justice as a universal. It also includes an evaluative judgment that unjust slights are bad because they injure one's prospects of flourishing—a judgment that requires reference to a conception of the good. Yet Thomas chooses not to characterize anger—or any other passion—as an intellective desire.

The reason is because the beliefs and evaluative judgments that partly constitute a passion like anger have their basis in immediate sense apprehensions, which elicit sense desires that take place in and through alterations in bodily states. "[T]he material element of anger" is the "commotion of the heat urging to instant action" (I–II 48.3 *ad* 1). Thomas quotes Pope Gregory I: "*the heart that is inflamed with the stings of its own anger beats quick, the body trembles, the tongue stammers, the countenance takes fire, the eyes grow fierce, they that are well known are not recognized. With the mouth indeed he shapes a sound, but the understanding knows not what it says*" (I–II 48.2). The sense desires of human beings can come under the governing influence of reason (I–II 46.4), but the point here is that they retain their organic quality.

As these comments on the passion of anger suggest, Thomas holds that the passions are not in themselves carefully formed and critically re-flected desires for the humanly good. Rather, they are sense desires for particular delectables—desires that are partially composed of bodily com-motions. Yet passions are more than thoughtless, knee-jerk responses to items that happen to make us feel good or bad at the time. At least, they are more than this when they occur in rational animals whose sense and intellective operations are well developed and well integrated. One could say that Thomas locates the passions between the ends of a sense-intellect continuum: Passions are caused and partly constituted by sense appre-hensions that come to be more or less informed by the judgment of "universal reason." They are caused and partly constituted by sense de-sires that come under the more or less compelling influence of the rational appetite or will (I 81.3).

This account of Thomas's understanding of human passion is suffi-ciently precise for our purposes, for we have distinguished passion from belief, perception, and intellective desire, and we are prepared to under-stand passion's influence on these during the deliberative process.

PASSION'S IMPACT ON CHOICE

In Thomas's scheme, passion can influence choice in both negative and positive ways. On the one hand, passion can so captivate a person's energy and attention that the intellective desires, as well as the beliefs and perceptions, which combine to constitute a given deliberative process do not get properly formed. First, passion can so distract the will that a person fails to feel and reflect upon a range of relevant desires prior to settling into one that will govern the deliberative process. This makes it likely that the person's governing desire (represented by the major premise of the practical syllogism) will not include, as it should, the intention to realize one among several, related ends, which are together constitutive of human happiness.

> [S]ince all the soul's powers are rooted in the one essence of the soul, it follows of necessity that, when one power is intent on its act, another power becomes remiss, or is even altogether impeded, in its act, both because all energy is weakened through being divided, so that, on the contrary, through being centered on one thing, it is less able to be directed to several; and because, in the operations of the soul, a certain attention is requisite, and if this be closely fixed on one thing, less attention is given to another (I–II 77.1).

Second, passion can so impede judgment that a person acquires distorted beliefs and perceptions regarding the best means for realizing a given end (represented by the minor premise). An inordinate attraction or repulsion of the sense appetite toward or away from a particular object causes a person to believe or perceive that object to be better or worse than it is. Mistaken beliefs or perceptions cause, in turn, an inaccurate presentation of the object to the (already distracted) intellective appetite, which elicits an inordinate movement of that appetite toward the object (represented by the conclusion of the syllogism) (I–II 77.1, 9.2).

On the other hand, ordinate passions directed toward appropriate objects strengthen the intellective appetite. They make it easier and more pleasant for this appetite (represented by the major premise) to drive the deliberative process in light of what is believed or perceived to promote human flourishing.[9] They also make it easier and more pleasant for the intellective appetite (represented here by the conclusion) to tend toward what is believed or perceived, as a result of deliberation, to be the best possible response to the situation.[10]

Ordinate passions also contribute to the overall goodness of moral character. It is good for a person to do the right thing, says Thomas, but it is better to do the right thing while, at the same time, feeling the right way. When one feels the right way, one gives expression to the fact that reason governs the whole of one's person, that it guides the use of all of one's powers:[11] "Accordingly, just as it is better that [a person] should both will good and do it in his external act; so also does it belong to the perfection of moral good, that [a person] should be moved unto good, not only in respect of his will, but also in respect of his sensitive appetite" (I–II 24.3).

Construed in light of his theory of the passions, Thomas's reflections on the deliberative process also suggest that ordinate passions make possible a more complete knowledge of particulars (represented by the minor premise). Consider, for example, Thomas's discussion of consent (*consensus*) in the *Summa*. Consent is an initial application and attachment of the intellective appetite to a range of possibilities that a person believes or perceives to be likely to promote a desired end. Before a person judges which of these possibilities is the best one, and before she applies and attaches her intellective appetite (in choice) to that possibility, she considers the possibilities plurally and, so to speak, tries them on for size. She entertains them in the sense that she gets an initial desiderative "feel" for them, a sense for which of them (as provisionally desired) resonates best with the desire or set of desires that is driving the current deliberative process. Precisely in being moved by the objects of consent, the person gains an intimate knowledge of the objects at issue.

> [S]ince the act of an appetitive power is a kind of inclination to the thing itself, the application of the appetitive power to the thing, in so far as it cleaves to it, gets by a kind of similitude, the name of sense, since, as it were, it acquires direct knowledge of the thing to which it cleaves, in so far as it takes complacency in it (I–II 15.1).

This "appetitive knowledge," Thomas implies, can help a person make a much better judgment than she would otherwise be able to make regarding which of the possibilities available to her is indeed the best.

Thomas is referring in the above passage to the *intellective* appetite and not to the *sense* appetite (wherein the passions are located). We have seen, however, that there is for Thomas a kind of continuum between those appetites that are more intellective and those that are more sensitive, between those that are more or less informed by "universal reason" and those that are more or less informed by immediate sense apprehensions. The fullness of Thomas's understanding of the passions as cognitive, as well as sensitive, seems to require the recognition of such a continuum. If a passion like anger, "in some measure reaches up to the higher appetite," as Thomas thinks that it does,[12] such a passion might be enough like an intellective desire in relevant respects to make a contribution to the knowledge of particulars that is similar to the contribution made by intellective desire.

Elsewhere, Thomas suggests that passion can contribute to our knowledge of particular persons with whom we are concerned in our deliberations. Thomas says that in passion—particularly in love (*amor*), which is a cause of every passion—an initial change is wrought in a lover's appetite that causes him to stand in relation to his beloved with a kind of familiarity, accustomedness, or complacency (*complacentia*) (I-II 27.1). In love's complacency, the lover senses that his beloved is like him and is, indeed, part of him.[13] Because the beloved is part of him, knowledge of the beloved approaches something like self-knowledge. It is a knowledge much more immediate, direct, and intimate than that possible via the exercise of intellect without passion.[14]

> Knowledge is perfected by the thing known being united, through its likeness, to the knower. But the effect of love is that the thing itself which is loved, is, in a way, united to the lover. . . . Consequently the union caused by love is closer than that which is caused by knowledge (I–II 28.1 *ad* 3).

This passage suggests that the initial movements of the appetite which constitute love's complacency contribute importantly to our knowledge of other persons. Loving another, enjoying an initial sense of kinship with her that is wrought in the attachment of our appetite to her, we know her in a deeper, more penetrating way than we could if we did not love her.

It could be that Thomas is referring here, as well, to intellective love and not to the love that is a cause of passion proper. Sometimes he refers to intellective love as passion "in a wider and extended sense" (I–II 26.2). Still, when we consider how similar some of the passions are in some respects to movements of the intellective appetite, there is reason to suppose that, for Thomas, some passions, some of the time, contribute to our knowledge of particular persons in ways that promote good deliberation. Thomas's theory of the passions leaves this open as a possibility.

I argue at various junctures in this project that passion *can* contribute to our knowledge of particular others. Passion's cognitions can contribute to our knowledge, but passion's desiderative and bodily components can contribute as well. By way of foreshadowing, consider an example which suggests that the physical sensations ingredient in passion can themselves be "knowing." I encourage readers to consider this example in light of similar experiences of their own.

An Example

It sometimes happens as I go about my day that I find myself riled up inside. I am clenching my jaw, my stomach is in knots, and it is not immediately clear to me why my body is in such a commotion. When I stop to reflect upon the commotion, I am usually successful at isolating certain beliefs and perceptions that seem to be partly at cause. Sometimes I am able to change these beliefs and perceptions and sometimes I am not. Sometimes a change in belief and perception elicits a change in the commotion and sometimes it does not. In any case, the bodily commotion that I suffer is a source of knowledge to me. Not only does the commotion inform me of certain beliefs and perceptions that I happen to be entertaining, which are constitutive of my knowing what is the case. The commotion itself is part and parcel of my knowing, such that without it I could not be said to know what I know as fully and as vividly as I do.

What, exactly, does the bodily commotion add to my knowledge? It adds a felt conviction that what I believe or perceive to be the case is important to me, and it gives me an indication of just how important it is. It adds a physical sensation of the attractiveness or the repulsiveness of that which holds my attention. My presumption is that the commotion is partly an embodied wanting, and the embodied wanting is partly an experience of the goodness or the badness of some object or state of affairs. We all know that our wanting is frequently mistaken about what is and is not of value. Still, it is clear that sometimes our wanting informs us that valued items in our lives are at stake—items that our intellect is bent on ignoring.

Pressing further, my bodily commotion informs me that something is amiss regarding something of importance to me. It is partly in my enfleshed attachment to that something that I am able to discern what that something is, what in its regard is amiss, and why and how much it matters to me. It is partly in my wanting that I begin to try various beliefs and perceptions on for size in an attempt to see which of them best "fit" the commotion and illuminate its intentional cause and content. It is partly in my wanting and in reflecting upon my wanting that the commotion begins to take on distinctive shape as this or that particular passion. Of course, as I experiment with possible cognitive contents, my wanting is liable to undergo change. Nevertheless, it remains a guiding source of knowledge.

To press into an interpersonal context, sometimes when I reflect upon what is contributing to the commotion in my flesh, I notice that my husband, Bryan, is upset about something. We have been in contact with each other all day and I have had plenty of opportunity to perceive his trouble, but it is only now that my body has become powerfully engaged that my perception is complete and forceful enough to make me stop what I am doing and take notice. My commotion is a source of knowledge about Bryan. It is not simply that it informs me of certain beliefs and perceptions that I was already entertaining implicitly, but of which I have now become more explicitly aware—beliefs and perceptions that are sufficient in themselves to capture the content of my knowing. It is, in addition, that the commotion itself is an aspect of my knowing. The commotion itself is a felt awareness that something is amiss regarding something I love. It is a bodily recognition that something of what I want in my love for someone else is being painfully frustrated or denied. Belief and perception can inform me of this, but they cannot, apart from a fully embodied mode of operation (in which desire, too, is engaged) impress upon the whole of me that and how deeply this frustration or denial matters to me.

Finally, as I seek to discern just what is amiss with Bryan, my bodily commotion serves as a guide in the inquiry, setting certain parameters regarding which beliefs and perceptions "fit" with what my flesh already "knows" to be the case. I sometimes discover partly in my bodily commotion that Bryan is suffering a similar commotion. We are sometimes able to draw on the experience of our shared commotion in discerning together what is bothering the both of us. We are sometimes able to uncover a more definitive intentional cause and content to what we feel such that our shared commotion gets identified more clearly as one passion or another. Once again, enfleshed wantings are often off the mark, but we sometimes come to know something of what another is suffering precisely in an embodied aching that we share with him or her. This aching is indispensable to the completeness of our knowing.

This example raises all sort of questions that we will be better able to pursue after we have explored the nature of friendship, but I introduce it here because it behooves us to have an intimation early on in our inquiry of the way in which passion can contribute to knowledge of particulars and, hence, to the making of good choices. I hope to show, especially in our discussion of compassion proper, that we can only perceive well what is required of us morally if we perceive with passion appropriate to the situation in which we find ourselves, that is, if we grasp relevant features of the situation in an embodied, desire-full way.[15]

. . . BOTH TO ACT AND TO FEEL

Acquired moral virtue is a habitual disposition concerned with choosing both to act and to feel.[16] For Thomas, as for Aristotle, the way we feel can and should be subject to choice. How can we choose to feel movements of the sense appetite or, more specifically, passions?[17] Thomas indicates that whether and in what manner we are attracted via our sense appetites toward a given sensible good depends on two factors.

The first factor is the way in which the sensible good is imaged, interpreted, and evaluated. Humans apprehend a sensible particular while entertaining a host of beliefs and perceptions concerning the sort of object that it is, its attractiveness or repulsiveness relative to other objects of sense or imagination, its bearing on human well-being, etc. As we have seen, passions are partly constituted by beliefs and perceptions like these.[18] To the extent that passion-constituting beliefs and perceptions are open to revision and to the extent that we want to make such revisions, in accordance with our intellective desire for human flourishing, we have some choice about what to feel and how to feel it (I–II 17.7).

We can often choose, upon feeling a particular passion, to talk ourselves out of the passion, to continue feeling it in the same way, or to continue feeling it, but in a different way, depending upon whether or not it is believed or perceived, upon reflection, to be appropriate to the situation at hand (I–II 10.3 *ad* 1, 24.1). Thomas says that sometimes a person, "by the judgment of his reason, chooses to be affected by a passion in order to work more promptly with the co-operation of the sensitive appetite" (I–II 24.3 *ad* 1). Of course, once we feel a particular passion, it is likely to skew (for better or for worse) our reflections about whether or not the passion itself is appropriate.

We can also choose, to some extent, to become certain sorts of believers and perceivers by deliberating about how we ought to regard our relationships with our fellow human beings and what our balanced responsibilities ought to be to ourselves and to others. We can deliberate about what sorts of things we ought to look for and focus on as significant in situations of moral import. We can choose over time to become persons whose passions are partly composed of realistic beliefs and perceptions that are informed by well-deliberated desires for the humanly good.[19]

There are obvious limitations to such an endeavor. One of these is imposed by bodily temperament (I–II 17.7). This is the second factor that influences whether and in what way we are attracted via the sense appetite to a particular sensible good, namely, the way in which the bodily organs are disposed to receive what is imaged, interpreted, and evaluated. Thomas holds, for example, that some people have physical constitutions that dispose them to hot-temperedness. They may dislike this disposition and set out to change it by carefully reexamining relevant beliefs, by questioning the way in which they value themselves and the esteem of others, by arriving at reasonable, realistic attitudes that mild tempered persons would endorse, and yet still be unable to change their temperament. Their failure could be due to assumptions that they hold, but of which they are not yet explicitly aware. It could be due to factors in their early upbringing that continue to influence them, but in a hidden way. Thomas insists, however, that it could also be due to the disposition of their bodily organs.[20] Our physical make up could, if Thomas is right, impose important constraints on our ability to choose how to feel—constraints that we might not be able to remove entirely.[21]

It is possible, then, to choose to feel movements of the sense appetite, but this possibility is a limited one. Following Aristotle, Thomas says that reason rules the passions, not as a master rules his slaves, but as a leader of a politic rules over free subjects, "who, though subject to the government of the ruler, have nevertheless something of their own, by reason of which they can resist the orders of him who commands."[22]

. . . IN ACCORDANCE WITH THE MEAN

Finally, acquired moral virtue is, for Thomas, a habitual disposition concerned with choosing both to act and to feel in accordance with the mean, where the mean relative to us is defined with reference to the rule of human reason. Once again, the mean of human action and passion is not an arithmetic mean discerned by calculating the midpoint between two extremes, each of which can be identified in the abstract. Attaining the mean requires steering a course between excess and deficiency, but this course will be steered differently by different people in response to different elements of different circumstances. Nor is the mean attained simply by applying universal rules to particular cases as though these rules could never be confounded by the new and idiosyncratic (I–II 94.4).

The mean is achieved by following a rule of sorts—the rule of practical wisdom or prudence: "[I]t belongs to the ruling of prudence to decide in what manner and by what means [a person] shall obtain the mean of reason in his deed" (II–II 47.7). Prudence is an intellectual virtue whose exercise consists in clear-sighted, realistic discernment of what is morally at stake in a situation; open, honest assessment of what the situation demands of us; and intelligence and foresight informed by years of our own and others' experience regarding how these demands can best be met (II–II 47.1, 47.3 *ad* 3, 47.9, 49.3).

Prudence is an intellectual virtue concerned preeminently with reasoning well about what is to be done, but for Thomas, reasoning well requires having well-ordered desires (I–II 58.5). Reasoning well about practical matters is not something that we do as disengaged, disembodied intellects. Rather, it is something that we do as whole, embodied persons with appetites. Achieving the proper balance and interaction of right reasoning and right appetite (as well as right action) requires habituation to the whole assortment of intellectual and moral virtues. In the exercise of virtue, the prudent person reasons cogently about what to do. At the same time, however, the prudent person's intellective and ordinate sense appetite give him a "feel" for the situation at hand, which assists him in making a sound judgment.[23] In Thomas's view,

> [R]ectitude of judgment is twofold: first on account of perfect use of reason, secondly, on account of a certain connaturality with the matter about which one has to judge. Thus, about matters of chastity, a [person] after inquiring with his reason forms a right judgment, if he has learnt the science of morals, while he who has the habit of chastity judges of such matters by a kind of connaturality (II–II 45.2).

Along the same lines,

> A [person] may judge in one way by inclination, as whoever has the habit of a virtue judges rightly of what concerns that virtue by

his very inclination towards it. Hence, it is the virtuous [person], as we read, who is the measure and rule of human acts (I 1.6 *ad* 3).

For someone who seeks to identify and highlight passion's positive contribution to the deliberative process, passages like these look promising. While the passages likely refer to inclinations of the intellective, rather than the sense, appetite, if we take seriously the way in which certain passions approximate the "higher appetite," there is reason to suppose that passions can prove indispensable to the person of practical wisdom's perception and evaluation of what is the case.

This suffices for a consideration of those elements of Thomas's theory of acquired moral virtue that are directly relevant to this inquiry. It should be clear that Thomas's account of acquired moral virtue is very much like Aristotle's account of character virtue, although we have taken the opportunity to explore a few avenues and make a few distinctions with Thomas that we did not do with Aristotle. Taken together, these accounts furnish us with a working understanding of moral virtue and the way in which belief, perception, desire, and passion interweave to constitute its exercise. We need this understanding if we are to discern how, according to Thomas, acquired moral virtue can be transformed in Christian experience.

Three
Thomas Aquinas on Theological and Infused Virtue

Recall that, for Thomas, there is a two-fold rule or measure for human action. In addition to the rule of natural law, which is the rule of reason toward which we are naturally inclined as rational animals (I–II 94.3), human beings are subject to the eternal law, the understanding of which "surpasses the natural reason, and requires the supernatural light of a gift of the Holy Ghost" (I–II 8.3 *ad* 3). Being perfectly virtuous, for Thomas, requires not only following the dictates of reason, but also becoming receptive to the gratuitous movement of the Holy Spirit in our hearts and in our minds (I–II 65.2, II–II 2.3). We have considered what it is to exercise virtue in accordance with the dictates of reason. We need presently to consider what it is to exercise virtue in response to the movements of grace.[1]

The kind of grace with which we are principally concerned here is habitual grace.[2] Habitual grace is a participation of the human being "in the Divine Nature, after the manner of a likeness, through a certain regeneration or recreation" (I–II 110.4). It is an infused quality of the soul "whereby the corrupted human nature is healed, and after being healed is lifted up so as to work deeds meritorious of everlasting life, which exceed the capability of nature" (I–II 109.9). Habitual grace manifests itself partly in the form of the theological virtues of faith, hope, and charity (II–II 23.2 passim and *ad* 1).

THEOLOGICAL VIRTUE

Faith, hope, and charity are virtues in that they are habitual dispositions to think, feel, and act well. They are "principles" by which human powers are ordered to their proper end. As theological virtues, they are distinct from acquired virtues in several respects. Whereas acquired virtues are habits that direct those who possess them toward a natural human happiness proportionate to human powers, theological virtues are habits that direct those who possess them toward a supernatural human happiness proportionate to humans only *qua* participants in the divine nature (I–II 62.1). Theological virtues are habits that are infused by God, "entirely from without," and cannot be acquired by means of deliberate human action (I–II 62.1, 63.1). They are habits that direct persons toward God, not simply as the distant "beginning and end of natural good," but as an intimate Friend with whom one shares "a certain mutual return of love, together with mutual communion" (I–II 62.1, 109.3 *ad* 1, 65.5). The reality of the theological virtues is made known to persons, not by means of "natural reason" alone, but by means of divine revelation contained in Scripture (I–II 62.1).

The theological virtues are accompanied in the Christian life by other contributions of habitual grace called "gifts of the Holy Spirit." Although the theological virtues dispose believers to think, feel, and act well in union with the Holy Spirit, persons who are thus disposed nevertheless "stand in continual need of being moved by the yet higher promptings of the Holy Ghost" (I–II 68.2 *ad* 2). They stand in need of additional habits by which "all the powers of the soul" become further disposed "to be amenable to the Divine motion" (I–II 68.1 *ad* 3). As Paul Wadell puts it, they stand in need of perfecting gifts that enable them to become "so disposed to God and so docile before God that God's will [becomes] the power by which [they act]."[3]

Thomas identifies seven gifts of the Holy Spirit: understanding, knowledge, fear, wisdom, counsel, piety, and fortitude. We will consider those gifts that are associated directly with faith, hope, and charity, namely, understanding, knowledge, fear, and wisdom. Such a consideration will begin to make manifest the ways in which the process of deliberative choice making can be altered in Christian experience.

FAITH AND ITS IMPACT ON CHOICE

Faith is defined by Thomas as a habitual disposition of the intellect, infused by God, to assent at the command of the will to simple and complex propositions about God, propositions that reason cannot of itself know to be true (II–II 4.5). In the absence of faith, the person of practical wisdom can and does contemplate the first cause of all things. She is able in contemplation to "know of God *whether [God] exists*, and . . . what must necessarily belong to [God], as the first cause of all things, exceeding all things caused by [God]" (I 12.12). In faith, however, "the intellect's natural light is strengthened by the infusion of gratuitous light" (I 12.13). While the person of faith still "cannot know of God *what [God] is*," she can know God "more fully according as many and more excellent of [God's] effects are demonstrated to us, and according as we attribute to [God] some things known by divine revelation, to which natural reason cannot reach, as, for instance, that God is Three and One" (I 12.13 *ad* 1).

Faith is supplemented and perfected with the gifts of understanding and knowledge. The gift of understanding concerns the direct apprehension of divine truths. It enables a person habitually to have a sound grasp of things that are proposed to be believed, to penetrate to the very essence of divine things (II–II 8.1 *ad* 6). "[T]he stronger the light of the understanding, the further it can penetrate into the heart of things. Now the natural light of our understanding is of finite power; wherefore it can reach to a certain fixed point. Consequently, [a person] needs a supernatural light, in order to penetrate further still so as to know what [he or she] cannot know by [his or her] natural light: and this supernatural light which is bestowed on [a person] is called the gift of understanding" (II–II 8.1).

The gift of knowledge concerns the sure and right judgment of what is proposed to be believed. It enables a person habitually to discern what is to be believed from what is not to be believed (II–II 9.1). In the person of practical wisdom who is without the gift of knowledge, sure and right judgment is reached by means of demonstrative reasoning. "On the other hand, in God, there is a sure judgment of truth, without any discursive process, by simple intuition . . . wherefore God's knowledge is not discursive or argumentative, but absolute and simple to which that knowledge is likened which is a gift of the Holy Ghost, since it is a participated likeness thereof" (II–II 9.1).

Faith and the gifts of understanding and knowledge are speculative in the kind of knowledge that they afford,[4] but they can have considerable impact on the way in which choices of character are made. Recall that the desire for some particular good is called into focus or elicited in a given situation, partly on account of what we believe or perceive human happiness to consist in. If we are functioning well as human beings, we will desire particular ends here and now that we believe or perceive to be productive of good human living. If we have faith and the gifts that perfect faith, if we believe accordingly that human flourishing consists partly in following the dictates of the eternal law and thereby enjoying a preliminary participation in the life of God, then certain desires rather than others will tend to be called into focus in a given situation, namely, desires for ends that we believe to promote supernatural happiness. For example, if I believe in faith that I can begin to enjoy an eternal friendship with God here and now partly by loving my neighbor as myself, I will likely be disposed to see certain situations as situations requiring loving response, and I will be disposed to desire in those situations the loving response.

Because faith forms the desires that set the parameters for and give focus to particular deliberative processes, faith gives determinative shape to our beliefs and perceptions about what is the case and how in this case a desired end might best be realized. In faith, I am likely to believe that the person before me is a neighbor whom I am called to love. In faith, I am likely to look to stories about Jesus for guidelines concerning what counts as a loving response to the neighbor (II–II 8.3, 8.5, 9.3).

HOPE AND ITS IMPACT ON CHOICE

Hope is a habitual disposition of the intellective appetite or will to be moved toward an arduous future good, namely, eternal happiness and the divine help by which it is obtained (II–II 17.4); "hope makes us adhere to God, as the source whence we derive perfect goodness, i.e. in so far as, by hope, we trust to the divine assistance for obtaining happiness" (II–II 17.6). The person of practical wisdom who does not possess the theological virtue of hope "hopes" in that she is likely now and then to undergo "a movement of the appetitive power ensuing from the apprehension of a future good, difficult but possible to obtain" (I–II 40.2). It is only with the infusion of habitual grace, however, that the practically wise person characteristically tends toward God "as to a good to be obtained finally, and as to a helper strong to assist" (II–II 17.6 ad 3).

Supplementing and perfecting hope is the gift of filial fear, which concerns the proper submission of the self to God.[5] In filial fear, says Thomas, the self submits to God as a child submits in affection to a loving father. The gift of filial fear enables a person habitually to be a nonresistant subject of the Holy Spirit's movement out of concern to avoid offending and thus being separated from God. A person fears sinning lest she alienate herself from a relationship whose enjoyment promotes her supernatural happiness. Of course, a person is naturally prone to fear the loss of important goods, but it is only with the infusion of habitual grace that she fears the loss of her beloved Father's affection and assistance (I–II 42.1, II–II 19.2 *ad* 3, 19.9 *ad* 1).

Like faith and its attendant gifts, hope and its attendant gift of fear can have considerable impact on the exercise of deliberative choice. Hope's longing for eternal fellowship with God and its trust in God's assistance toward this end will tend to direct a person's attention to certain features of a situation rather than others. One who hopes will likely attend to features of a situation that have reference to her eternal happiness.[6] Moreover, she will desire particular ends, in response to these features, insofar as these ends promote the ultimate end of her fellowship with God. Her longing for and trust in God will set limits to the means by which the particular ends can be realized, as the means themselves must contribute to the realization, not only of immediate ends, but of the final end as well (II–II 17.2 passim, *ad* 2, and *ad* 3, 17.4).

CHARITY AND ITS IMPACT ON CHOICE

Lastly, charity is a habitual disposition of the intellective appetite or will to be united with God in a love that has the character of friendship (II–II 23.1). "[C]harity makes us adhere to God for [God's] own sake, uniting our minds to God by the emotion of love [*affectus amoris*]" (II–II 17.6). The person of practical wisdom who does not possess the theological virtue of charity has a "natural desire for God"[7] in that he "desires for his ultimate end . . . his perfect and crowning good," which is his perfection (I–II 1.5). He may desire as constitutive of his perfection a knowledge and love of God as God is in Godself. It is only with the infusion of charity, however, that a person desires and seeks this knowledge and love as someone who already shares an intimate union with "the Holy Ghost, Who is the love of the Father and the Son" (II–II 24.2).

We will not be in a position to discuss the nature of charity as friendship with God or the relationship between friendship with God and friendship with humans until we are further along in our inquiry. We can only indicate at this point that in friendship with God, as Thomas conceives of it, the believer begins to share in the very life of God, and in this shared life, he begins to know and to love as a participant in the knowing and loving of God. The rest of this chapter is, in effect, a preparation for understanding the way of knowing and loving that is possible for fully embodied persons in friendship with God and the way in which this knowing and loving can alter deliberative choice making.

The gift of the Holy Spirit that is associated with charity is wisdom, which concerns the judging and setting in order of all things "according to Divine rules, by reason of a certain connaturalness or union with Divine things" (II–II 45.1, 45.4). The gift of wisdom enables a person to feel so at home in the presence of God that, as Etienne Gilson phrases it, she can "peer right into God" and judge divine things in genuine sympathy with God, "instinctively sensing what is true long before grasping its demonstration."[8] Distinguishing the wisdom that is possible without the gift of wisdom from that which is possible with the gift, Thomas says,

> Accordingly it belongs to the wisdom that is an intellectual virtue to pronounce right judgment about Divine things after reason has made its inquiry, but it belongs to wisdom as a gift of the Holy Ghost to judge aright about them on account of connaturality with them: thus Dionysius says (*Div. Nom.*ii) that *Hierotheus is perfect in Divine things, for he not only learns, but is patient of, Divine things*" (II–II 45.2).

This strikes a familiar chord. We saw in our discussion of Thomas on acquired moral virtue that a right intellective (and perhaps sense) appetite can promote our knowledge of particular persons. Tending toward a person according to a bond of affection, we become partly a reception of and response to that person, such that we are able (to a limited degree) to know that person as we know ourselves (I–II 28.1 *ad* 2). Now we see that intellective love can contribute to our knowledge of God as well. Tending toward God in love, we "[attain] to God . . . intimately by a kind of union of the soul with [God]" (II–II 45.3 *ad* 1). We attain to God's *logos* such that we become partial embodiments of that *logos* who know and follow it as our most fundamental insight and inclination. We do so habitually, with pleasure and with ease. Thomas is clearly pointing to something "higher" here than our participation in the divine *logos* by means of the natural law. He is pointing to a "supernatural elevation" of our capacity to know (II–II 45.1 *ad* 2).

The wisdom that contemplates and consults divine things as they are in themselves is speculative,[9] but it is of practical import insofar as the wise person judges human acts by divine things and directs human acts according to divine rules (II–II 45.3, cf. 45.3 *ad* 1). In wisdom, desires for particular goods will be elicited in a given situation, not simply on account of beliefs regarding what God wills (as we find with faith and its attendant gifts), but on account of connaturality with God's will, i.e., participatory knowledge of and love for what God wills. What we desire in wisdom will be in matter and in manner what God wills for us. Such desire will, in turn, drive and direct in a distinctive fashion our reflections regarding what in this situation will contribute best to the end desired.

We can gather that charity, too, is of practical significance in Thomas's view, for it is in friendship with God that the person with charity desires, perceives, and believes everything. It is in friendship with God that she loves and reasons about what is of value and about what must be done to promote what is of value. As we have seen and shall explore further in what follows, the friend of God will not only love and reason about different things for different reasons (relative to persons who lack charity), but she will do so in a different way.

INFUSED VIRTUE

Faith, hope, charity, and their associated gifts orient persons toward the attainment and enjoyment of our highest end, "i.e., to God [Godself] immediately. But the soul needs further to be perfected by infused virtues in regard to other things, yet in relation to God" (I–II 63.3 *ad* 2). Hence, God provides humans with other infused habits, such as infused prudence and infused temperance. Like the theological virtues and the gifts of the Holy Spirit, the infused virtues dispose us "in a higher manner [than the virtues that we can acquire through our own acts] and towards a higher end, and consequently in relation to some higher nature, i.e., in relation to a participation of the Divine Nature (I–II 110.3). They dispose us to be ordered in a supernaturally elevated way, but specifically with regard to everyday matters.

Thomas seems to write of the infused virtues as though they are a parallel set of virtues which, once infused gratuitously, coexist alongside the acquired virtues (I–II 63.3, 63.4). It appears that a person with charity is someone who is in a position to exercise, at any given moment, either set of virtues. She can choose to exercise one or more virtues that have their basis in "supernatural principles" that are infused by God. Or she can choose to exercise one or more virtues that have their basis in "certain natural principles pre-existing in us" (I–II 63.3). Or, perhaps, she can choose to exercise a mixed set of infused and acquired virtues. Perhaps she can exercise infused prudence with regard to "matters necessary for salvation," and she can exercise acquired prudence with regard to matters necessary for realizing finite human ends (II–II 52.1 *ad* 1).

A problem with this rendering of the relationship between infused and acquired virtue is that it does not capture Thomas's understanding of the unity of the moral life in charity. True, Thomas says that the Christian is bound by a two-fold rule for human action and passion. She is to follow the dictates of both supernaturally elevated reason and natural reason. But it makes the most sense for Thomas to say that once a person gains access to the rule of supernaturally elevated reason—once her capacity for natural reason is supernaturally elevated into the *logos* of God—then she will no longer be disposed to exercise merely natural reason (unless she sins mortally and loses charity). Even concerning the affairs of this world, she will be disposed to exercise a rational capacity that has become fundamentally qualified by her received capacity to reason in a supernaturally elevated way. Things necessary for natural human happiness will perforce be perceived and reasoned about in light of things necessary for supernatural human happiness.

Thomas says that charity is the "form" of the virtues in that, once infused, charity "directs all other virtues to its own end" (II–II 23.8 *ad* 3).[10] It does so by transforming the will itself. It "superadds" to the natural power of the will a "habitual form" that inclines the will toward the highest end for human beings and disposes it to seek this end with pleasure and with ease (II–II 23.2). Thus, charity (in concert with the other theological virtues and their associated gifts) "perfects" the very powers with which acquired virtue is exercised.[11] It would seem, therefore, to perfect whatever acquired virtue we happen to possess at the time of infusion. If we have not acquired any virtue prior to the time of infusion, then charity perfects the powers with which we may or may not cultivate such virtues in the future.

The implication of this reading is that, with the infusion of charity, already functioning acquired virtues are, in effect, transformed into their infused counterparts. This is not to say that already functioning acquired virtues are prerequisite to the infusion of charity and thus prerequisite to the reception of infused virtue. Thomas makes clear that they are not. It is just to say that the infusion of charity transforms the whole of the person, such that she becomes oriented fundamentally toward the attainment of supernatural happiness. Even when she chooses to act and to feel in such a way that she will attain to natural human happiness, she necessarily sees natural human happiness as subordinate to (and thus qualified by) her vision of supernatural human happiness. She always chooses both to act and to feel *sub specie aeternitatis*.[12]

It may seem odd to suggest that Thomas construed the life of charity as one that does not require and, technically speaking, does not even allow the acquisition of merely acquired virtue, particularly given the amount of energy he expended explicating for his predominantly Christian audience the nature and value of this sort of virtue. Upon reflection, however, it does not seem so odd. The life of charity remains, according to this reading, a life whose realization requires immense human initiative and effort. Doing well at living the life of charity requires working in intimate relationship with God to cultivate habits that one has first received from God. To be sure, infused habits are "infused in us wholly from without"; still, those who receive these habits must choose freely, again and again, to act and to feel in accordance with them. Without a kind of practice that one would expect to resemble the practice of cultivating acquired virtue, these habits remain "ours" in only a limited sense.[13] This account of the relation between infused and acquired virtue will have to suffice for present purposes. As Jean Porter notes, Thomas does not himself "offer a satisfactory account of the relation of the infused to the acquired virtues in the history and character of the individual whose virtues they are."[14]

Thomas does make clear that the infusion of "the moral virtues . . . together with charity" (I–II 65.3) can alter the exercise of moral agency. It can alter the deliberative processes in which we choose to engage and the ways in which we choose to engage in them (relative to the processes we would carry out in the presence of acquired virtue alone). Making use of the model of the practical syllogism again, it is likely that we will, in the exercise of infused virtue, begin a given piece of deliberation with a different major premise. Receiving and responding to particulars on the basis of different beliefs about the meaning and value of human life, we will begin with different intentional desires for the immediate or long-term realization of this meaning and value.

As Thomas frames it, we will intend a different end in the exercise of infused virtue:

> For a [person's] health and a horse's are not of the same species, on account of the difference between the natures to which their respective healths are directed. In the same sense, the Philosopher says (*Polit.* iii.3) that citizens have diverse virtues according as they are well directed to diverse forms of government. In the same way, too, those infused moral virtues, whereby [persons] behave well in respect of their being *fellow-citizens with the saints, and of the household* (Douay,—*domestics*) *of God* (Eph. ii.19), differ from the acquired virtues, whereby [persons behave] well in respect of human affairs (I–II 63.4).

Whereas acquired virtue aims at the perfection of human nature and the enjoyment of natural human flourishing, infused virtue aims at the perfection of a supernaturally elevated human nature and the enjoyment of a supernatural human flourishing in fellowship with God. It aims, accordingly, at mediate ends that will promote this ultimate end.

As we will likely begin a given deliberative process with a different major premise in the exercise of infused virtue, so too we will likely arrive at a different minor premise. Viewing particulars against a different horizon of intentional desire, we will look at potential contributors to our ends from a different angle, noticing and focusing on different things for different reasons, counting different things to have different degrees of moral salience, supposing them to promise different kinds and degrees of success in promoting the ends that we desire most.

Taking temperance as an example, Thomas argues that we will discern and observe a different mean in the exercise of infused virtue than we would in the exercise of acquired virtue alone:

Now it is evident that the mean that is appointed in such like con-
cupiscences according to the rule of human reason, is seen under a
different aspect from the mean which is fixed according to the Divine
rule. For instance, in the consumption of food, the mean fixed by
human reason, is that food should not harm the health of the body,
nor hinder the use of reason: whereas, according to the Divine rule,
it behooves [a person] to *chastise* his *body, and bring it into subjection*
(1 Cor. ix.27), by abstinence in food, drink, and the like. It is therefore evident that infused and acquired temperance differ in species;
and the same applies to the other virtues (I–II 63.4).

Those actions and passions that we believe or perceive to be productive
of a natural human flourishing will thus likely differ from those actions
and passions that we believe or perceive to be productive of a supernatural human flourishing.

Finally, in the exercise of infused virtue we will likely conclude our
deliberations differently. We will conclude them in clear-sighted recognition of and passionate desire for our elevated ends and the different
means judged best for promoting these ends. In short, even if the chosen
actions and manifestations of passion appear outwardly to be the same in
the exercise of infused virtue as we imagine they would be in the exercise
of acquired virtue alone, they will in infused virtue mean something quite
different to the agent who performs them. They will have a different sense
in the context of a different understanding and experience of the self in
relation to what is ultimate.

An important element of this divinely wrought transformation of
moral agency in charity is the infusion of prudence.[15] In the exercise of
infused, rather than merely acquired prudence, a person will deliberate
about and choose how to act and to feel on the basis of different intentional desires, perceptions, and beliefs, but she will also deliberate and
choose with supernaturally elevated capacities to reason and to love.[16]
She will reason about what is to be done with a more perfect "*memory* of
the past, *intelligence* of the present, *shrewdness* in considering the future
outcome, *reasoning* which compares one thing with another, [and] *docil-
ity* in accepting the opinions of others" (II–II 53.3). What is more, the
person with infused prudence will reason about what is to be done as one
who is in love with God—as an active participant in the outpouring of

God's love for Godself and God's creation. She will reason lovingly, inclined and attentive to what is good and true, and she will choose to act and to feel in love with what God loves.

For additional assistance, the person with infused prudence will receive the perfecting gift of counsel, by which she will be enabled, as a matter of habit, to anticipate the singular and contingent things likely to occur in the process of committing a proposed course of action. Infused with the gift of counsel, the person will enjoy a kind of foresight possible only in intimate friendship with a God who comprehends all things (II–II 52.1 *ad* 1).

INFUSED VIRTUE'S IMPACT ON PASSION

In faith, hope, charity, infused prudence, their associated gifts, and with the addition of yet other gifts, we would expect all of the virtues that we have managed to acquire through the exercise of our own moral agency to be transformed in the matter and manner of their exercise. Of special interest with respect to this project is the way in which Thomas thinks that we will choose to *feel* in the exercise of infused virtue. It is easy to get the impression from passages like the following that we will choose to feel no passion at all:

> For a life of pleasure consists of two things. First, in the affluence of external goods, whether riches or honors; from which [a person] is withdrawn,—by a virtue so that he uses them in moderation,— and by a gift, in a more excellent way, so that he despises them altogether. Hence the first beatitude is: *Blessed are the poor in spirit*, which may refer either to the contempt of riches, or to the contempt of honors, which results from humility. Secondly, the sensual life consists in following the bent of one's passions, whether irascible or concupiscible.[17] From following the irascible passions [a person] is withdrawn,—by a virtue, so that they are kept within the bounds appointed by the ruling of reason,—and by a gift, in a more excellent manner, so that [a person], according to God's will, is altogether undisturbed by them: hence the second beatitude is: *Blessed are the meek*. From following the concupiscible passions, [a person] is withdrawn,—by a virtue, so that [a person] uses these passions in

moderation,—and by a gift, so that, if necessary, he casts them aside altogether; nay more, so that, if need be he makes a deliberate choice of sorrow; hence the third beatitude is: *Blessed are they that mourn* (I–II 69.3).

Another similar passage is also worth quoting at length:

> But since it behooves [a person] to do his utmost to strive onward even to Divine things . . . we must . . . place some virtues between the social or human virtues, and the exemplar virtues which are Divine. Now these virtues differ by reason of a difference of movement and term: so that some are virtues of [persons] who are on their way and tending towards the Divine similitude; and these are called *perfecting* virtues. Thus prudence, by contemplating the things of God, counts as nothing all things of the world, and directs all the thoughts of the soul to God alone;—temperance, so far as nature allows, neglects the needs of the body; fortitude prevents the soul from being afraid of neglecting the body and rising to heavenly things; and justice consists in the soul giving a wholehearted consent to follow the way thus proposed.—Besides these, there are the virtues of those who have already attained to the Divine similitude: these are called the *perfect virtues.*—Thus prudence sees nought else but the things of God; temperance knows no earthly desires; fortitude has no knowledge of passion; and justice, by imitating the Divine Mind, is united thereto by an everlasting covenant. Such are the virtues attributed to the Blessed, or, in this life, to some who are at the summit of perfection (I–II 61.5).

These passages point to an interesting tension in Thomas's ethical thought. Thomas wants to say that being perfectly virtuous requires both following the dictates of reason and being receptive to the movements of the Holy Spirit in our hearts and in our minds (II–II 2.3). Grace does not overcome the acquired virtues; rather, it "perfects" them (I 2.2 *ad* 1). Moreover, it does so incrementally as we gain, in ongoing conversation with God, a deeper and deeper understanding and love of our highest end (II–II 2.3, 17.2 *ad* 1). The difference between the virtue that we exercise in accordance with natural reason and that which we exercise in accordance with supernatural reason would seem to be, in a sense, quantitative.

Of course, a supernatural orientation is qualitatively different from a natural orientation in that it orders us to a formally different end. But once we are initiated by God into the pursuit of our supernatural end, we will have to be educated toward this end. As we are educated toward this end, we will be re-educated toward our natural human end, which means that our ordinary understanding and experience of ourselves and the ultimate significance of our chosen action and passion will be altered. We would expect this alteration to effect changes in our habits of action and passion. But we would not expect these changes to be radical in persons who already possess a significant amount of acquired virtue. Nor would we expect the infusion of habitual grace to remake persons who already have rationally ordered bodily appetites and passions into persons who simply "cast [these] aside" in order to have "no knowledge of passion."[18]

Thomas seems to say as much elsewhere in the *Summa*. For example, he says that our concern in acquired virtue to tend well to the health of the body is not cast aside with the infusion of charity; rather, it is directed toward a higher end. "[O]ut of the love of charity with which we love God," he says, "we ought to love our bodies also." We ought to love them in order to place ourselves in a position of being able to serve God well as embodied creatures. Quoting Paul's letter to the Romans, Thomas exhorts us to "Present . . . [our] members as instruments of justice unto God" (II–II 25.5).

Regarding the passions, in particular, Thomas says that, "just as it is better that [a person] should both will good and do it in his external act; so also does it belong to the perfection of moral good, that [a person] should be moved unto good, not only in respect of his will, but also in respect of his sensitive appetite" (I–II 24.3). This is a clear statement of Thomas's integrative understanding of the flourishing body-soul composite.[19] The fact that he refers here to the perfection of *moral* good does not mean that he is not also referring to the perfection of *spiritual* good. For he goes on to say, "according to Ps. lxxxiii.3: *My heart and my flesh have rejoiced in the living God*: where by *heart* we are to understand the intellectual appetite, and by *flesh* the sensitive appetite" (I–II 24.3). Thomas makes manifest that it belongs to the perfection of moral *and* spiritual good that the whole person—in soul and in body, in reason and in passion—be ordered toward the enjoyment of God in this life.

Admittedly, Thomas says elsewhere that "our bodies are unable to enjoy God by knowing and loving [God]." But he continues: "by the works which we do through the body, we are able to attain to the perfect knowledge of God. Hence from the enjoyment in the soul there overflows a certain happiness into the body. . . . Hence, since the body has, in a fashion, a share of happiness, it can be loved with the love of charity" (II–II 25.5 *ad* 2). The body's ability to share in and thus to complete the soul's enjoyment of God ought therefore to be valued and promoted.

Accordingly, it would be a mistake to neglect the good of the body "so far as nature allows" and to cast aside the embodied passions of the soul in order to enjoy more completely the goodness of God. As long as we are embodied creatures, the complete enjoyment of any good will have to be embodied, and it will have to be empassioned. Hence, it behooves us to care for our bodies and to maintain in good working order the passions that orient us toward the embodied enjoyment of our moral and spiritual good.

Perhaps the tension at issue can be eased by saying that, for Thomas, the infusion of virtue effects a transvaluation of human value. Looking with the help of supernaturally elevated reason toward our highest human happiness in the life to come, we achieve a renewed perspective on what is ultimately worthy of pursuit in this life. Much of what natural reason deems to be of value will still be valued in charity, but it will be valued partly because its pursuit contributes to our knowing and loving of God. Much that attracts our sense appetite apart from charity will continue to attract us under the influence of charity. It will do so, however, in a way that draws us, not simply toward an enjoyment of finite objects themselves, but also toward an enjoyment of the Power in which these objects have their being and their goodness.

Thomas says that the body and its passional movements can contribute to our knowing and loving of God by adding a certain fullness to our experience of God, but in the end, it seems that this contribution is not all that crucial for him. It can and should be sacrificed "if necessary" and "according to God's will" (I–II 69.3). The contribution is, after all, only indirect. The body and its passional movements contribute to our knowing and loving of God only insofar as the body suffers movements of the sense appetite *qua* overflow from movements of the intellective appetite (II–II 25.5 *ad* 2).

PASSION'S IMPACT ON CHOICE

Could passions of the soul, which take place in and through changes in bodily organs, partly in response to the apprehension of sensible particulars, ever contribute directly to our knowing and loving of God? As Thomas sees it, most passion undermines our knowing and loving of God by turning our attention away from God and attaching it to temporal goods, focusing our attention on pleasures of sense that we enjoy without reference to God as the highest end for human beings (I–II 77.4).[20] But what about passion that begins in sense apprehension, yet opens us up to the apprehension of Absolute Mystery in the world? What about passion that originates as a movement of the sense appetite (in Thomas's scheme), but elicits a resonance in an intellective appetite in love with the will of God? What about passion that is evoked in faith, hope, and charity, such that it emerges into explicit consciousness as partially constituted by beliefs and perceptions that refer created goods to the good of the Creator? We pressed Thomas in the previous chapter to appreciate that passion can, according to its own, proper movement, contribute to our knowledge of sensible goods, our knowledge of ourselves and of other persons. We need now to press Thomas to appreciate that passion can, according to its own, proper movement, contribute to our knowledge of God. For this reason, it ought not to be "cast aside" in an effort to "strive onward even to Divine things" (I–II 61.5).

Recall that, in Thomas's scheme, passions are partly caused and constituted by "sense apprehensions" that include evaluative judgments. Often, these judgments are not made explicitly. We discover ourselves to be feeling a physical commotion and it is not until we reflect upon this commotion that we begin to make explicit the judgments that partly comprise it, such that the commotion begins to be identified and described by us as a particular passion and not simply a physical disturbance like a stomach ache. Still, it seems clear that our passional commotions are partly caused and constituted by judgments. A given commotion just is a reception and an evaluative response that focuses our energy on a particular object, focuses our attention on the object (once we begin to attend consciously to the primordial pulls of appetite), and keeps our attention focused on that object as we begin to reflect explicitly upon what the commotion is about.[21]

Once this is understood, it becomes clear that passion can contribute to our knowledge of God. For if we habitually apprehend whatever we apprehend *in* faith, hope, and charity, then the initial evaluative judgments that cause and partly constitute a given passional commotion will likely have implicit reference to God as object. So will the thoughts, perceptions, and desires by means of which we feel this commotion more fully and reflect upon its meaning and significance more explicitly. So will the passion with which the commotion is eventually identified. To reflect upon the commotion, then, is in part to reflect upon God and our passionate relation to God.

It is not simply the cognitive reflection upon a given commotion that contributes to our knowing of God. The commotion itself contributes to our knowing. It stimulates, drives, and focuses our reflections. It sets limits upon which of our cognitions will illuminate our "hot" or "cold" relation to what is currently at issue. Certain cognitions will "fit" the commotion, clarify, intensify, and enrich the commotion, giving it shape that makes sense out of our experience, and others will not. It is the feeling of the commotion that guides the inquiry, even as that feeling changes in response to the inquiry.

Nor is it simply the initial beliefs and judgments partly composing the commotion that contribute to our knowing of God. The physical aspect of the commotion contributes as well. It provides a powerful, visceral sense that a given object or end matters to us and that it matters immensely. It gives us a bodily sense of being attracted to or repulsed by an object or end that bears importantly on our weal and woe. True, some reflection will be required in order for a particular bodily sensation to be understood as, say, a desire for the physical presence of Christ. Still, the bodily sensation itself, in such a case, would be integral to our knowing how much this presence matters to us as body-selves. It would be a component part of our knowing of God.[22]

As we can sometimes come to *know* God more fully in feeling and reflecting upon our passions, so we can come to *love* God more fully. Believing, perceiving, and desiring whatever we believe, perceive, and desire in faith, hope, and charity, our deepest drives, our strongest appetites for various goods emerge upon reflection as intentional desires that have reference to God. Over time, we come to love sensible objects *in* God. This means that we become participants in the movement of divine love such that we love whatever we love, including sensible objects, in and through this participatory movement. This also means that we apprehend sensible objects as having their goodness from God, and we are attracted to them as such. We may also come to love God *in* sensible objects, which is to say that we may come to taste, to feel, to suffer, or to relish, for example, the physical presence of Christ in an object like the Eucharistic meal. Again, it is not simply the interpretation of our appetitive drives that enables us to love God more fully. The drives themselves, even before we describe and interpret them to ourselves, set the stage for the inquiry, determining which kinds of description and interpretation will make good sense of the drives, which will open us up to the full enjoyment of the drives and to the experience of the divine in this enjoyment.

We will have the opportunity to explore further the way in which the whole of passion contributes to the knowing and loving of ourselves, one another, and God when we look at the particular virtue of compassion, but this gives us a start. Already we have pressed further than Thomas, to my understanding, was willing to go in affirming the importance of fully embodied passion to the pursuit of friendship with God.[23] We have pressed, however, in a manner that is consistent with Thomas's broad understanding of the passions as desiderative discernments of value. The moves we have made are necessary if we are to capture the full significance of certain aspects of compassion.

In sum, whether we exercise acquired moral virtue or the infused virtue of the Christian, we will be well disposed, in Thomas's view, to choose how to act and to feel. In the exercise of infused virtue, however, we will be disposed to choose within the context of different descriptions and, hence, experiences of human reality, its ultimate meaning and significance. Infused virtue, for Thomas, does not overcome or oppose acquired virtue, but perfects and elevates it. The infusion of habitual grace, in its many forms, enables us to assent with certainty to revealed truths that we cannot completely comprehend. It enables us to love wholeheartedly a perfect good that we cannot completely possess. In this knowing and loving, we find our rational faculties being pressed beyond their natural limits, borne in a mysterious way by the Absolute Mystery that is trusted to be the uncreated cause and final telos of human being. It is, I think, this understanding of openness to Mystery and the ways in which this openness alters the experienced content and interaction of belief, perception, and desire in the moral life that makes Christian ethical accounts of good human living and of compassion, in particular, so provocative.

Four

Aristotle on Friendship

We have begun to examine the nature of virtue and the ways in which virtue can be understood and experienced differently when Christian beliefs, perceptions, and desires come into play. Our next task is to explore the relational context within which virtue is exercised. Human beings are social beings.[1] To the extent that we acquire virtue at all, we learn what virtue is, we learn that it is fine (*kalon*), and we learn to love and exercise it as fine, as persons who are embedded in an intricate web of relationships. We do so as daughters, sons, sisters, brothers, mothers, fathers, lovers, partners, colleagues, fellow citizens, and the like. All such relationships have a hand in shaping the moral agencies with which we seek, attain, and enjoy the humanly good.

One relationship that conditions the exercise of moral agency in profound ways is friendship. Our concern throughout Part II will be to delineate some of the ways in which friends share their lives together, such that they become habitually disposed to exercise virtue *as* friends in relation to friends. We will begin with Aristotle's account of character-friendship and its impact on the cultivation of acquired moral virtue, then proceed with Thomas Aquinas's Christian Aristotelian account of friendship and its impact on the cultivation of infused moral virtue. Our concern will be to plumb for an understanding of what it might mean for a Christian who shares a life with God to exercise virtue in friendship with God and in friendship with those whom God has befriended or wishes to befriend.

FRIENDSHIP DEFINED

Aristotle defines friendship (*philia*)[2] as a relationship between separate beings (1161b28)[3] consisting in affection and well-wishing (1155b29), where this affection and well-wishing are reciprocal (1155a33, 1155b29) and mutually known (1156a5), and where each friend wishes the other well "for his own sake" (1155b31).[4] The account of friendship given in the *Rhetoric* includes as a feature of friendship an inclination to bring about the good that we wish for our friends, as far as this is possible.[5] In other words, friendship is a relationship of mutually known and reciprocated affection and well-wishing in which each person wishes and does good to the other for the other's own sake.

Friendships arise and persist, in Aristotle's view, because two people perceive something good in each other that makes them lovable in each other's eyes. The good in question might be the other's usefulness, pleasantness, goodness of character, or some combination of these (1156a8 ff.). Ideally, affection and well-wishing between friends should be proportionate to each other's objective usefulness, pleasantness, or goodness of character. It should reflect "the comparative worth of the friends" (1158b28, 1159a36).[6]

Friendships that arise and persist primarily on the basis[7] of the enjoyment or expectation of advantage or pleasure tend to be unstable and short-lived: "And so these sorts of friendships are easily dissolved, when the friends do not remain similar [to what they were]; for if someone is no longer pleasant or useful, the other stops loving him" (1156a19). Friendships based on advantage or pleasure also tend to be superficial in that they are based on partial, incomplete understandings of the persons involved: "Those who love each other for utility love the other not in himself, but in so far as they gain some good for themselves from him. The same is true of those who love for pleasure; for they like a witty person not because of his character, but because he is pleasant to themselves" (1156a12).

Advantage-friendships and pleasure-friendships are incomplete in their instability and superficiality, but they are still friendships. To say that one advantage- or pleasure-friend loves another not in himself, but in order to gain some good from him is not to say that the one is simply using the other for his own benefit and without regard for the other's own good. If this were the way in which Aristotle understood advantage-

and pleasure-friendships, he would not have characterized them as friendships. Friendships, by definition, involve wishing each other well for each other's own sake.

The advantage- or pleasure-friend does wish his friend well for her own sake. It's just that he conceives of her according to a narrow description of who she is relative to him, such that he is attracted to her and wishes good to her *as* someone who is of help to him or someone whose company brings him pleasure. If the person ceases to be helpful or pleasing then the affection that brought the advantage- or pleasure-friends together in the first place and motivated its continuation will dissolve. So will the occasion for mutual well-wishing.[8]

The best friendships in Aristotle's view are those that arise and persist primarily on the basis of the friends' excellence of character.[9] These friendships are stable and lasting: "[T]he friendship of good people . . . lasts as long as [the friends] are good; and virtue is enduring" (1156b6–13). These friendships are also more intimate in that they are based on a more complete knowledge of the persons involved. Character-friends are attracted to one another *as* virtuous, which is to say that a character-friend is compelled by his friend's conception of the good, her desires and plans for realizing elements of that good, her habits of perception, the things she finds pleasant and painful, and so on. These are the particulars that, in the deepest sense, make the friend who she is, and to love them is to love the friend *as she is in herself.*[10] Character-friends find one another useful and pleasant to be with, but this is precisely because they are good (1156b13–25).

The kind of friendship with which we are concerned in this chapter and the next is character-friendship. We are also concerned with friendships between family members that can influence from an early age the formation and cultivation of a person's moral agency. Aristotle has little to say about whether friendships between parents and children, sisters and brothers, and wives and husbands, tend to be friendships of character or whether they tend, instead, to be friendships of utility or pleasure.[11]

He seems to hold that friendships between brothers and those between wives and husbands are closely akin to friendships of character (1162a10–15, 1162a25–28). Friendships between parents and children, too, appear akin to friendships of character, although Aristotle does not specify how a parent can be said to love a child on the basis of the child's excellence of character when the child is too young to have acquired much character. In any case, of both the love between adult persons of similar, well-developed virtue and the love of fine parents for their children, Aristotle says that the adults love their others as "other themselves" (1161b28, 1166a30). What does this mean? Surely, the sense in which we love other adults of similar, well-developed virtue as "other ourselves" differs from the sense in which we love our daughters or sons as "other ourselves," but how? Pursuing these questions throughout Part II should prepare us well to explore, throughout Part III, what it means (and how it is possible) to suffer the pain of another self as one's own.[12]

LOVING THE SELF

Love for a character-friend is, according to Aristotle, an extension of love for the self (1168b5). Loving ourselves, we love those whom we regard as part of ourselves and we love them as we love ourselves. We love ourselves, not only as extended selves in union with others, but as separate selves in distinction from others. Hence, we love our friends as "other ourselves" who, like ourselves, function as separate and unique centers of chosen action and passion. Our account of Aristotle on friendship needs to hold all of this together. As we explore some of the central features of Aristotelian friendship in this chapter and the next, we will focus on the nature of our love for ourselves, the way in which this love is extended to "other ourselves," the senses in which we are one and the same relative to "other ourselves," and the senses in which we are separate and different.

As we have seen, friendship for Aristotle is a relationship of mutually known and reciprocated affection and well-wishing in which each person wishes and does good to the other for the other's own sake. Because affection for others and the wishing and doing of good to others for their own sakes is understood to be an extension of affection for ourselves and the wishing and doing of good to ourselves for our own sakes (1166a10–20, 1168b1–6), it would be helpful to consider what it is, for Aristotle, to have affection for ourselves and to wish and do good to ourselves for our own sakes.

To wish and do good to ourselves for our own sakes is, in Aristotle's teleological scheme, to wish for and do what contributes to our human flourishing, which is to wish for and do what promotes our active exercise of complete virtue. This much follows in a straightforward way from Aristotle's eudaimonism and his theory of character virtue. Wishing for and doing what promotes the active exercise of virtue is a matter of reflecting on the good life and the ways in which its component parts can best be cultivated and integrated. It is a matter of planning and carrying out activities that will enhance our understanding of ourselves and the world around us, our keenness of perception, our attentiveness and responsiveness to particulars, and so on. Wishing and doing good to ourselves is a matter of wanting to be and becoming fully human. It is a matter of actualizing our distinctively human potential in all of its abundance: "What is pleasant is actualization in the present, expectation for the future, and memory of the past; but what is pleasantest is the [action we do] in so far as we are actualized, and this is also most lovable" (1168a13).

Having affection for ourselves, in turn, is a matter of being attracted to and delighting in the good that we wish for and do in the pursuit of our actualization. It is a matter of being attracted to and delighting in our own good selves—our values, our desires, our pleasures and pains, our past actions, our future plans and goals—as we envision, embody, re-envision, and re-embody these through decision-making processes. As self-lovers, we want to flourish as human beings in the exercise of complete virtue, we do what we can to promote this flourishing, and we thoroughly enjoy ourselves in the process. We enjoy our wanting, we enjoy getting what we want, we enjoy being who we are and actively becoming more fully who we are, simply because it is good that we should flourish.

Being attracted to and delighting in ourselves is, at its best, not a matter of stepping back from ourselves, assessing what is objectively lovable about ourselves, and being rationally compelled to delight in ourselves on the basis of what we deem to be lovable. It is, for Aristotle, more a matter of delighting in the activity of being ourselves: "And living is choiceworthy, for a good person most of all, since being is good and pleasant for him" (1170b2–6, 1166a19). It is also a matter of delighting in the activity of being with the persons we perceive ourselves to be: An excellent person "finds it pleasant to spend time with himself, and so wishes to do it. For his memories of what he has done are agreeable, and his expectations for the future are good, and hence both are pleasant" (1166a23–27).

LOVING THE RELATIONAL SELF

Loving ourselves, we wish and do good to ourselves for our own sakes, and we enjoy ourselves in the activity of wanting and attaining what is good. To complicate matters, however, we do all of this as persons in relation. As Aristotle says, "a human being is political, tending by nature to live together with others" (1169b19, 1097b11). We cannot pursue Aristotle's theory of moral education here,[13] and we need not do so in order to be aware of the fact that, for Aristotle, it is in intimate relation with others that we learn what the good is, that this knowledge becomes second nature to us, and that we come to love thinking, feeling, and acting in accordance with what is good (1179b5–32, 1147a19–22, 1104b10–13, 1179b24–32, 1161a16–19). It is in intimate relation with others that we learn, in particular, what it is to wish for and do good to ourselves and to delight in ourselves. It is in relation with others that this wishing, doing, and delighting become activities that are constitutive of our being fully ourselves. An excursion into the nature of one familial relationship, namely, friendship between young siblings who are close together in age, will begin to reveal what it means to say that, from the day we are born, we are persons in relation who understand, love, and conduct ourselves as such.

Three comments before we begin: First, it is obvious that not all of us grow up living together with brothers or sisters who are close to us in age. Some of us lead home lives in which we do not even have the opportunity to live consistently with one parent or another. Nevertheless, all of us are persons in relation. All of us who manage to survive to adulthood have role models, teachers, neighbors, friends, and so on, who take care of us (however minimally), teach us a language (however poorly), communicate to us a vision (however short-sighted and distorted), and show us how to love (or that love is impossible). Our concern here is simply to take a limited philosophical look at one kind of relationship in which many of us participate in our youth, namely, intimate sibling friendship, in order to specify some of what it might mean for one human being to share a life with another human being at an early age. This analysis is not based on scientific study, and it does not purport to reflect the current self-understanding of all or even most human beings; it is an idealized and simplified conceptual analysis intended to contribute in a limited way to a normative account of relational selfhood.

Second, not all of us are male. Because Aristotle discusses, not relations between siblings, but relations between brothers, without so much
as a mention of girls' relationality with girls or with boys, the implicit
assumption seems to be that girls' relationality is of little or no moral significance: friendship between boys is paradigmatic of "our" earliest human
relationality. On the one hand, this poses a problem for us. Carol Gilligan
has conducted psychological studies which indicate that girls tend to
relate to people differently than do boys. She argues that taking boys' relationality as paradigmatic has led many theorists of psycho-social and
moral development to misunderstand and misjudge girls' relationality,
concluding that it is abnormal or inferior, rather than simply different.[14]

On the other hand, however, many of the limited sorts of things that
Aristotle has to say about friendships between brothers in ancient Greece
seem to me, as a woman with sisters and a brother, as a mother of both a
girl and a boy, and as an ordinary observer of other people's familial relationships, to apply in a general way to friendships between brothers,
between sisters, or between sisters and brothers, even today.[15] More to the
point, what he says about brothers seems to me, as an ethicist who seeks
to say something truthful about the nature of relational human existence,
to apply in considerable measure to boys and girls, men and women,
alike. In what follows, I simply disavow Aristotle's sexism and address
some of the ways in which relations between siblings, in broadest outline,
can be thought to promote in siblings habits of exercising their moral
agencies as persons in relation. My failure to attend to recent psychological research regarding differences between boys' and girls' relationality
may be a limitation, but it is a necessary one within the framework of this
project. I do not wish to make or defend any empirical claims about
gender-specific differences between males' and females' capacities to befriend intimately or to be compassionate.[16]

Third, Aristotle has little to say about sibling friendship that speaks
explicitly to the issue of what it is to be a moral agent who exercises her
moral agency within the context of a delicate web of relationships. However, if we consider certain passages in the *Nicomachean Ethics* regarding
friendship between brothers in light of Aristotle's theory of character
virtue, and in anticipation of what Aristotle says about adult character-
friendship (to be addressed in the next chapter), these passages prove
suggestive. They provide us with a place to start and an angle from which
to pursue the topic.[17]

SIBLING FRIENDSHIP

Let us consider a few passages on sibling friendship and allow ourselves to press well beyond them, but in a manner that is broadly consistent with Aristotle's ethic of virtue.

In Aristotle's words,

> The friendship of brothers is similar to that of companions, since they are equal and of an age, and such people usually have the same feelings and characters (1161a27–28).

> Brothers love each other because they have come from the same parents. For the same relation to the parents makes the same thing for both of them; hence we speak of the same blood, the same stock and so on. Hence they are the same thing, in a way, in different [subjects]. Being brought up together and being of an age contributes largely to friendship; for two of an age [get on well], and those with the same character are companions. That is why the friendship of brothers and that of companions are similar (1161b30–37).

> Friendship between brothers has the features of friendship between companions, especially when [the companions] are decent, or in general similar. For brothers are that much more akin to each other [than ordinary companions], and are fond of each other from birth; they are that much more similar in character when they are from the same parents, nurtured together and educated similarly; and the proof of their reliability over time is fullest and firmest (1162a10–15).

Aristotle makes clear that siblings close together in age who are born of and raised by the same parents in the same household will tend to be similar in character on account of their similar relations with their parents. What is not made clear is the way in which the sibling relation itself generates a sameness of character in the siblings that contributes to the intimate sharing of a life. Unclear is the way in which the sharing of a life becomes a context within which the siblings learn to exercise virtue.

Coming from the same parents, siblings who are close together in age will benefit from similar parental nurture and education. Where the parents are persons of fine moral character who are committed to "living well and doing well in action," siblings will grow up together listening to their parents talk about what is of value to them, what kind of life is worth living, and what makes for human happiness. Siblings will watch their parents pursue what is important to them, expressing joy and satisfaction at success, sorrow and frustration at failure. They will listen to their parents decide what to do in situations that they deem to be of particular significance. They will watch their parents deliberate in light of what they care about, choose in accordance with their deliberations, carry out their decisions, and accept responsibility for the consequences. Siblings will see their parents do all of this in (more or less) intimate relation with each other.

Encouraged to emulate their parents (i.e. gaining the pleasure of abundant love when they do and suffering the pain of threatening anger when they do not), siblings who benefit from similar parental nurture and education will tend to have similar senses of what counts as humanly good, similar interests in pursuing perceived goods, similar responses to situations that call for decision, and similar pleasures and pains. Much more than this, however, Aristotle suggests that siblings will tend to share a life in common.[18]

SHARING A LIFE

Sharing a life in common means having similar visions of human flourishing, similar senses of what it is that makes life worth living, and similar notions of the sorts of people they want to be. Young siblings who are close together in age generally have different ideas about what they want to be when they grow up, but at the same time, they tend to have similar ideas about what counts as excelling at whatever they choose to do. Sharing a life in common means more, however, than having *similar* visions of the good. It means *sharing* a vision of the good.[19]

Part of what young siblings deem to be of value in their lives is their very agreement over what is of value to them. Siblings value the fact that their separate lives are lived together against the same horizon of meaning and significance—a horizon that they have "inherited" from their parents but which, to some degree, they seek to test, refine, and redefine through the medium of conjointly reflected experience. If one sibling begins to alter his understanding of the good life in distinction from the other, both siblings are likely to sense, however vaguely, that the meaning and significance of their lives is being called into question. Both are likely to try to persuade each other back into substantial agreement, changing or resisting change together. Where disagreement is sustained, it will be important to the siblings that they construe their differences in a way that allows for the preservation of their bond.[20] There is an impression on the part of many siblings that they are, in a sense, all each other has—that nonfamilial friends will come and go, but familial friends, for better or for worse, will be bound together for life. Hence, the stakes of basic agreement concerning what is important in life are high.[21]

Of course, siblings must reach an age of reason before they are able to reflect critically about the content of *eudaimonia* and the difference it makes to them that their conceptions of *eudaimonia* are shared. Even before they reach such an age, however, siblings share games, songs, stories and other imaginings, all of which function partly to constitute a shared world of meaning and value in which they can dream about and experiment with the notion of "living happily ever after."

Sharing a life in common also means having similar interests in pursuing what contributes to good living. It means wanting to do, feel, and experience many of the same things in life—to get equal servings of ice cream, to play with the same toys, to play with the same friends, to enjoy the same closeness and camaraderie with those friends, and so on. More than having *similar* interests, however, sharing a life in common means *sharing* interests in private and shared goods.[22]

For our purposes, private goods are goods that a person desires simply because she takes them to be good, irrespective of whether anyone else desires these goods for or with her. Shared goods are goods that persons desire partly or wholly because one or more others desire these goods for or with them. Private goods become shared goods when the person who desires the private goods perceives that one or more others desire these same goods for or with her, and when she then comes to desire these goods partly because one or more others desire them in this way. Shared goods become private goods when one or more people who had desired goods for or with someone else cease to desire the same goods in the same way, and when that someone else perceives the change, but continues to desire the goods anyway.

Sharing an interest in *shared* goods involves jointly cultivating and sustaining an interest in certain goods partly because both parties want to desire goods in common. Part of what young siblings want in desiring certain goods is that the other desire the same goods, that the two of them pursue and enjoy the same goods together, that they be bound up with each other in their desiring. To take a simple example, very young siblings sometimes ask each other what kind of candy they will choose for a treat, in a way that indicates on both siblings' parts a want to desire the same treat. They will sometimes choose something other than their favorite treat because it strikes them as an added treat to desire the same treat as the other. The anticipated sweetness of shared desire plays a significant role in their deliberations.

Sharing an interest in *private* goods involves jointly cultivating and sustaining an interest in each other's pursuit and enjoyment of his own, distinctive goods. Sharing an interest in each other's private goods easily yields to the generation of shared goods as each sibling realizes that the other wants for or with him the goods that he once desired alone, and each takes the other's wanting to be an additional reason for his own, continued wanting. But sometimes sharing an interest in each other's private goods simply amounts to sharing an interest that each other enjoy his own goods for and with himself. Siblings can share an interest in each other's wanting and enjoying of certain goods even though each is unable to understand or appreciate the other's attraction to those goods, and each cannot bring himself to desire those goods for or with the other. Siblings can also share an interest in each other's continuing to want and enjoy his own goods irrespective of sibling incredulity. What makes this interest in private goods shared is the fact that both siblings want to want in common that each other attain and enjoy his own, unique goods, and both siblings give shape and impetus to this metawanting by continually seeking to assay and extend each other's loyalty in its regard. For example, sometimes young siblings neglect to question each other about the candy they will choose and simply choose what suits their own, particular desires. Yet, after choosing their candy, they show an obvious interest in each other's choices. What is more, they show immense delight in the fact that each of them appears to be interested in the other's choice.

To proceed, sharing a life in common also means having similar ideas about what, in a particular situation, actually contributes to good human living. With siblings who have reached an age of reason, it means looking at the same situation from a similar angle with a similar passional response, deliberating in light of similar beliefs, perceptions, and desires, reaching similar conclusions about what ought to be done, and feeling similar commitments to do what ought to be done. More than this, however, sharing a life in common means *sharing* perceptions, deliberations, and choices.[23]

Young siblings share perceptions in that they frequently come to understand the significance of a given situation in conversation with each other, taking note of what aspects strike the other as relevant and important and finding those aspects relevant and important for the very reason that they strike the other as such. Siblings who share perceptions construct an interpretation and an understanding of a situation together, in light of each other's gut reactions, initial impressions, and past histories of reception and response. Over time, repeated incidents of side-by-side perception generate shared habits of perceiving, i.e., habits of perceiving, as it were, with one eye, knowing just what each other is noticing in a given situation, from what angle, and why, without a word having to be spoken.

Siblings often share deliberations and choices as well. It is partly in conversation with each other that siblings learn how to think, learn what counts as a good reason for doing something, and learn what it means to take responsibility for their actions. Confronting a situation of moral import together, siblings who share a life will share a perception of what is at issue in the case at hand. Drawing from a stock of experiences that they have undergone together or otherwise communicated to each other over the years, siblings will construct an imaginative vision of what will likely happen if they do this or that with respect to what is at issue. They will have a shared interest in realizing certain outcomes rather than others and they will jointly commit themselves to doing what will promote the outcomes desired. One sibling's deliberations with the other will often seem like deliberations with herself, as if the voice of the other is simply one of the voices that she discovers within herself. The commitment made on the basis of this shared voice will be significantly univocal. The siblings will act as one person, of one will and mind.

In her novel *Sula*, Toni Morrison captures beautifully some of what I have been describing. Reflecting as an adult upon the return of her dear childhood friend, Sula, Nel has this to say about the manner in which she and Sula have shared a life:

> Sula's return . . . was like getting the use of an eye back, having a cataract removed. Her old friend had come home. Sula, who made her laugh, who made her see old things with new eyes, in whose presence she felt clever, gentle and a little raunchy. Sula, whose past

she had lived through and with whom the present was a constant sharing of perceptions. Talking to Sula had always been a conversation with herself.[24]

Where there are disagreements in deliberation and choice, sibling friends will likely wrestle with these disagreements in a way that continues to promote the relationship to which they continue to feel bound.

Finally, sharing a life in common means being similarly pleased and pained by the same things. More than this, however, it means *sharing* pleasures and pains.[25] Part of what siblings will be pleased at in a given situation is that they are both pleased. If one sibling ceases to be pleased at the situation or becomes pained by it, the other will often find herself enjoying it less or ceasing to enjoy it altogether. Each sibling is pleased and pained with reference to the other. Both want to share pleasure in shared goods, such that their enjoyment of these goods is multiplied and powerfully qualified. Both want to share pleasure in private goods, such that they can enjoy each other's enjoying, even though they cannot understand how each other could possibly enjoy the peculiar goods that he enjoys.

With respect to pain, it may be too much to say that young siblings *want* to share pain in shared and private evils. It is not too much to say, however, that siblings want that their own pain be shared by the other, at least in the sense that their pain elicit in the other some pain *at* their pain, i.e., some recognition that they are in pain and some acknowledgement that it matters. Young siblings do not ordinarily want to be alone in their pain. Nor is it too much to say that someone who is pained at a sibling's pain sometimes experiences an intimacy that she finds curiously compelling. Although children are often oblivious to a sibling's pain or afraid of it (especially if they caused it), they are sometimes drawn into that pain in a way that elicits in them a remarkable tenderness that carries over into the playful moments subsequent to the pain's alleviation.

Conceptions of *eudaimonia*, interests, deliberations and choices, pleasures and pains, and much more come to be shared in the activity and conversation that go into living together over time. By the time a child is old enough to realize reflectively that he is a person in relation, he is already embedded in several life-shaping relationships. One of the first things my son, Ben, used to ask me when he got up from his nap was, "Hannah up? Daddy at work?" Even at the age of three, his younger sister, his father, and I were so much a part of him and his life that he could not dream of beginning a project or playing a game without first finding out if the rest of the family was around to watch or to share in his activity. Already, Ben exhibited a deeply rooted, inchoate habit of living in relation—a habit of thinking, feeling, and acting in light of what others close to him were thinking, feeling, and doing. It is with continued reference to what others are thinking, feeling and doing that Ben has slowly come to discover and learn to reflect philosophically upon who he is, what is expected of him, what can be expected of others, what he wants out of life, and so on.

AN EXAMPLE

It would be a mistake to suppose that the activities that promote shared conceptions of good living, interests, deliberations, choices, pleasures, and pains are principally intellectual and verbal. Physical activities, too, generate sameness of character in subtle, interesting ways.[26] I think, for example, of my husband, Bryan, and his brother, Ross, who are two years apart in age. They wrestled together in their youth at home and on the same wrestling teams at school. They still wrestle together now and then. In the aggressive interplay of their bodies, a profound brotherly intimacy is revealed. The intimacy is, in part, a physical one. Their bodies move spontaneously in response to the movement of one another's limbs, as if these were their own limbs, as if their bodies were one body struggling with itself. The intimacy is also emotional. Their physical activity becomes the medium through which otherwise hidden emotions find expression.

In the act of pinning Ross, for example, in feeling Ross's body make its last, futile struggle for escape, collapsing in utter exhaustion under the weight of Bryan's body, Bryan understands Ross's vulnerability, his weakness, and his sense of loss at being pinned in a way that he would not, say, in conversation about how Ross feels as he is being pinned. He also understands something of the deeper feelings of vulnerability, weakness, and loss that frame Ross's experience of loss at being pinned. For vulnerability, weakness, and a sense of loss are, in part, feelings in our limbs, and when Bryan feels Ross's limbs give way, he feels an integral component of Ross's emotional life. Just as the feeling of heaviness and relaxation in Ross's limbs elicits relaxation in Bryan's limbs, so some of Ross's vulnerability, weakness, and sense of loss are communicated to Bryan through Ross's limbs, eliciting similar feelings in Bryan.

It's not that Bryan reflects explicitly at that moment about the vulnerability and weakness that he and his brother share and the losses that both of them have sustained over the years. It is more that the feeling of heaviness and relaxation in Ross's limbs elicits a gentle, playful camaraderie on the part of Bryan, a lightheartedness that uplifts the heaviness in Ross that Bryan now experiences vaguely as his own. Bryan delights in his victory, but it is as if he cannot fully enjoy his victory as long as Ross is unable to enjoy it with him. The feeling of Ross's limbs, then, provides Bryan with a special kind of access to his brother's inner life.

Obviously, what Bryan feels in feeling Ross's limbs give way is interpreted. It is itself, in part, an interpretation that is informed by the look on Ross's face, by his moans and groans, and by years of experience gained in previously shared activity and conversation. Nevertheless, it is a physical feeling that contributes importantly to Bryan's understanding of Ross. The sharing of physical activity is just one of the many threads that knits the lives of Bryan and Ross together, but it is a central one. It makes it possible for the brothers to know each other more intimately which, in turn, makes possible a deeper, more complete sharing of conversation and activity. Shared activities of many sorts promote the sharing of conceptions, interests, deliberations, choices, pleasures, and pains, all of which contribute to siblings' shared experience that "they are the same thing in a way in different [subjects]."

As siblings mature and their circles of association and experience are enlarged, they may find themselves growing more and more distinct from one another in their ways of perceiving, thinking, feeling, and acting, but they will never leave behind entirely those early-established patterns of perceiving, thinking, feeling, and acting in light of what others are perceiving, thinking, feeling, and doing. They will never leave behind entirely those habits of valuing and enjoying things more when they are valued and enjoyed by others, constituting their perceptions in light of others' passions, deliberating with themselves as they deliberate with others, deciding what to do at the same time that they are reflecting upon what others would do. The others in question may become, more and more, friends other than siblings with whom they have more in common and in whose presence they find themselves delighting more, but the basic patterns persist. The challenge, of course, is for youths to find their own distinctive visions and voices amid the plethora of visions and voices that together contribute to a world of shared meaning and value. The challenge is to give deliberate shape to their own unique characters precisely in conversation with others.

We began this discussion of sibling friendship in an attempt to understand better what it means to wish and do good to ourselves and to have affection for ourselves for our own sakes. Our principal concern has been to show that the self that we love is fundamentally a self in relation, a self that is entangled in and supported by a web of relationships from the start. The self that we love is, as Nancy Sherman puts it, an extended self. It is a self that is extended through attachments to others, a self whose good is extended to include the good of others as partly its own.[27] Loving ourselves, then, means loving our already extended selves, which means loving others who are already part of us. Simply in loving ourselves, then, we love other selves *as* ourselves.

For children who grow up in the company of a sibling friend, the other who is confronted day in and day out is someone with whom we are stuck, so to speak. It is someone with whom we have little option but to spend most of our time. The sheer number of hours that we play with such a sibling guarantees that we will one day find her to be (for better or for worse) inextricably part of us, inescapably loved and attended to in our loving and attending to ourselves. It is different with friendships between adults who have not grown up together. As we shall see, there is an element of choice in adult friendships that is absent or less prominent in the sibling friendships of youth. Yet it is fair to say that sibling and other early friendships, even if these are not the ones that we would choose for ourselves upon reflection, encourage at a very young age the development of enduring patterns of thinking, feeling, and acting in light of the good of others, patterns that come to have a profound effect on how we relate to others as adults.

There is never a time when we choose, as adults, to become persons in relation. Nevertheless, we do reach an age when we become capable of embracing or trying to reject our relationality. We become capable of giving deliberate shape to the particular network of attachments in which we find ourselves lodged. Obviously, the choices we make as adults regarding the shape of our relationality are deeply influenced by our earliest relationality. In the next chapter, we will consider how, as adults, we can extend ourselves more deliberately toward others as friends and the role that choice plays in this extension.

Five

Aristotle on Friendship and Choice

Aristotle says that brothers are "the same thing, in a way, in different [subjects]" (1161b33). A brother loves his brother, not simply as someone who happens to be like him, but as someone with whom he has come to share a life. He loves his brother as someone with whom he has come to share conceptions of the humanly good, interests, patterns of perception, deliberations, choices, and pleasures and pains.

What of the love with which an adult loves a nonfamilial friend? It is one thing to extend the self's love for itself to someone who has always seemed to be part of the self—someone who has been raised in much the same way, by the same caretakers, in the same home. It is another thing to extend the self's love of itself deliberately to another whose conceptions of the good life, interests, and so on, are notably separate and distinct. Aristotle says that an adult of fine moral character "is related to his friend as he is to himself, since the friend is another himself" (1166a31). In character-friendship, an adult extends his self-love to "another himself" with whom he shares a life.

In this chapter, I consider what it is to regard someone as "another oneself" such that one is able to exercise virtue as an extended, inclusive self. I do so with an eye toward eventually making the case that it is within the context of relationships with "other ourselves" that the virtue of compassion, in particular, is best cultivated and extended toward those whom we might not ordinarily regard as "other ourselves." Our main concern in what follows is with adult character-friendship and its impact on the exercise of moral agency, but let us consider first what Aristotle has to say about the friendship of a parent for his or her child. In Aristotle's view, an adult loves his or her child much as he or she loves his or her adult friend of good character, namely, as "another himself" or "another herself" (1161b28). Yet, as I mentioned previously, the sense in which one's child is "another oneself" seems different from the sense in which a fellow adult of similar character is "another oneself." Attending to differences and similarities in these senses should enrich our account of what it is for an adult to share his or her life with a friend and to exercise virtue *qua* friend.

PARENT-CHILD FRIENDSHIP

What Aristotle says about a father's friendship with his child differs, in certain respects, from what he says about a mother's friendship with her child. Again, I note but reject antiquated stereotypes, picking up on some of Aristotle's ideas and expanding them in a more egalitarian spirit. I do discuss briefly the friendship that pregnant women can sometimes have with their fetuses. A discussion of maternal-fetal friendship should bring into better focus than discussions of friendships between physically discrete selves some important elements of what it means to regard someone as "another oneself."

Regarding the relationship between parent and child, Aristotle has this to say in the *Nicomachean Ethics*:

> Friendship in families also seems to have many species, but they all seem to depend on paternal friendship. For a parent is fond of his children because he regards them as something of himself; and children are fond of a parent because they regard themselves as coming from him. A parent knows better what has come from him than the children know that they are from the parent; and the parent regards his children as his own more than the product regards the maker as its own. For a person regards what comes from him as his own, as the owner regards his tooth or hair or anything; but what has come from him regards its owner as its own not at all, or to a lesser degree.
>
> The length of time also matters. For a parent becomes fond of his children as soon as they are born, while children become fond of the parent when time has passed and they have acquired some com-

prehension or [at least] perception. And this also makes it clear why mothers love their children more [than fathers do].

A parent loves his children as [he loves] himself. For what has come from him is a sort of other himself; [it is other because] it is separate. Children love a parent because they regard themselves as having come from him (1161b16–29).

Again, let us explore and extend some of these reflections in a way that is broadly consistent with Aristotle's ethic of virtue.

LOVING A CHILD AS ANOTHER ONESELF

As we have seen, love for a friend is, in Aristotle's scheme, an extension of self-love. Loving oneself is a matter of wishing and doing good to oneself for one's own sake. It is a matter of actualizing oneself as a person of complete virtue.[1] Loving oneself is also a matter of having affection for oneself. It is a matter of being attracted to and delighting in one's own actualization as a person of complete virtue. Extending one's love for oneself to another, then, will be a matter of wishing for and doing what contributes to another's flourishing for the other's own sake, but where the other's flourishing is regarded as part and parcel of one's own. It will be a matter of being attracted to and delighting in the other's own actualization, but where this actualization is experienced as an aspect of one's own, extended self-actualization.

For Aristotle, a fine parent who takes seriously the task of parenting wishes for, does, and delights in whatever promotes the flourishing of his or her child. To begin with, the (biological) parent wishes for, does, and delights in the bringing of his or her child into existence: "[F]or the parent conferred the greatest benefits, since he is the cause of their being" (1162a6). According to Aristotle's biology, a father is the cause of his child's being in a different sense than a mother is the cause of her child's being. As Nancy Sherman puts it, "the mother's body is regarded [by Aristotle] as merely the accidental matter in which the form, carried by the father's sperm, is instantiated. As such, it is the father, and not the mother, who bears the essential biological relation to the child."[2] Still, both contribute some part of their flesh to their offspring, whether it be semen or nutrients, and Aristotle seems to have something like a fleshly contribution in mind when he says that a child comes from a parent like a tooth or hair.

Of more interest, I think, is the notion that the child comes from her parents as a product from some craft. A parent wishes for, does, and delights in the production of his or her child as a craftsman or an artist delights in the production of an *oeuvre* (1167b34–1168a5). On the one hand, the child is chiefly the work of the male, in Aristotle's view. "The male contributes the principle of movement," actively imparting form to a woman's passive material "by means of the motion he sets up."[3] A woman's matter is needed for the growth and development of the embryo, but it is the male principle that is likened to craftsmanship and artistry: "For the carpenter must keep in close connection with his timber and the potter with his clay, and generally all workmanship and the ultimate movement imparted to matter must be connected with the material concerned, as, for instance, architecture is *in* the buildings it makes."[4]

On the other hand, Aristotle acknowledges that a woman labors hard to produce a child and that this labor gives her a stronger sense than a male has that the product of her labor is indeed hers:

> Besides, everyone is fond of what has needed effort to produce it; e.g. people who have made money themselves are fonder of it than people who have inherited it. And while receiving a benefit seems to take no effort, giving one is hard work.
> This is also why mothers love their children more [than fathers do], since giving birth is more effort for them, and they know better that the children are theirs (1168a23–27).

Aristotle may recognize that a woman labors over the creation of her product even before giving birth at 1161b25, where he suggests that a mother's active relationship with her child begins during pregnancy: "The length of time also matters. For a [male?] parent becomes fond of his children as soon as they are born while children become fond of the parent when time has passed and they have acquired some comprehension or [at least] perception. And this also makes it clear why mothers love their children more [than fathers do]."[5]

A parent thus loves his or her child as a producer loves a flesh and blood product that partially replicates the producer's being and reveals the creative efforts of that being. A parent also loves his or her child as a benefactor loves a beneficiary. A parent wishes for, does, and delights in whatever benefits his or her child. Aristotle addresses the way in which a benefactor regards his or her beneficiary at 1168a5:

1. Being is choiceworthy and lovable for all.
2. We are in so far as we are actualized, since we are in so far as we live and act.
3. The product is, in a way, the producer in his actualization.
4. Hence the producer is fond of the product, because he loves his own being. And this is natural, since what he is potentially is what the product indicates in actualization.

Aristotle is trying to elucidate why a producer or a benefactor loves the product he creates or the person he benefits more than the product or beneficiary loves him. He wants to say that the reason is, in part, because in loving the beneficiary, the benefactor understands and experiences the beneficiary to be himself, his own, or part of him in a way that the beneficiary, in return, does not understand or experience the benefactor. In loving the beneficiary, the benefactor stands to his beneficiary as to "another himself," but what does this mean?

The benefactor who loves his own being, loves being beneficent. He loves the action in which his potential for beneficence is actualized. Indeed, he loves the person whom he benefits because, in being benefitted, that person contributes to the actualization of the benefactor's own best self. In being benefitted, the beneficiary becomes an inextricable part of the benefactor, able to indicate to and on behalf of the benefactor what the benefactor is unable to indicate alone, namely, that he is beneficent. The beneficiary becomes a part of the benefactor's actualizing self most notably when the beneficiary, by continuing to receive and reflect the benefactor's beneficence, makes possible the cultivation of that beneficence over time.

Parents who love their children are like benefactors who benefit themselves in the act of benefiting their child. The way in which the well-being of a parent-benefactor is bound up with the well-being of the child-beneficiary can be elucidated with reference to the relationship that a pregnant and birthing woman can have with the fetus whom she benefits in her labor. A healthy pregnant woman of fine character who wants her fetus and has the wherewithal to give birth to and nurture a baby extends the network of affection within which she is already embedded to her fetus early on in her pregnancy. She becomes explicitly a person in relation to her fetus. She begins to wish and do good to her fetus by watching what she eats, avoiding the drinking, eating, and inhaling of intoxicants, getting regular exercise, talking and singing to her fetus, and so on. She begins to delight in her fetus as it somersaults and kicks, seemingly in response to her mood, movement, or voice.

Precisely in benefitting her fetus, the woman benefits herself. To begin with, she benefits herself as a person apart from her fetus. For example, treating her fetus well has the effect of providing her with some good habits—habits that she might have been unable to acquire previously, but can now continue to cultivate with relative ease well beyond the time of parturition.[6] What is more, she benefits herself as a person who is, "in a way," her fetus—a person who is becoming her own best self partly in relation to this "other herself." As she contributes to the actualization of her fetus, she contributes to her own actualization as a person in love with this fetus. She becomes more and more embedded in this intimate relationship and she assumes more and more initiative and responsibility in its regard. As she delights in her fetus, she delights in the activity that is bringing her fetus into the fullness of human being, which is to say that she delights in the activity that is part of her own actualization as a person in relation to this fetus: she delights in herself. She delights in a self that has become and will always remain partly a self with this child.

The interweaving of mother's good and fetus's good can come to a remarkable fullness in birthing, under certain circumstances. Birthing her child naturally, a woman can experience herself to be fully her own self in the actualization of potentialities that are especially important to her (e.g. her hidden physical strength, her courage in the face of pain, her trust in her own creative powers). Yet she can experience herself, at the same time, to be fully with this child who potentiates her actualization, partly by moving through her as an extension of her own body and partly by moving through her as other-than-her-body. She can experience herself as being actualized with another in undergoing and contributing actively to movements within her body that are both familiar and foreign, captivating and frightening, at once like and unlike movements within her body that are strictly her own.[7]

Obviously, the relation between maternal and infant activity and actualization is more complex than we can capture here. For one thing, there are other relationships that contribute to the mother's identity and have an impact on her changing sense of "mineness" and "otherness" relative to her fetus or infant. Sometimes what is best for the fetus who is partly her/s and yet partly other than her/s is not what is best, overall, for her. Sometimes her fetus's actualization threatens to cause her injury or even death. But sometimes, in pregnancy and birthing, the activity and actualization of a woman and her infant can be brought into a remarkable coincidence empirically and experientially—a coincidence that can be difficult to maintain or, for others, to achieve once the infant is separated from the woman's body. It is therefore worth special attention.

As many committed parents testify, this way of understanding and experiencing another to be part of oneself and her good to be partly one's own continues after the birth of a child as parents seek to nurture and educate the child. Precisely in benefitting their child as an included other, the parents benefit themselves. For example, in seeking to educate their child morally—in seeking to communicate through their own example a vision of good living, an understanding of its component parts, a passion for its pursuit, and a joy in its promotion—parents cultivate within themselves and inspire in each other character traits that can be difficult to acquire apart from the peculiar challenges of parenting (e.g. patience, forgiveness, and tenderness toward what is dependent). The parents are benefitted most when they seek to reveal to their child through their own example what it is to exercise complete virtue as persons in relation—as persons who are finally only "self-sufficient" in their "self-realization" relative to their "other selves" whose good is included in their own.

LOVING A CHILD AS ANOTHER BUT SEPARATE SELF

To love a child as "another oneself" is, for Aristotle, to love the child as an extension of one's body, as an embodiment of one's defining creative efforts, as a beneficiary in whom one's beneficence is realized and revealed. It is, in effect, to love the child as an extension of one's own interests.[8] At the same time, however, it is to love the child as separate from oneself—as someone who has interests that extend well beyond and, in some cases, differ from one's own. It is to wish for, do, and delight in the child's attainment of her own interests for her own sake (1166a1–9). Aristotle says, for example, that "friendship seems to consist more in loving than in being loved. A sign of this is the enjoyment a mother finds in loving.

For sometimes she gives her child away to be brought up, and loves him as long as she knows about him, but she does not seek the child's love, if she cannot both [love and be loved]. She would seem to be satisfied if she sees the child doing well, and she loves the child even if ignorance prevents him from according to her what befits a mother" (1159a27). Implicitly, Aristotle suggests that a parent's love for her child consists partly in letting go of the child and encouraging him to think, feel, and act separately and differently, indeed to live his life apart from her, if this is what best promotes the child's distinctive flourishing.[9]

It seems that for Aristotle this loving of the child as separate is not in a straightforward way a sacrifice for the parent. Even if the parent feels pain in letting go of her child, there is a sense in which she can be said to flourish in her pain, so long as her child is benefitted by the separation that causes the pain. First, if her child is indeed benefitted by the separation, then so, in a way, is she. Insofar as that part of her extended self is benefitted, she becomes an extended beneficiary of her own beneficence. This is not to say that her pain is erased; rather, the pain experienced in this part of her extended self is qualified by the perception that that part of the self is doing well. Second, in benefitting her child, she flourishes in the actualization of her potential for beneficence. The very pain that she feels in letting go of her child can be regarded as a passional component of a proper act of beneficence. To feel due passion in the exercise of an excellence *is* to do humanly well.

Here it is especially clear that, from an Aristotelian perspective, the end of human life is not happiness as *eudaimonia* is often translated, but human flourishing. Human flourishing is accomplished, not in simple and pure pleasures, but in the pursuit and enjoyment of complex and often bittersweet pleasures that leave us vulnerable to and pained by loss, but without which our lives are less than fully human because they are less than fully relational.[10]

Just as a parent loves her child as separate from herself such that she regards her child's good as worthy of promotion for its own sake, a loving parent loves herself as separate from her child, such that she regards her own good, too, as worthy of promotion for its own sake. In fact, a parent will only be able to love her child as separate from her if she first loves herself as separate from her child. This is implied by Aristotle's understanding of the primacy of self-love (1166a12–b2). The parent who loves herself loves that which is best in her, which includes her rational agency and the excellences of mind and character through which her rational agency is exercised. Her agency and its exercise is, of course, shaped by the network of relationships within which she is embedded as a social, political creature, but these relationships do not fully determine or define it. A parent must understand herself to be a unique center of rational and passional activity, and she must delight in this very activity if she is to understand that her child, too, is a unique center of rational and passional activity, and if she is to delight in her child as such, molding the child to a significant degree, but ultimately with the aim of teaching the child how to mold herself—to think, feel, and act responsibly for herself.

In sum, Aristotle suggests that a child is "another but separate self" in the sense that she is partly constituted by contributions of parental flesh, creative and moral effort, and education. A child whose claylike lump of potentiality is shaped deliberately by her parent is a part of that parent's extended body who shares many of his or her loves and pursues these loves with and apart from the parent, actualizing through her own pursuits aspects of the parent that the parent cannot actualize apart from the child. A child is also a part of a parent that is other than what the parent regards as most intimately "himself" or "herself." She has potentialities to shape and loves to pursue that sometimes strike the parent as foreign. Still, the parent feels compelled to make at least some of these loves his or her own, such that the parent is able to become, in the act of promoting his or her child's own interests, something more and other than what he or she thought himself or herself to be.

A parent and a child can come to share a life in much the same way that we have already seen it possible for siblings to share a life. There are, however, two important differences between the sense in which parent and child tend to share a life and the sense in which siblings tend to share a life. First, young siblings who are friends do not have a strong sense of each other *as* other. They tend not to promote each other's rational agencies as separate as well as shared. Parents of good character, on the other hand, seek to benefit their children precisely by providing them with the goods they will need in order to flourish as separate and distinct agents of virtue.

Second, young siblings have relatively undeveloped capacities for practical rationality, but these capacities are relatively equal when the siblings are close together in age. The same cannot be said with regard to a parent and a young child. Although a parent will think, feel, and act inescapably in light of her child's thinking, feeling, and acting, her child is not likely to mold her to the degree that she will mold her child. Her child will have much less influence over the shaping of her deepest visions, values, and habits (most of which are already firmly entrenched in her character) than she will have in shaping her child's. This important inequality makes genuine mutuality of love difficult to achieve between parent and child, at least until the child becomes an adult himself.[11]

CHARACTER-FRIENDSHIP

Aristotle's account of friendship between adults of similar character combines the regard for another's separateness that is apparent (but not likely as sharp) in a fine parent's love for a child with the equality and mutuality of influence that is foreshadowed in sibling friendship. Let us consider, at last, the sense in which an adult friend of good character can be said to love his or her friend as "another himself" or "another herself." What is perhaps most distinctive about adult character-friendship is the role that choice plays in the formation and cultivation of the relationship. Siblings, and parents and their children, are largely stuck with each other. If they want to live good and pleasant lives, each of them has to learn to get along with the other who is already and inextricably part of him, at least until one or the other reaches a point at which he can leave home and cease to spend his days with the other.

The case is different with adult character-friends. As adults, we are to a greater extent free to spend time with whomever we please. If we find that our characters clash with one another's, if we find that we are not good for each other or do not enjoy each other's company, we can to a greater extent choose to spend our time with other people. Of course, this can be a difficult choice to make, especially if the persons involved are a parent and an adult child, grown siblings, spouses, or lovers. Still, some choice is possible and this is important, for (in modern terms) it means that we can be held responsible for the friendships we pursue and for pursuing well those friendships in which both friends thrive.

Choosing to Love a Friend as Another but Separate Self

To love an adult character-friend as "another oneself" is to wish for, do, and delight in the good of someone with whom one chooses to share a life. To choose to share a life with someone is, in part, to choose to spend our days in someone's company (1172a2). Aristotle says that if we are good, we choose to spend our days in the company of people who are good in themselves, good for us, and pleasant to be with (1158a26–27).

We choose to spend time with people who are good in themselves, because it is naturally the good, or the apparent good, that human beings find lovable (1155b18–27, 1156b6–12). We also choose to spend time with people who are good for us, people who are likely, particularly in sharing with us a conception of *eudaimonia*, interests, deliberations, choices, pleasures, and pains, to encourage and participate in our own flourishing.

John Cooper discusses two arguments that Aristotle gives in the *Nicomachean Ethics* regarding the way in which a good friend can contribute to our own flourishing. First, Aristotle argues at 1169b28–1170a4 that human flourishing consists partly in the achievement of self-understanding, and it is in conversation and other activities shared with good friends that self-understanding is best achieved. As Cooper interprets him, Aristotle argues "that to know the goodness of one's life, which [Aristotle] reasonably assumes to be a necessary condition of flourishing, one needs to have intimate friends whose lives are similarly good, since one is better able to reach a sound and secure estimate of the quality of a life when it is not one's own."[12]

Second, Aristotle argues at 1170a4–11 that good living requires the enjoyment of continuous activity, and continuous activity is best enjoyed in sharing one's activity with friends. As Cooper interprets Aristotle, "he argues that the fundamental moral and intellectual activities that go to make up a flourishing life cannot be continuously engaged in with pleasure and interest, as they must be if the life is to be a flourishing one, unless they are engaged in as parts of shared activities rather than pursued merely in private; and given the nature of the activities that are in question, this sharing is possible only with intimate friends who are themselves morally good persons."[13]

Continuous activities engaged in with friends of similar, good character contribute to good living in three principal ways. First, "they provide one with an immediate and continuing sense that what one finds interesting and worthwhile is really so," since someone whom one values finds the same things interesting and worthwhile. Second, "they enhance one's attachment to and interest in one's own personal, direct activities," by putting them within the larger framework of joint activities that are themselves a source of pleasure and interest. Third, "they expand the scope of one's activity," by making it possible for one to be (indirectly) active in and through the activities of friends.[14]

For Aristotle, the kind of activity that we need most to enjoy continuously in order to flourish as human beings is the activity of practical reason. The activities of perception and understanding, in particular, are central to the exercise and enjoyment of human excellence (1170a19). Friendship contributes to human flourishing partly in that it promotes the sustained development of the friends' capacities for perception and understanding. Let us expand on Aristotle's explicit reflections.

Adult persons of good character have reasonably firm, stable values and commitments that consistently inform their perceptions of particulars. Adult friends of similar, good character are attracted to one another largely on account of the fact that they have what appear to be similar values and commitments that inform in similar ways their perceptions of contingent singulars. In the sharing of conversation and other activities, friends give frequent expression to what they perceive in the world around them and this expression serves as an occasion for character-building conversation.

One friend, for example, might perceive a given situation from a different angle than the other. When she realizes this difference in perception, she is likely to examine whether or not her perception is in accordance with her deepest values and commitments, and whether it is consistent with the information available to her. If she finds her perception to be, upon reflection, consistent with her well-formed habits of perceiving as well as with the facts, she will likely challenge her friend to explain and justify his alternative perception. Rising to the challenge, her friend will likely reflect similarly on his own perception, questioning whether it is consistent with his deepest values and commitments, and whether it is consistent with the information available to him.

Upon reflection, the friend may discover that his perception does not quite fit with his deepest values—values that he and his friend have come to share. He may alter his perception accordingly, re-imaging the situation before him in accordance with a different description designed to elicit a different passional response. He may, instead, find that his perception is so acute and moving that it forces a reshaping or overhaul of his values. He may defend his different perception, finding that it is based on some piece of information available to him, but not to his friend or some piece of information available to both, but only brought into consideration as relevant by him. He may discover that his values are basically the same as his friend's, but that he ranks them in a different fashion. As he defends his own perception, he may succeed in altering his friend's perception, in turn.

Back and forth, back and forth. The process is familiar enough to all of us. It is the process of defining ourselves morally in relation to our friends and encouraging our friends to do the same. It is the process of becoming fully who we are by testing and refining our characters in conversation with people who are able, through the exercise of their own moral agencies, to reflect the best and the worst of us back upon ourselves for critical evaluation. It is the process of enabling our friends to do the same testing and refining of their own characters relative to us, such that each of us serves simultaneously as (our own) light and (each other's) mirror. As I hope to make clear throughout this project, the fullest exercise of our capacities for imaginative and passionate perception, as well as for deliberation and commitment to chosen action, is possible precisely in friendship.

Paul Wadell argues along similar lines that, for Aristotle, "[F]riendship stands not just as a single virtue, but also as the relationship by which people become good; it appears as exactly the activity in which we are trained and tutored in the virtues. By spending time together with people who are good, by sharing and delighting with them in our mutual love for the good, we are more fully impressed with the good ourselves."[15] Wadell drives home the point that we *must* spend time with friends who are good, for we cannot become good apart from them.[16]

We must resist the notion that loving a friend as "another oneself" involves one person "losing her identity" in the other, or that it involves "merging" identities in such a way that one or the other of the friends cannot perceive, think, feel, and act for herself. We must also resist the notion that loving a friend as "another oneself" involves doing violence to the other's uniqueness by subsuming it under the category of "the same." These effects can and do occur in friendships as we know them, but they ought not to. In the best of Aristotelian character-friendships, the kind of friendships with which we are concerned in this project, both parties encourage themselves and each other to become fully their own unique selves in intimate relation with each other. Indeed, the best of friends will, in spending their days together, discover that they often see with one eye, feel with one heart, and think with one mind, but each will contribute actively and equally, over time, to the exercise of this one eye, heart, and mind. And each will actualize her own distinctive potential as a rational agent partly in making this contribution. As Aristotle says, "the friendship of decent people is decent, and increases the more often they meet. And they seem to become still better from their activities and their mutual correction. For each moulds the other in what they approve of, so that '[you will learn] what is noble from noble people'" (1172a10–14).

To choose a friend who is good for us, then, is to choose to spend our days with someone who, simply in being herself and seeking to flourish as the relational self that she is, enables us to flourish in relation to her. Notice that, according to this picture, we flourish as persons and as friends partly by encouraging our friends' own flourishing. This is not to say that we encourage our friends to do well simply for our own sakes. Aristotle insists that we encourage them to do well for their own sakes, and one proof of this is that we encourage them to excel at being who they are even when this encouragement threatens to precipitate the dissolution of our friendship by highlighting and exacerbating differences in vision or value.[17] We encourage our friends to flourish primarily because it is good that they should flourish (1168a34). We also encourage them to flourish, however, because we have a deep and personal interest in the well-being of those who are part of us. When they do well—even if it turns out that they do best apart from us—part of us does well as a result.

The claim that our motives for seeking the good of friends are always mixed in this way concerns persons who like to think that the best human loves are selfless.[18] As we proceed, it will become apparent that the idea of selfless love or compassion is highly problematic. The presence of mixed motives in all human loves is an inescapable fact of human psychology. Denying the goodness of mixed-motive love encourages inappropriate feelings of guilt and/or acts of self-deception aimed at denying (while nonetheless suspecting) that one has anything to feel guilty about. It is in excelling at being human in relation to other humans that the greatest enjoyment is found. Those of us who enjoy ourselves enjoy being with people who bring out the best in us. We enjoy being with people who help us excel at being ourselves.

Choosing to Share a Life

If we are good, we choose as friends people who are good, good for us, and pleasant to be with, but what does it mean to *choose* such people as friends? What does it mean to choose to share a life with them such that we become for each other "other ourselves"? We cannot simply choose to meet people who are good, good for us, and pleasant. Even if we do meet people of this sort, we cannot simply choose to make them love us in return. To say that we choose our friends sounds so controlling, when in fact what is involved is one of the most vulnerable of human activities.

Consider a case in which two persons meet and hit it off from the start. If both parties are interested, they choose to spend some time getting acquainted with each other. As Aristotle says, friends "need time to grow accustomed to each other; for as the proverb says, they cannot know each other before they have shared the traditional [peck of] salt" (1156b26; cf. 1157b20–24, 1158a6–11). It is only in spending time together that they can discover whether or not it is likely that, through exercising their rational agencies in association with each other, these agencies will truly come into their own. For Aristotle, "living to its full extent would seem to be perceiving or understanding (1170a17–19). . . . Perception is active when we live with [our friend]; hence, not surprisingly, this is what we seek" (1171b32–35).

In the course of spending their days together, character-friends who take each other to be good and pleasant share activities that weave their lives together: "Whatever someone [regards as] his being, or the end for which he chooses to be alive, that is the activity he wishes to pursue in his friend's company. Hence, some friends drink together, others play dice, while others do gymnastics and go hunting, or do philosophy. They spend their days together on whichever pursuit in life they like most; for since they want to live with their friends, they share the actions in which they find their common life" (1172a1).

Friends who share a life in common "agree about what is advantageous, make the same decision, and act on their common resolution" (1167a27); "they are in concord with themselves and with each other, since they are practically of the same mind; for their wishes are stable, not flowing back and forth like a tidal strait. They wish for what is just and advantageous, and also seek it in common" (1167b5). Central to the activity of sharing a life, in Aristotle's view, is choice: "reciprocal loving requires decision, and decision comes from a state; and what makes [good people] wish good to the beloved for his own sake is their state, not their feeling" (1157b30); "decision is proper to a friend and to virtue" (1164b1).

Let us extend what Aristotle says here about friendship and choice by developing a line of inquiry begun with the discussion of sibling friendship. We need to grasp the role that choice plays in coming to stand to a friend as to "another oneself." We also need to consider the limits of choice. In the long run, these reflections should aid us in articulating what it is, and the extent to which it is possible, to choose to feel compassion toward "other ourselves," as well as toward those whom we might not ordinarily regard as such.

Choosing to Share a Vision of the Good

Friends who choose to spend their days together choose to share a conception of *eudaimonia*. Unlike young siblings and unlike parents and their young children, adults of similar, sound character usually come together with already well-developed visions of good living. In fact, it is largely these ready-made visions, as they are glimpsed in the friends' earliest conversations and activities, that initially attract the friends to one another. Still, the conceptions of good living that each of the friends have developed in relation to significant others in their lives remain conceptions in relation, conceptions open to criticism and contribution from persons whose opinions they value. In living together, friends' conceptions of *eudaimonia* are discussed, challenged, changed, and developed. Most significantly, they are expanded and enriched. For what is important to our friend, who is so much like us and yet whom we respect as separate from us, becomes important to us. Even when our friend values something that conflicts with what we value, it is still likely to be experienced by us as important, worth attending to, and worth trying to reconcile with our own values, because it is of value to someone who is part of us.

Adult character-friends choose to share a vision of good living in that they choose to engage in conversation and activity that reveals, makes more explicit, and challenges one another's conceptions, looks for connections, draws them out, tests them, and seeks lovingly to persuade toward substantial agreement. Friends may sustain important differences in their respective visions, but to the extent that they share a vision in common, these differences are somehow bridged. Friends carry on with the assumption that their differences can and eventually will be mediated with regard to deeper points of agreement. Differences will be understood, appreciated, and even respected as features of a variegated, but unified frame of moral reference.[19]

Choosing to Share Interests

Friends who choose to spend their days together also choose to share interests with one another. One friend may choose to cultivate an interest in something that is already of interest to her friend just so that they can spend more of their time together more pleasurably. One friend may find a private interest of her friend's difficult to understand or appreciate, but she may nevertheless choose to take an interest in the way that that peculiar interest impinges on the other's exercise of her rational agency. Both friends may cultivate new interests together that neither had outside of the friendship, picking up on experiences that both of them have found enjoyable and that provide the opportunity for both of them to expand their minds, hearts, vision, and skills together.[20]

It is significant that, in Aristotle's view, a wife and a husband can be character-friends who share interests in common, even if women's presumedly inferior capacity for rational agency keeps such a friendship from being, in his judgment, as good as exclusively male friendships can be. He notes that children, in particular, can be a common interest that binds the lives of spouses together: "Children seem to be another bond, and that is why childless unions are more quickly dissolved; for children are a common good for both, and what is common holds them together" (1162a26).[21]

Cultivating new interests in order to become more fully involved in a friend's life can be difficult. That which pleases and pains us is fundamental to our character and it is not a simple matter to choose to be pleased by something that we do not already and naturally find pleasing. It is possible, however, for adults to meet with some success in the development of some interests by re-imaging the object or activity in question, by imaginatively redescribing it to ourselves in such a way that it begins to resemble in important respects objects or activities in which we are already interested.

To take a simple personal example, I had never been much interested in professional basketball in my youth, but when I chose to marry a man who loves basketball, it seemed appropriate that I attempt to cultivate an interest in it so that we could enjoy the sport together. What I did was to take note of significant similarities between basketball players and dancers, between the sport of basketball and the art of dance. Re-imaging the play of ball and bodies on the court as a graceful dance, I began naturally to be moved by the players' agility, flexibility, strength, and skill, the choreography of intentional, coordinated movement, and the mutual understanding of and love for the art of basketball among the committed players. Through time, the re-imaging became habitual, it became a spontaneous pattern of perception that engendered spontaneous enjoyment. I could not simply choose to love basketball as I originally perceived it, but I could choose to perceive it in such a way that I would naturally begin to love it, just as I love dance.

Aristotle himself recognizes that we can in some ways choose how we perceive. For example, he says that "What the erotic lover likes most is the sight of his beloved, and this is the sort of perception he chooses over the others, supposing that this above all is what makes him fall in love and remain in love" (1172a29), as if the erotic lovers might, instead, be character-friends if they chose to perceive each other principally as rational agents, attending more to each other's characters than to their outward appearances.

Obviously, there are limits to the possibilities of re-imaging and imaginatively re-perceiving. I could not, for example, re-image boxing as a dance, as some people seem able to do, because the deeply ingrained perception of boxing as physically and morally repulsive is too strong for me deliberately to overcome. Nor would I want to overcome this perception.[22]

Choosing to Share Deliberations and Choices

Friends who choose to spend their days together also choose to share deliberations and choices. Like young siblings, adult character-friends discover as they spend considerable time in each other's company that each deliberates about issues that matter to both of them partly as the other would deliberate on her own, as if the other's voice has become one among a choir of voices that each friend takes to be her own. The way in which deliberations come to be shared between adult character-friends, however, is more intentional, partly because it has to be. For such friends generally come to the friendship already possessing their own ways of knowing, feeling, and reasoning. They have already developed their own styles and habits of deliberative activity, and these styles and habits are bound to differ in significant ways.

Adult character-friends sometimes find themselves focusing on different aspects of a situation as relevant and significant, reasoning differently about those aspects, perhaps with different emphases on logic and gut reaction, drawing on different emotion-laden experiences, counting different reasons and motives for choice to be the more binding. Aristotle does not say so explicitly, but surely he would agree that part of what makes character-friendship so significant to good living is that in it, friends choose to engage each other rationally and passionally in knowledge and appreciation of these differences. Still, friends who choose to spend their days together choose to deliberate with each other as though they were coparticipants in a single deliberative process. They choose, for example, to communicate to each other their unique perceptions of particular situations in ways that are likely to elicit in the other a reaction similar to their own—a reaction that contributes to a full-bodied understanding between them. They choose to reconstruct their own perceptions and ideas in ways that are likely to elicit within themselves a reaction similar to their friend's, making it possible for them to perceive and reason about a given situation from more than one perspective at a time.

As friends engage each other as partners in a common deliberative activity, their separate capacities for perception, thought, and passion are expanded. Each friend entertains the expressed thinking and feeling of the other. Both eventually come to take the other's unique perceptions, thoughts, and passions as seriously as their own. Both find that in time they just notice, not only the things that they used to notice, but also the things that they know the other person notices. They will count as a *prima facie* good reason or motive what they would not otherwise count as such, except that the other counts it as good.

Because this process is mutual and the friends contribute to it equally in the best of friendships, we can see that neither friend "loses her identity" in the other; rather, both extend and enhance their identities by adding to or including the other's identity in their own, attaching themselves deliberately and, eventually, habitually to the other's ways of perceiving and understanding just as they remain attached to their own. Obviously, parts of their old identities will be overhauled and parts of the new identities that they entertain as their own will be rejected. What is important to note is that this process is deliberately chosen by the friends over time. In so choosing, the friends flourish.

Friends who choose to deliberate together also choose to choose together. They do not simply find themselves choosing univocally as young sibling friends often do; they aim at this univocity deliberately. They aim at a sharing of commitment to action in which each friend understands and experiences the commitment as the other understands and experiences it, as the perceptions, thoughts, and feelings that they deliberately share largely compel it. This sharing of commitment in which both friends find their motivations multiplied in kind and, some of them, increased in intensity is something that friends aim at by choosing to share conceptions of good living, interests, deliberations, and so on, because it is one more way in which they can enlarge their own unique capacities for choice at the same time that they feel one another to be intimately part of themselves.

Choosing to Share Pleasures and Pains

Friends who choose to spend their days together also choose to share pleasures and pains. Aristotle says that each character-friend takes pleasure in the other's good (1171b14) as though the other's good were her own. Presumably, there is an element of choice at work even in the sharing of pleasure. It is not simply that one friend perceives the other's pleasure and upon perceiving that pleasure chooses to enjoy it as her own. It is more that both friends form their own characters over time in such a way that they are prone to be delighted at what delights the other and/or at the other's delight, where the pleasure in question is deemed appropriate. That is to say, they choose through a series of well-crafted decisions to become people whose ways of valuing general ends and attending to particular goods set them up to be spontaneously and immediately pleased by the same things that please their friends and/or by their friends' being-pleased.

For example, good character-friends recognize that envy toward one another undermines their capacity for shared enjoyment and they

deliberately seek to uproot it from their characters. One way to do
this is to uproot the beliefs and judgments that partly constitute this
passion—uproot them, reject them, and creatively replace them with
other beliefs and judgments that are equally consistent with the facts, but
more consistent with the passion for intimate friendship. Friends may
recognize that envy includes the belief that the internal and external
goods that they desire for themselves are limited in quantity, such that
when one friend acquires these goods, there are less of these goods to go
around. The friends may, upon reflection, become convinced that the
goods that they desire for themselves are not, strictly speaking, limited
in quantity, and that one friend's acquisition of these goods can actually
contribute to the other's enjoyment of the same (if only vicariously). The
friends may, accordingly, choose together to become persons whose characters are well formed by this insight.

The sharing of pain between friends is the topic of Part III, but it is
worth noting here some of what Aristotle has to say about it. Aristotle
says that a noble person chooses to share the pain of his friends. He
chooses, presumably, to develop habits of reason-guided, passionate reception and response that dispose him to be pained at what pains his
friends, or at least at his friend's being-pained.[23]

Strikingly, Aristotle says that a noble person chooses to suffer with
friends in their pain, but he does not allow his friends to suffer with him
in his pain.

> The very presence of friends is also pleasant, in ill fortune as well
> as good fortune; for we have our pain lightened when our friends
> share our distress. Hence indeed one might be puzzled about
> whether they take a part of it from us, as though helping us to lift a
> weight, or, alternatively, their presence is pleasant and our aware-
> ness that they share our distress makes the pain smaller. Well, we
> need not discuss whether it is this or something else that lightens
> our pain; at any rate, what we have mentioned does appear to
> occur.
>
> However, the presence of friends would seem to be a mixture [of
> pleasure and pain]. For certainly the sight of our friends in itself is
> pleasant, especially when we are in ill fortune, and it gives us some
> assistance in removing our pain. For a friend consoles us by the
> sight of him and by conversation, if he is dexterous, since he knows

our character and what gives us pleasure and pain. Nonetheless, awareness of his pain at our ill fortune is painful to us, since everyone tries to avoid causing pain to his friends.

That is why someone with a manly nature tries to prevent his friend from sharing his pain. Unless he is unusually immune to pain, he cannot endure pain coming to his friends; and he does not allow others to share his mourning at all, since he is not prone to mourn himself either. Females, however, and effeminate men enjoy having people to wail with them; they love them as friends who share their distress. But in everything we clearly must imitate the better person (1171a28–1171b13).

Even if we overlook the sexism expressed in these passages, many of us will judge Aristotle's perspective on the sharing of pain to be seriously misguided. Extolling the solitary suffering of one's own pain as "manly" serves to disguise and perpetuate an all too common fear of relational vulnerability.[24] Sharing one's pain with a friend does require becoming exposed to that friend, revealing some of the deepest and darkest secrets of one's soul to him or her, and surrendering control over how he or she reacts to those secrets. Perhaps he or she will think one crazy, weak, burdensome, bad, too intense, too demanding. Perhaps when he or she finds out what is really in one's heart he or she will love one less, thereby increasing the pain that one already feels. To the extent that one refuses to take a risk and reveal one's pain to a friend, however, one makes it impossible for that friend to share one's life. One fails to contribute adequately to the intimacy of the friendship.

If both friends "imitate the better person" and choose not to allow the other to share their pain, compassion will not likely occur between them.[25] Both persons will be deprived of the lightening of pain that the sharing of pain can accomplish, both will be deprived of the active exercise of complete virtue, and both will fail to understand and love each other for who they really are. If only one person "imitates the better person," then the relationship will be deeply unequal and the person who alone is willing to bare her soul will rightly lose patience with and trust in the other—unless she loves the other as a therapist and not as a friend whose own development of character is of interest and importance to her.

As Martha Nussbaum makes manifest throughout *The Fragility of Goodness*, Aristotle distinguishes himself from other ancient philosophers in encouraging his readers to acknowledge and even value the ways in which certain human vulnerabilities condition the choices of character. While he recognizes the value of being vulnerable vis-à-vis friends in suffering their pain as our own, however, he fails to recognize the value of being vulnerable in sharing our pain with them. He neglects to make clear that both types of sharing contribute to the intimacy and, hence, the value of our friendships. We would all agree that there are certain pains that are inappropriately shared in certain ways with certain friends at certain times for certain reasons. Rather than reject outright the notion of sharing one's pain with others as "unmanly," however, it seems better to pursue the mean. We will explore this possibility in Part III.

CHOOSING TO FEEL IN FRIENDSHIP

As we have seen, character-friends choose to spend time together, and in spending time together they choose to share conceptions of *eudaimonia*, interests, deliberations and choices, and pleasures and pains. They choose to regard each other as "other themselves" in that they contribute deliberately as separate and distinct centers of rational and passional activity to the exercise of a common, extended moral agency. They choose to wish for, contribute to, and delight in the good of each other, partly from the perspective of what remain their own, separate agencies, and partly from the perspective of what has become a web of jointly coordinated and cultivated habits of perceiving, thinking, feeling, and valuing.

Just as choice is at the center of the individual's rational activity, choice is at the center of those friendships in which individuals flourish as rational agents. Good friends choose to give impassioned, intelligent shape to their friendships. We ought not to get the impression, however, that friendship is a shared activity wholly constituted by reciprocal acts of will. Clearly, it is not. As Aristotle recognizes, mutual good will is necessary for friendship, but it is not sufficient, "since it lacks intensity and desire, which are implied by loving" (1166b33). It also lacks an acquired familiarity with and enjoyment of each other's presence, both of which are typical of friendship (1158a9). Aristotle points to the deep fondness that develops in familial and nonfamilial friends as they continue to spend their days together, a fondness that consists partly in mutual understanding, accustomedness, and trust (1158a15, 1161b25–28,

1162a12–13, 1171a12). He also likens the love of character-friends to erotic passion in that both are a kind of "excess" that can only be felt toward a few people at a time (1158a12–13, 1171a12).

It is unfortunate for us that Aristotle did not take the opportunity to explore in more detail the passional component of character-friendship and its relationship to the erotic. We cannot pursue the topic here, partly because it would require defining and defending an account of the erotic. But if we take the erotic to be more (and sometimes other) than the narrowly genitally sexual, and take it to be something like a fullness and intensity of physical as well as emotional feeling that permeates the whole of our thinking, perceiving, and feeling as persons in relation,[26] then we will surely want to recognize that the best of character-friendships have an erotic dimension. Intimate character-friends not only respect each other's goodness and experience a kind of "intellectual pleasure" in the sharing of conversation and other activities. They also long for each other's physical company. They are physically and emotionally stirred and delighted by each other's embodied presence (where these feelings may or may not have a genitally sexual component).

But if friendship is understood to be, in part, an intense, passionate, mutual attraction toward and delight in one another, can one really be said to choose a friend? Can either friend choose to become attracted and attached to the other with this sort of affection? Aristotle's ethic of character implies that we can choose to be attracted to what is good partly by choosing to be good ourselves. Insofar as *we* are good, we will be attracted to others who are good and we will enjoy ourselves in their presence. But does this sort of attraction amount to anything more than a feeling of admiration? It appears that, for Aristotle, character-friends feel more than admiration for each other in their goodness. They enjoy in each other's company an intimate sense of communion that, at some point in the sharing of a life, transcends the rational calculation of relative goodness. Can this sense of communion itself be chosen?

To eliminate the elements of passional spontaneity, vulnerability, and luck from an account of our closest character-friendships would be un-Aristotelian. It would reduce these friendships to something "cool and institutional,"[27] something that Aristotle did not, in my judgment, intend to do. Still, Aristotle's ethic of character implies that the powerfully passionate aspects of friendship are themselves, to some extent, subject to choice. Friends can and do choose, for example, to engage in activities that bring them sheer delight in each other's embodied presence. They can and do choose to take up new activities with each other when the fire in their relationship begins to smolder. They can and do choose to culti- vate ways of perceiving each other that highlight each other's most attractive intellectual, emotional, and physical qualities. True enough, character-friends are attracted to each other chiefly on the basis of each other's character, but it cannot be denied that a person's character often finds partial expression in things like her physical appearance and her level of physical fitness. Friends can and do choose, to some extent, to attend in their passionate perceptions to those physical expressions that bespeak what they take to be each other's most lovable qualities of char- acter. They can and do choose, to some extent, to regard tenderly those expressions that bespeak each other's deepest vulnerabilities and weak- nesses.[28]

We will have more to say about the passional dimensions of character-friendship when we turn in the next two chapters to Thomas Aquinas's account of friendship. Before we make this move, however, a final comment on Aristotle's account is in order. Aristotle does not en- courage friendship between persons and gods. A god is so superior in goodness to a person that the sharing of a life between them is not to be expected. Friendship can only be expected between relative equals in virtue (1158b33–1159a1). Moreover, human beings are so constituted that their becoming fully human involves their continuing to need friends. A god, on the other hand, does not need friends (1159a5–14). As we shall see, Thomas insists on the Christian God's transcendence relative to God's creation, but he maintains that friendship between God and persons is nevertheless possible and worthy of pursuit.

To sum up, we have seen in this and the previous chapter that for Aristotle, the self's love for a friend is an extension of its love for itself. The self is an already-relational self who comes to know and to love itself in knowing and loving others who know and love it in return. It is a rela- tional self that learns rather early on in life to extend its love of itself deliberately to its "other selves," some of whom are in a position to con- tribute with the self to the construction of a shared moral agency and some of whom are not. The self who participates with an adult other in the co-construction of a shared moral agency retains the sense of itself and its other as distinct seats of thinking and feeling. At the same time, however, it acquires an uncanny sense that its thinking and feeling are part of a larger movement of integrated thought and passion, a movement over which it does not exercise complete control. The self who participates in this larger movement has the sense that the other contributors to this movement are its "other selves" in that the self and these others to some extent think the same thoughts and feel the same feelings, extending and altering these thoughts and feelings through shared conversation, much as the self extends and alters its own thoughts and feelings through its own processes of rational reflection.

Recalling our discussion of parent-child friendship, we can conclude that, like a parent in relation to her child, the adult character-friend regards her friend as "another herself" partly in that she makes creative contributions to the formation of his character, much as a craftsperson gives form to her craft. But in the case of adult character-friendship, these contributions are made by both friends with approximate equality and mutuality of power and influence. It is especially evident in the case of adult friendship that part of what the friends love in each other is what becomes of their contributions to each other when these contributions are received, altered, and reflected back as altered by separate centers of rational and passional activity.

Like a parent in relation to her child, the adult character-friend also regards her friend as "another herself" in that she is able to realize and reveal, in benefiting her friend for his own sake, excellences that she cannot realize and reveal apart from him. But in the case of adult character-friendship, once again, the deliberate benefiting and the enjoying of extended self-actualization is approximately equal and mutual. It is most evident in the case of adult character-friendship that when friends seek to benefit each other mutually, they gain in each other's company a sense of trusting community that enables them to recognize and actualize potentialities that they did not even know they had.

The sense in which a friend stands to her friend as to "another herself" is something that we shall pursue throughout the rest of this project. Aristotle's insights will have to be stretched further than we have already begun to stretch them if they are to provide us with a grasp of relational selfhood that is adequate to account for the phenomenon of compassion. As a step in the right direction, let us return once again to the thought of Thomas Aquinas. Thomas's reflections on friendship extend Aristotle's reflections on "other selfhood" in powerful ways.

Six

Thomas Aquinas on Friendship

Thomas embraces much that Aristotle has to say about friendship, but goes on to give it a distinctively Christian twist. Actually, the story is more interesting than this, for Thomas attends in the *Summa Theologica* to an aspect of friendship with which Aristotle only scarcely deals, namely, its passional aspect. Thomas focuses in a way that Aristotle does not on the manner in which a lover is passionally moved by his or her beloved in friendship. As we have seen, Aristotle says that friendship is more than wishing well to each other for each other's own sakes; friendship includes "intensity and desire, which are implied by loving" (1166b33). Aristotle has little to say, however, about the nature of this intensity and desire. Examining what Thomas contributes on this score will deepen our understanding of what it is to love a friend as "another oneself," and will thus prepare us to discuss what it is to exercise a virtue like compassion *qua* friend.

FRIENDSHIP DEFINED

According to Thomas, "that which is loved with the love of friendship is loved simply and for itself" (I–II 26.4). A friend "wishes and does good to his friend, by caring and providing for him, for his sake" (I–II 28.3). A friend wishes and does for his friend what will promote his friend's attainment and enjoyment of his own, proper good (I–II 26.4), and of course, friendship's well-wishing and doing are reciprocal (I–II 28.2).

A friend wishes and does good to his friend as he wishes and does good to himself because he stands in relation to his friend as he stands in relation to himself. He stands in relation to his friend as though his friend "were himself or part of himself" (I–II 28.1 *ad* 2, 26.2). "Hence a friend is called [one's] *other self* [*alter ipse*] (*Ethic.* ix.4), and Augustine says (*Confess.* iv.6), *Well did one say to his friend: Thou half of my soul*" (I–II 28.1).

A friend "stands to the object of his love, as to himself," says Thomas, on account of a certain "bond of affection" that exists between them (I–II 28.1). What is the nature of this bond? Taking the point of view of the lover, Thomas speaks of it as a "dwelling" of the beloved "in" the lover or a "dwelling" of the lover "in" the beloved (I–II 28.2). On the one hand, the beloved is said to be "in" the lover,

> inasmuch as [the beloved] is in [the lover's] affections, by a kind of complacency: causing him either to take pleasure . . . in [the beloved's] good, when present; or, in the absence of the [beloved], by his longing, to tend . . . towards the good that he wills to the beloved, . . . not indeed from any external cause, . . . but because the complacency in the beloved is rooted in the lover's heart.

On the other hand, the lover is said to be "in" the beloved,

> inasmuch as [the lover] reckons what is good or evil to his friend as being so to himself; and his friend's will as his own, so that it seems as though he felt the good or suffered the evil in the person of his friend. Hence it is proper to friends to desire the same things, and to grieve and rejoice at the same, as the Philosopher says (*Ethic.* ix.3 and *Rhet.* ii.4).

The beloved is "in" the lover insofar as the lover "wills and acts for his friend's sake as for his own sake, looking on his friend as identified with himself." The lover is "in" the beloved insofar as the lover "reckons what affects his friend as affecting himself" (I–II 28.2).

The bond of affection that is characterized by Thomas as a "mutual indwelling" is an effect of "love" (*amor*), where "love" refers to the passion of love, proper (I–II 26.2). The passion of love is an initial change wrought in a person's sense appetite by a sensible object that is perceived to be delectable. In a wider sense, love refers also to a change wrought in a person's intellective appetite or will by an object that is believed or perceived by the intellect to be good. In either case, the nature of this change in appetite is difficult to nail down.

Thomas says that, when a lover perceives his beloved, his appetite is changed by the beloved in such a way that it acquires a kinship (I–II 27.4), aptness (I–II 27.4), or adaptation (I–II 26.2) toward the beloved. The lover's appetite is acclimated to the beloved in such a way that the lover enjoys a sense of natural suitability (I–II 26.1 *ad* 3) or connaturality (I–II 27.1) with the beloved. Thomas distinguishes carefully the passion of love from the movements of desire and joy:

> whatever tends to an end, has, in the first place, an aptitude or proportion to that end, for nothing tends to a disproportionate end; secondly, it is moved toward that end; thirdly, it rests in the end, after having attained it. And this very aptitude or proportion of the appetite to good is love, which is complacency in good; while movement towards good is desire or concupiscence; and rest in good is joy or pleasure (I–II 25.2).

Love as complacency is a moment in the love of friendship (*amicitia*) that precedes the desire to spend time with the beloved in the enjoyment of shared activity. It is a moment of reception in which the lover's attention is gently captivated by and attuned to the beloved, such that the lover feels accustomed to the beloved and begins to soak the beloved's presence in with pleasure.[1]

The principal cause of love as complacency is the likeness of the beloved to the lover. As Thomas indicates,

> For the fact that two [human beings] are alike, having, as it were, one form, makes them to be, in a manner, one in that form: thus two [human beings] are one thing in the species of humanity, and two white [human beings] are one thing in whiteness. Hence the affections of one tend to the other, as being one with him (I-II 27.3).

When the other is perceived to be like the self in respects that are important to the self, the self has the impression that it is already apportioned to the other. The self has the impression that it has already received the other as he is in himself by virtue of the fact that the other is, in a way, already present in the self. The love that the self has for itself is extended with ease and with pleasure to that which is so much like the self that it seems already to *be* the self.[2]

In sum, friends wish and do good to each other as they wish and do good to themselves because they are bound to each other by a kind of affection. The affection that we are considering here is not, strictly speaking, the desire "to live together, speak together, and be united together in other like things," although friends certainly do wish for and do what promotes the sharing of a life in common (I–II 28.2 *ad* 2). The affection that we are considering is something prior and prerequisite to such desire. It is a receptivity to the desires, the pains, and the joys of the other. It is a way of receiving the desires, pains, and joys of another into the self, such that they seem to the self to become partly the self's own. Friends wish for and do what promotes each other's good, all the while bound to each other's good as they are to their own.

Recall that, for Thomas, love for a friend is an extension of love for the self. Broadly speaking, the complacency, the desire (including the well-wishing), and the joy that one feels toward a friend is an extension of the complacency, the desire, and the joy that one feels toward oneself. In the remainder of this chapter, we will deepen our grasp of the affection that binds friend to friend by exploring the way in which the self is bound in self-love's complacency to itself, and the way in which the self is able, on account of being thus bound, to extend its complacency toward another. I believe that understanding self-love's complacency is basic to understanding what it is to share a life and, indeed, a self with "another oneself," according to Thomas.[3]

COMPLACENCY IN THE RELATIONAL SELF

Thomas does not describe in any detail the aspect of the self's love for itself that we are calling complacency in the self, but what he says, in general, about complacency can serve as a foundation upon which to build. As we have already begun to see, complacency is a kind of refiguring of the self's appetite (I–II 26.2 *ad* 3). It is a restructuring that takes place as a beloved object penetrates the self, introduces itself into the self's intention, impresses itself upon the self's appetite, and takes root therein (I–II 26.2, 28.2, 28.2 *ad* 3). It is a reorienting of the self's appetite according to which the self apprehends the beloved object as belonging to its own well-being (I–II 28.1). As the Latin term *complacentia* suggests, a certain pleasure attends the adaptation of the self's appetite toward the beloved. The complacent self enjoys an initial sense of agreeableness and at-homeness vis-à-vis the beloved.

Accordingly, we can say that self-love's complacency is an altering of the self's appetite in which the self receives an impression of itself, finds the impression agreeable, and feels at home with the self so perceived. In self-love's complacency, the self becomes familiar with some of its deepest and most characteristic beliefs, values, and passions as well as its more spontaneous meanderings of thought, will, and feeling. It assents to and takes repose in the self's orientation and activity with an implicit trust that the self is well disposed to pursue and enjoy its distinctive human good.

The self that rests in the reception of its perceived self rests also in the reception of others who are perceived to be like it in important respects. Receiving an impression that another's chosen or spontaneous patterns of perceiving, feeling, reasoning, valuing, acting, and enjoying are consonant with its own, the self simply perceives the other *as* its own. It receives the other in such a way that the other seems to the self to be, together with the self, part of a single, extended self. The other's good appears to the self to be included in its own good, such that the self is set up to desire the other's good in the act of desiring its own. Loving the other as part of itself, the self quiesces in its inclusive self, gently embracing and enjoying a sense of connectedness and accustomedness to the other, resting assured that the inclusive self is fit to pursue the good of both self and included other well.

Of course, the self in which the complacent self rests is a dynamic self. Apart from the included other, the self is a desiring self that is never completely at rest in itself. It is a desiring self that is always captivated by and drawn toward some further good of the self. Accordingly, resting complacently in the self will involve becoming alert to the self's natural dynamism, attending to some of the desires that contribute to this dynamism, becoming familiar with these desires, and assenting to their pull. It will also involve trusting the mysterious, ineffable source of this pull, quiescing in the power of being that animates the self's desire.[4]

Similarly, resting complacently in the self *qua* inclusive of another will involve being impressed by something of the other's peculiar dynamism. It will involve taking in, or being taken in by, desires that seem to have seeped through the porous bounds of the other's self and become partly one's own, multiplying, intensifying (or perhaps, diminishing by contrariety) what one desires apart from the other. It will also involve being impressed by the power of being that incites the other's dynamic being, as if the other's inclusion in the self brings with it a further inclusion of this power, a more extensive participation therein. It will involve feeling pleasantly at home in this extensiveness.

If we recognize in the love of self and its included other not only a quiescence in particular beings, but also a quiescence in the power that animates particular beings, then we can imagine how it is that one self can sometimes have an unusually direct access to the experience of another self. Self-love's complacency is a moment in which the self's deepest and most basic manner of heeding and consenting to the power that enlivens it can come into step with that of another. It is as if self and other are placeholders for the same power, and the self is able, by virtue of its characteristic accustomedness to this power, to slip spontaneously into the place of the other, as it were, from the ground (of being) up, so as to share to some extent the place of the other (without necessarily losing its previous place). Where the slippage occurs on the part of both selves and in relation to each other, the selves enter into and meet in a common, extended space, the boundaries of which are defined for them by their shared resting in being's initiative toward them.

The self encounters in this slippage a *distinctive* other. It is taken up into being's propulsion as it meets with and animates the other in his particularity. It is captured by the other at the base of his personality, where finally unique configurations of desire emerge from the abyss of subjectivity. Where the slippage is mutual, each self is caught up in and compelled by something of the other's peculiar reception and response to being's drive.

In the resultant synchronicity of desire, the lover seems to "stand to the object of his love as to himself." He participates in the other's appetitive movements in a direct and immediate way, such that there seems to him to be no discernable gap between the movement of appetite in which he participates and the implicit sensing or understanding of that movement as his own. When the lover reflects explicitly upon the movement in which he participates, he then comes to understand and, if appropriate, assent to that movement explicitly, just as he understands and assents to movements of appetite that are strictly his own. When he reflects upon the particular nature of these movements, he then begins to interpret and define them, in accordance with what he perceives to be the case and in accordance with the way has learned to label desires that arise within himself.[5] Prior to reflection, however, the movements of which we speak are best described as inchoate and undefined lurings or propulsions.

We have begun to describe the nature of self-love's complacency as it extends to include the other. This is one way of approaching the sense in which friends can sometimes be "in" each other such that they find themselves feeling, wanting, willing, and even thinking with some degree of synchronicity. We have pointed to an enduring moment in the love of friendship wherein a lover is captured by and quietly assents to the movement of being in its enlivening and informing of a particular other. This is a moment in which the boundaries between separate selves are experienced to be porous and permeable and the lover finds herself slipping, as a participant in being's movement, into the unique movement of another, allured or impelled to a limited extent as the other is allured or impelled. In such a moment, it becomes ambiguous and perhaps irrelevant who is "in" whom, for the lover experiences herself with the other to be one, extended self. In friendship, of course, this experience is mutual.[6]

As we illuminate the self's complacency in itself and the way in which this complacency opens the self up to the experiences of other selves, we inevitably run into the movement of desire and the joy that attends the fulfilling of desire. The love of friendship toward the self and toward its "other selves" includes, not only the movement of love, but also the movements of desire and joy. Clearly, love, desire, and joy, along with a range of other passions, will often be felt at the same time with respect to different dimensions of a complex situation that are attracting attention and eliciting response.

It is worthwhile, however, to isolate the moment of love as reception because it calls attention to the fact that reception conditions response. It enables us to discern that a failure to respond well to another person often has its roots in a failure to receive well. It also enables us to discern that receiving well is largely a matter of being open, vulnerable, permeable, and pliable vis-à-vis the other. It is a matter of comporting oneself so that one is readily captivated by a particular other and made fit to respond to her as she is in herself.[7]

Notice that the change wrought in love's complacency does not take place initially by means of reflective, rational judgment and evaluation. It takes place by means of the more immediate pull of appetite. This insight is crucial to the construction of a realistic theory of the passions. As we have seen, a passion like anger is partly caused and constituted by cognition—by perception, belief, judgment, and evaluation. But explicit, passion-defining cognition tends to emerge only on the heels of more or less immediate apprehensions of sense. These immediate apprehensions can elicit desire well before we are able to identify and specify the intentional content of our desire.

To be sure, there is no impression upon appetite without perception, and all perception of which we are aware is to some extent interpretation. Hence, even the initial reception that we have been highlighting will have some implicit, if not explicit, cognitive content. However, there is much to a given passion that precedes the more reflective evaluative judgments by which the passion comes to be defined. There are primitive, inchoate impressions made upon the appetite, which elicit a spontaneous assent to and participation in the movement of being in its animation of particular beings. By the time we are reflectively aware of these impressions, they have already begun to become something other than gut reactions. They have begun to be formed with the help of further cogitation into a particular passion.

COMPLACENCY AS THE CRADLE OF DESIRE

We slide right past complacency and into the movement of desire when that in which we are complacent is a desiring human being—when reception of another's desire spontaneously elicits the sharing of desire. Yet there is a distinction between the sharing of desire in complacency and the subsequent movement of the self's own desire that needs to be brought out and kept in mind. Thomas does not elucidate the distinction as I do, but what he says about complacency and desire seems to be consonant with this distinction.

In love's complacency, "the foundation and possibility in the structure of the will for the transcendence of the distinction between self and other" is established.[8] In complacency, the self flows into and out of the other freely and with ease—taking in, or being taken in by various elements of the other's changing desiderative bearing. The complacent self desires something of what the other desires as a participant in the other's desiring.

Desire, on the other hand, is more than a passive reception of the desire of another. It is an active response to the reality of another, made by a self that is more than the included other. In loving another, the self's own, separate desires that have not been taken up into consonant movement with the other's desires make themselves known. They call attention and affection to the fact that self and other are not identical. For as much as their desires may overlap, self and other are constituted *as* self and other partly by virtue of the fact that they embody different configurations of desire.

As we shall see and pursue further in Part III, it is this difference and the experience of it that provides the self with some of the perspective on the other's desire that it needs in order to assess wisely what can and ought to be done to benefit the other in her particular predicament. This perspective is not present in complacency. Still, complacency provides the self with something that desire cannot provide, namely, an immediate (albeit partial) access to the other as she is in herself. It may be that this access only amounts to a foggy impression of the other's experience that cannot be articulated without loss of felt meaning. Nevertheless, this impression is of considerable moral value. It serves as the cradle of love's desire in that it helps to form, support, and nurse developing desires within the self in such a way that they remain attentive and responsive to the desires of the other.

A friend who desires a beloved's good for the beloved's own sake deliberately works to accomplish this good (I–II 28.2), but attentive and responsive wishing and working, too, are cradled in love's complacency. Conditioned by complacency, a friend wishes and works so as to benefit the other partly *as* a participant in the other's wishing and working to benefit herself. Caught up in the wishing and the working of another, a friend will sometimes come to reflect explicitly, "I have been responding to my friend as though I were her (or she were me)! For a moment there, I was so much a part of her (or she was so much a part of me) that we seemingly ceased to be separate selves!"

The order here is significant (I–II 28.1). A person does not, in Thomas's judgment, enter into the love of friendship by explicitly judging that another person is so like him in respects that are important to him that she constitutes another himself, and by concluding that he ought therefore to love the other as he loves himself, whereupon the appropriate feeling, thinking, willing and acting are engendered. Rather, a person is passively taken by another upon perception of the other. He is taken up spontaneously into another's wanting and working, and it is only upon reflection that this takenness is explicitly noticed and acknowledged. Indeed, the lover receives the beloved as like him, but he receives her more by means of an immediate sense of kinship and accustomedness than by means of explicit judgment.

In calling attention to the priority of complacency in the love of friend for friend, Thomas adds a depth dimension to Aristotle's account of friendship. Aristotle enables us to construct a rather thick account of what it is to share a life with someone. He helps us to conceive of how we can share beliefs, perceptions, deliberations, choices, actions, pleasures, and pains so as to stand to our friends as to "other ourselves." But what Thomas enables us to do is to look behind or beneath these activities of shared living at some of the more passive and amorphous goings-on between friends. He helps us to conceive of the way in which we must take each other in, or allow ourselves to be taken in by each other passionally if the intimate sharing of a life is to be possible. He points with subtlety to the vulnerability, pliability, and trust that are crucial to our relational self-comportment. He points to a needed openness toward the power of being itself that prepares us to be captivated and penetrated by a particular other's being, allowing careful reason to be momentarily caught off guard.

COMPLACENCY WITHIN THE CONTEXT OF CHARITY

For further reference to the self's love of friendship toward itself and the extension of this love toward others, we must turn to Thomas's treatment of charity in the *Summa*. As we have seen, charity is a theological virtue. It is a habitual disposition of the intellective appetite to be united with God in a shared love of friendship. Thomas also speaks of charity simply as friendship with God.[9] Just as friendship with God transforms acquired moral virtue, friendship with God transforms the ways in which we love ourselves and each other. In what follows, I continue to explore what it is to love the extensible self with a love of friendship, only now I focus on what it is to do so within the context of a friendship with God.

From what we have said about the love of friendship toward others, we can surmise that, for Thomas, the love of friendship toward ourselves includes a resting with complacency in ourselves and, within the context of this complacency, a wishing and a doing of good to ourselves and an enjoying of ourselves for our own sakes. We can also say, in a broadly Thomistic vein, that as such, the love of friendship toward ourselves includes a familiarizing of ourselves with and an assenting to the power of being that courses through our body-selves and allures us out of bed each morning. It includes a responding to this power in a way that promotes our distinctive human flourishing.

Of course, as soon as Christian beliefs and affections come into play, shaped as these will be by the theological virtues and their attendant gifts, this power of being in which we become complacent is identified and experienced as the Power of Being (i.e. the divine being), and the actions and passions in which we flourish acquire implicit or explicit reference to this Power. Let us consider what self-love might look like for Thomas within a Christian context. Thomas says surprisingly little explicitly about the shape that self-love takes in a good Christian life, but what he does say provides us with a basis for further reflection.

Thomas says that, to the extent that we enjoy a friendship with God, we love ourselves "out of charity," i.e., with a love for God that is extended to include all whom God embraces as God's own (II–II 25.4, 26.3). He says that we enjoy "a certain union in relation to God," which entails that we have "a share of the Divine good" (II–II 26.4), and in charity, we assent to ourselves as partakers of this good. Assenting to ourselves, we assent to the Power that propels us into being ourselves. We become accustomed to the Power that seems in some ways to be other than us and yet so much a part of us that apart from our relation to it, we would simply cease to exist.

Complacent in ourselves, we rest in the reception of our God-related selves. Thomas admits that, strictly speaking, we cannot be said to be friends with ourselves because friendship implies union between separate beings, whereas we are identical with ourselves "which is more than being united to another" (II–II 25.4). Yet in charity, we love ourselves as friends of God (II–II 25.4), which means, in part, that we rest in the reception of ourselves from Another who is separate from us and yet so like us in important respects that we take our reception of the Other to be the very inception of ourselves. It may not be the case that we love ourselves as "other ourselves," but it *is* the case that we love ourselves in the restful reception of ourselves from Another, where the Other is one in relation to whom we stand in the act of standing in relation to ourselves.

Recall that, with the infusion of charity (as well as faith, hope, and the attendant gifts) we receive from God a supernatural orientation. We conceive a desire for supernatural human happiness, and we are made "proportionate" or fit to attain the object of this desire by means of the "elevation" or enhancement of our capacities to know and to love. We are taken up by God into a preliminary participation in the *logos* and love of God by which God knows and loves Godself. In a sense, then, we receive in charity "higher" selves to whom we assent in a "higher" way. We *do* receive "other ourselves" to whom we assent with deepened knowledge and intensified passion as our own, renascent selves.

Pressing Thomas to extend his understanding of love as complacency to the love of self as God's enables us to identify in the self's love of itself a moment of self-reception prior to self-response—a resting in the reception of our elevated selves prior to exercising our elevated capacities for realizing our elevated end. In this quiescence, we gain a peculiar access to the Source of our new selves. Moreover, we gain access to other selves who are conceived (and elevated) by the same Source. Resting in our received selves, we rest in the Conceiver (and Elevator) of selves, which allows us to rest, to some extent, in God's conception (and elevation) of selves other than our own. We are poised, as co-participants in the knowing and loving of God, to be caught up spontaneously in certain of our neighbors' movements of (elevated) knowing and loving.

Resting in ourselves, then, we come to rest in God's knowing and loving of us. Resting in the knowing and loving of God for God's creatures, it becomes possible for us to know and to love these creatures with a depth and intimacy akin to God's. By pressing Thomas to account for an aspect of complacency in the love of the self as God's, we can identify and begin to articulate a moment of reception prior to the responsive pursuit of supernatural happiness in which we simply soak in the Presence that makes the pursuit of such happiness possible. Absorbing that Presence, we are prepared to absorb something of the presence of others who too have their being and their good in that Presence. Pressing Thomas in this way, we can locate a moment of reception in which we are made fit to share in the life of God and to share in an enhanced way in the lives of others. Surprisingly, we see that all of this is accomplished simply in loving ourselves well.

I am pointing here to a connection between the Power of Being and all of that Power's created human beings, which permits humans to undergo as partly their own certain of each other's experiences of being human. A Christian ethic must uphold the notion that if we do not, in loving ourselves, experience ourselves to be more than ourselves, opened up to a Horizon larger than our own egos, vulnerable and receptive to the presence of other persons within this Horizon—and instead, we experience ourselves to be absorbed and enclosed in our own self-concern and self-enjoyment, oblivious to the needs of others—then we are loving ourselves in the wrong way, not loving ourselves at all, or loving the wrong selves. From a Christian ethical point of view, genuine self-love is prerequisite to love of others at least in part because it is in self-love that we discover that we are already embedded in others, that others are embedded in us, and that all of us are embedded in God.

CHARITY'S IMPACT ON DESIRE

Moving beyond complacency, Thomas indicates that loving ourselves is a matter of wishing, doing, and enjoying what contributes to the good of ourselves (II–II 25.7). Because we are God-related selves, the content of our good is properly conceived with reference to God. Thomas agrees with Aristotle that human flourishing consists, in part, in the exercise of complete virtue, but as we have already discussed, Thomas insists that complete virtue is exercised, not only in respect of the rule of reason, but also in respect of the divine measure. Moreover, it is exercised with divinely enhanced capacities for attaining that measure. In short, wishing, doing, and enjoying in self-love what promotes our well-being means pursuing in friendship with God those activities of reason and passion that constitute our highest possible perfection in this life—those excellences that constitute our preliminary engagement of God as friend.

For Thomas, friendship with God depends ultimately on God's free gift of Godself (II–II 24.3), but graced with God's presence in the form of infused habits and gifts, we are moved and enabled to embrace a fuller and fuller participation of this presence by exercising our (elevated) rational nature in the pursuit of good and the avoidance of evil, remaining receptive to God's continued instruction and assistance, and allowing God to reform ever more completely our vision of the good and our commitment to its realization (II–II 24.4, 24.5, 24.6). Open to God's perfecting presence, we are directed and empowered in our rational nature to submit ourselves more and more completely to the will of God, allowing charity "to have a greater hold on the soul and the likeness of the Holy [Spirit] to be more perfectly participated by the soul" (II–II: 24.5 *ad* 3).

We are directed and empowered in our rational nature to love God above all things, to subject ourselves to God entirely by referring all that we have and are to God, to follow God's commandments, and to make "an earnest endeavor to give [our] time to God and Divine things, while scorning other things except in so far as the needs of the present life demand" (II–II 24.8). We are directed and empowered to give our "whole heart[s] to God habitually, viz., by neither thinking nor desiring anything contrary to the love of God" (II–II 24.8).

Because our pursuit of friendship with God is, in Thomas's understanding, an activity of our graciously elevated rational nature, Thomas concludes that it is preeminently to the perfection of this rational nature that we must attend in loving ourselves well (II–II 25.7). Our sensitive and corporeal nature ought to be of secondary concern. Distinguishing between proper and improper love of self, Thomas says:

> Those who love themselves are to be blamed, in so far as they love themselves as regards their sensitive nature, which they humor. This is not to love oneself truly according to one's rational nature, so as to desire for oneself the good things which pertain to the perfection of reason: and in this way chiefly it is through charity that [a person] loves himself (II–II 25.4 *ad* 3).

Interestingly, Thomas reckons that the self and the self's body are two separate things to be loved in two different ways (II–II 25.12 *ad* 2). He also reckons our souls to be more ourselves than our bodies are. Accordingly, he deems our souls to be the more lovable (II–II 25.7). What is more, Thomas says that our neighbors' souls are more closely associated with our souls than our own bodies are, "as regards the participation of happiness"; hence our neighbors' souls are to be loved by us more than we love our own bodies (II–II 26.5, 26.5 *ad* 2).

THE EMBODIMENT OF COMPLACENCY AND DESIRE

While we would indeed wish to articulate an intimate connection that exists between separate persons who share in the same life of God, we must appreciate that this connection is one between whole persons in their embodied subjectivities. Keeping our focus on self-love and returning for a moment to complacency, we must be sure that self-love's complacency is construed as an embodied complacency. As we receive our new selves from God in the inception of our elevated subjectivities, we receive embodied selves whose bodies, too, are elevated by God and made capable of a fuller, richer experience of the divine in our lives. Resting in the reception of our wholly new selves, we experience a renewal in our very flesh and bone.

Accordingly, as our enfleshed self-assent opens us up as whole persons to the Power that animates and elevates the whole of ourselves, we receive and assent to this Power, too, with the whole of ourselves. This means that our complacency in God is in part a change wrought in our bodies; it is in part a change wrought in our sense appetites. Thomas opens a window to this possibility when he says that, "it is natural to the soul to be united to the body; it is not possible for the perfection of the soul to exclude its natural perfection" (I–II 4.6). Hence, "the soul desires to enjoy God in such a way that the enjoyment also may overflow into the body, as far as possible" (I–II 4.5). Although Thomas is speaking here of the joy that attends the fulfillment of desire, what he says of joy has implications with respect to the principle of that joy, which is complacency (I–II 25.2). If the perfection of joy requires the "charm and perfection" of bodily good, then the perfection of complacency requires a bodily-appetitive fitness for this charm and perfection (I–II 4.6 *ad* 1).[10]

Within the context of an embodied complacency in the self as God's, loving ourselves well means wishing, doing, and enjoying holistically what contributes to an embodied friendship with God. The whole of ourselves are made fit in charity to seek and enjoy God and the whole of ourselves are called to respond accordingly. This means that we love ourselves well in the divinely inspired and assisted pursuit of physical and passional, as well as intellectual and volitional, excellence. It means that each of these activities, properly balanced and integrated with the others and referred to God as ultimate end, make necessary, valuable contributions to our flourishing as friends of God.

Enjoying our newly embodied selves with God, we are gifted with an intimate knowledge and love of God. We are gifted with a gut level conviction that God is indeed God-with-us, a God who is involved in the whole of our fleshly lives and reveals, in our most exhilarating pleasure as well as our most excruciating pain, that we are deeply embedded in and warmly embraced by a larger Horizon of meaning and value. I believe that our pleasures and our pains can themselves be modes or aspects of our knowing and loving of God-with-us. In order for us explicitly to experience them as such, they must be interpreted, but we must not reduce the knowing and the loving to the interpreting and the being-moved in interpreting. Unless the interpretation is partly constituted by the pleasure or the pain itself, it will lack a viscerally felt sense that the interpretation is true (and too, that the interpretation cannot entirely capture the truth). And unless the affective response to the interpreting of the pleasure or the pain is in part constituted by the original pleasure and pain, this response will lack a sense of its embeddedness in our most primitive movements relative to Being's creative initiative.

Pressing Thomas to view the God-related self as a unified self, we can conclude that loving ourselves well means seeking and enjoying as well-developed, well-integrated, well-balanced selves whatever promotes the sharing of these selves with God. We shall pursue further in the following chapter the sense in which we can share our selves with God as friend. Before we can do this, however, we need to pursue further the sense in which we can share our selves with humans as friends, only now within the context of charity. In Thomas's scheme, an understanding of God as friend is modeled after an understanding of human friendship, just as an understanding of human friendship is modeled after an understanding of self-love.

Seven
Thomas Aquinas on Friendship and Choice

In loving her friend, a person wishes and does good to her friend as she wishes and does good to herself because she stands to her friend as she stands to herself. We have explored the way in which the self-loving self stands in relation to itself, with a focus on the way in which it rests with complacency in itself. Because the self is a relational self that loves other selves partly in the act of loving itself, our exploration of the self's complacency in itself has already prompted some consideration of the way in which complacency orients the self vis-à-vis others. In what follows, we shall explore further the way in which the self-loving self stands in relation to other selves and extends its love of itself toward them. We will consider first what it is, for Thomas, to regard a friend as "another oneself" and to love him as such. We will consider second what it is to regard God as a friend and to love God as such. Our discussion of friendship with God will prepare us to consider finally what it is—and how it is possible—to extend the self's love of itself toward strangers and even enemies.

LOVING A FRIEND AS ANOTHER ONESELF

Thomas says that the self regards as its "other selves" beings who are like it in important respects and who communicate this likeness to it through the sharing of conversation and other activities over time. The self regards as its "other selves" beings who commune with it, particularly in respect of features of the self that seem to the self to make it distinctively who it is.

IN THE COMPANY OF SIMILAR BEINGS

To begin with, Thomas says that similitude is a constitutive cause of friendship. The similitude that he has in mind is partly similitude of "species":

> [T]he very fact that two [human beings] are alike, having, as it were, one form, makes them to be, in a manner, one in that form: thus two [human beings] are one thing in the species of humanity, and two white [human beings] are one thing in whiteness. Hence the affections of one tend to the other, as being one with him; and he wishes good to him as to himself (I–II 27.3).

Similitude of species implies similitude with respect to the basic qualifications that make human beings what they are. It implies, for instance, likeness with respect to the capacities or the potentialities to envision, desire, and seek deliberately the good of human flourishing (II–II 25.3).

From Thomas's Christian perspective, similitude of species implies likeness in being created by God to "attain to [our] last end by knowing and loving God" (I–II 1.8). All human beings belong to God and receive from God an invitation to participate with God in the fellowship of everlasting happiness (II–II 23.1 passim and *ad* 2). Hence, "from the very fact that we share along with our neighbor in something received from God, we become like . . . our neighbor" (II–II 26.2 passim and *ad* 2).

Thomas also seems to have in mind similitude with respect to other, more particular characteristics. He appears to take for granted that friendship requires "some sort of proportion in the accidental qualities pertaining to the species, some equality of intellectual endowment, some similarity of appetites, some parity of temperament, of character, even of social status."[1] He notes, for example, that different sorts of friendship are based on different sorts of similitude: "friendship among blood relations is based upon their connection by natural origin, the friendship of fellow-citizens on their civic fellowship, and the friendship of those who are fighting side by side on the comradeship of battle" (II–II 26.8). Thomas acknowledges Aristotle's distinctions between friendships of character, utility, and pleasure, and he seems to take for granted that friendships of character are based upon similitude of visions, loves, patterns of perceiving particulars, habits of deliberating and choosing, and so on (II–II 23.1 *ad* 3, 23.3).

Again from Thomas's Christian perspective, similitude of particular characteristics would seem to include similitude with respect to explicit desires for God, interests in and commitments to study, worship, prayer, the increase of charity, and service. That is to say, a believer who "makes an earnest endeavor to give his time to God and Divine things"—a believer who "gives his whole heart to God habitually, viz., by neither thinking nor desiring anything contrary to the love of God"—will most readily regard as "another himself" someone who has a similar kind and level of commitment (II–II 24.8). Thomas cites Jerome as saying, *"True friendship cemented by Christ, is where men are drawn together, not by household interests, not by mere bodily presence, not by crafty and cajoling flattery, but by the fear of God, and the study of the Divine Scriptures."*[2]

It is one thing to say that two selves are the same in that they possess many of the same formal or accidental qualities. It is another thing, however, to say that two selves who are the same or similar with respect to such qualities constitute the same self. In other words, it is one thing to stand to someone as to "another self," but it is another thing to stand to someone as to "another oneself." Thomas indicates that parallel sameness cannot generate "mutual indwelling" unless there is "some kind of communication" between the separate selves (I–II 28.2, II–II 23.1)—some kind of community or fellowship that is made possible by the deliberate and sustained sharing of conversation and other activities (II–II 23.1 *ad* 1, 25.3). Friends' lives interpenetrate only when friends choose to "seek a suitable and becoming union;—to live together, speak together, and be united together in other like things" (I–II 28.1 *ad* 2).

IN THE COMPANY OF ANOTHER "I"

There is yet another kind of similitude prerequisite to friendship that Thomas points to only implicitly in his discussion of complacency. Robert Johann has given this kind of similitude eloquent expression in *The Meaning of Love*.[3] Johann reminds us that similitude is a cause of friendship only because love of the other is an extension of self-love. If we did not love ourselves, then we would not love others whom we perceive to be like us. We love ourselves as *objects* with a definitive set of universal or particular characteristics, but we love ourselves also and more basically as *subjects* of our own, characteristic activity. And we love our friends in the same way. What does this entail?

Qua subject, says Johann, the self

> is a subsistent plenitude revealed to itself in its own immanent activity; a generous abundance of being open to itself, not indeed as a pure datum of introspection, capable of being isolated and determined by a collection of attributes, but as affirmed and attained in the act by which it poses itself. This profound source is, therefore, unequaled by the knowledge had of it. It is a wealth, a richness, an expansive power of action, present indeed, but never wholly rejoined, never exhausted; always experienced as capable of new manifestations, new revelations. And it is this original and subsistent value, seized in the existential act of giving itself to itself, that I love when I love myself.[4]

If we love ourselves in receiving and assenting to our unique, irreplaceable, and ultimately incommunicable subjectivities,[5] and if we love others in the manner that we love ourselves, then part of our love for our "other selves" will consist in our receiving and assenting to *their* unique, irreplaceable, and incommunicable subjectivities. But how can we become complacent relative to a subjectivity that, like a horizon, recedes from our grasp every time that we make a move in its direction?

Other selves must be taken in and made "one" with us if we are to rest in their subjectivities as we rest in our own, and yet other selves must be taken in as somehow separate from us if they are not simply to be appropriated by us as objects *for* us. To put the matter differently, we must be taken out of ourselves and transported ecstatically into the self-presence of other selves if we are to be united with them as they are in and to themselves (I–II 28.3). "If the other has to be one with myself for me to love him as myself, he will have to be so in his very otherness. That very trait which irreducibly separates him from me must also unite us; in our very diversity there must be sameness."[6]

What trait do human beings possess that unifies us with our "other selves" even as it distinguishes us from them? Johann refers to it as the "plenitude of Being, present in every being by reason of immanence." He argues that, in relation to our "other selves," our most profound identity in difference consists in our own and each other's unique—and uniquely human—participations in the inexhaustible wellspring of Being: "with its unique subsistence thus rooted in, and constituted by, the creative presence of the one Absolute, each creature, in its very uniqueness, becomes one by likeness with every other."[7]

Taking each other in or being taken in by each other as unique manifestations of the same Power of Being means acquiescing in the Power itself as we make it present in and to ourselves and each other.

> God the Creator, present in all, is loved in all and above all. But this unique Value, as participated, is indistinguishable from that core of reality proper to each creature, its own subsistence. It is the presence of this Value in the creature that is the creature. Hence each creature is a unique value, yet communing in its uniqueness with every other creature in the Unique Value. Since, therefore, what I love in being is the presence of the Absolute, I can love it in the other as well as in myself. And since as in myself it is myself, and in the other it is himself, so my own proper good, loved in myself, can be found by likeness in the other in the very trait that irreducibly distinguishes him from me, his proper subsistence.[8]

As participants in the same Power of Being, persons who love each other as "other themselves" stand to themselves and to each other as to one Self that reveals in separate and uniquely embodied subjectivities different sides of the same Face. Captivated by and attuned to the one side (themselves), they are, at the same time, captivated by and attuned to the other (each other).

Once again, parallel sameness is not the same as "mutual indwelling." To become "one self" with respect to each other, separate selves must communicate to each other something of the unfathomable depths of their subjectivities, and they must be gripped by each other's communications such that they become present to each other as I and Thou. In Johann's words,

> I am not present to the *self* in the other if I see in him merely a variety of impersonal qualities and attributes that might equally well be found in others. Rather must I somehow grasp the presence of a living and original intention, the profundity of personal consciousness. . . . To love the other directly, I must somehow be present to

that unique principle of action which he is in himself, to the veritable subject with all his depth and mystery. It is to this inexhaustible source that my love looks, to this subsistent plenitude whose "very presence enchants me" and to whom I would supply whatever is needed for his complete development.[9]

When separate selves encounter each other as I and Thou, they not only touch in each other that which makes them irreducibly who they are as separate selves, they also touch the Unity in which their separate selves are mysteriously grounded.

Selves can encounter each other as I and Thou momentarily without even intending to do so, but the love of friendship would seem to require intentional, reciprocal, repeated encounters that add up to an enduring sense of community. To use Martin Buber's language, "the pure relation can be built up into spatio-temporal continuity only by becoming embodied in the whole stuff of life. It cannot be preserved but only put to the proof in action; it can only be done, poured into life." When separate selves choose to encounter each other in the midst of their shared activities as I and Thou, life for them "becomes so permeated by relation that this gains a radiant and penetrating constancy in it. The moments of supreme encounter are no mere flashes of lightning in the dark but like a rising moon in a clear starry night."[10]

To summarize, the self-loving self regards as its "other selves" beings who have the same nature, the same basic capacities for realizing a variety of human excellences, the same interests in human flourishing, and the same rootedness in the Power that makes human being and flourishing possible. The self regards as its most intimate "other selves" those beings who engage it in dialogue and other character-building activities that transform parallel sameness into a community of being.

BENEFITING THE OTHER "I"

Similitude and communion, as we have seen, are constitutive causes of friendship. Thomas says that together, similitude and communion generate a "union of affections," according to which friends regard each other as belonging to each other (I–II 28.1). Similitude, communion, and (mutually known) mutual affection are not, however, sufficient in themselves to constitute friendship. In order for friends to become, in the requisite sense, "one self" vis-à-vis each other, they must also be bound together in (mutually known) mutual benevolence. For Thomas, friends stand to each other as to "other themselves" insofar as each of them wills the good of the other and works for it, just as she wills and works for her own good. Friends stand to each other as to "other themselves" insofar as each of them wills and works for the other's good, for the other's own sake, with the sense that the other's sake is included in her own sake (I–II 28.3 *ad* 3, 28.2).

In light of our discussion of similitude and community, we can begin to grasp how this wishing and doing are possible. It is possible to wish and to work for another's good as we wish and work for our own because it is possible to regard another's good as part and parcel of our own good. In Johann's words, the other's good consists in "his complete unfolding and expansion in being, the full development of that power to love which he is."[11] But this unfolding is, in a sense, an aspect of our own unfolding. More precisely, it is an aspect of the unfolding of the Self in whom each of us has our source. Each of us flourishes as we *and* our "other selves" emerge more and more fully, in our unity as well as our diversity, from the depths of our common Source.

While we naturally seek to benefit our friend partly for our own (extended) sake, we can still be said to seek his benefit for his own sake.

> I tend to [my friend], not as to an object to be possessed, but as to a subject to be cherished for himself. The charm with which he envelops me comes from the sole fact that *he exists*. If my love has an ambition, it is to render him infinitely lovable; its one goal, his total flowering in existence. If I am enriched by his goodness, and I am more than words can describe, it is precisely because somehow I attain it in itself, as unique.[12]

The other's good and my good are separate in that each of us is destined to reveal another aspect of the Power of Being, but the other's good and my good are the same in that both goods are, at bottom, aspects of the divine good.

A friend wishes and works for the benefit of her friend for her friend's own sake, but where her friend's sake—her friend's flourishing— is regarded as integral to her own flourishing. To recover Thomas's mode of expression, a friend wishes and works for the other that the other "may be in God" (II–II 25.1), i.e., that she may enjoy with God and with the rest of God's befriended "the fellowship of the spiritual life, whereby we arrive at happiness" (II–II 25.2 *ad* 2). In light of our discussion of Thomas on theological virtue, we can say that friends will wish and work for what contributes to each other's perfection in charity (II–II 24.8). They will engage each other in conversation and activity that is designed to help each other love God as much as possible, love subordinate ends only to the extent that they contribute to the love of God, understand God's will more clearly, reason more lucidly about how God's will might be carried out, and commit more strongly to the carrying out of that will. They will seek to provide each other with the help they need to avoid sin and its causes, namely, ignorance, unruly passion, and malice (I–II 76, 77, 78).

In sum, the love of friendship toward another self "denotes a certain union of affections between the lover and the beloved, in as much as the lover deems the beloved as somewhat united to him, or belonging to him, and so tends towards him," wishing and doing good to the beloved for the beloved's sake, with the sense that the beloved's sake is ingredient in his own (II–II 27.2). The union of affections that Thomas has in mind is a union that is effected on the basis of certain commonalities that we have with all rational creatures, but it is a union that is effected also on the basis of commonalities that we have with only a few. The commonalities are ones that we cultivate by pursuing in the company of particular others "some fellowship in life"—some fellowship in which the commonalities that we share make possible a profound communion (II–II 25.3). As Johann makes clear, the communion that Thomas's ethic points to, if only obliquely, is a communion in which separate selves are able to discover, to disclose, and to develop—face to face—the uniquely two in the same One.

LOVING GOD AS FRIEND

Charity, says Thomas, is "a certain spiritual union" with God that "makes us adhere to God for [God's] own sake, uniting our minds to God by the emotion of love" (I–II 62.3, II–II 17.6). It is "a kind of friendship of [human beings] for God" (II–II 23.5). If charity is indeed a friendship between human beings and God, then it must be a relationship of mutual affection between human beings and God in which humans wish and do good to God for God's own sake and God wishes and does good to humans for humans' own sakes. It must be a relationship that constitutes, between humans and God, the intimate sharing of a life. But how is it possible for human beings to have a relationship of this sort with that which "transcends [human being] on all sides"?[13] Is the notion of human friendship with God a meaningful one?

Leo Bond tackled this question decades ago in his article, "A Comparison between Human and Divine Friendship." It will be helpful for our purposes to recall his analysis. Bond begins by making the point that, within a Thomistic framework, speaking about God as a friend requires speaking analogically: "any relationship which is spoken of as existing between [humans] and God is understood to exist, really and formally, only in [humans], since real non-subsistent relation is something which pertains to the created order only."[14] Accordingly, "the term 'friend' applied to God and to [humans] is of necessity an analogous one, as is every term that is applied to both God and [humans]."[15] Nevertheless, analogous predications can be true ones, and Bond attempts to show that between a fine human being and God, "there exists a true friendship, friendship according to the commonly accepted and literal sense of the word."[16]

GOD AS SIMILAR BEING

Bond proceeds by considering the principal prerequisites of human friendship and by explicating the sense in which these prerequisites can be predicated of human friendship with God. As we have seen, friendship between humans requires, to begin with, similitude. It requires similarity of species, similarity with respect to certain accidental qualities pertaining to the species, and similarity in the possession and exercise of ineffable moral agencies that have their source in the same transcendent Mystery. Is there a comparable similitude between humans and God that can justify referring to a relationship with God as a friendship? Bond maintains that, for Thomas, there is.

First, persons are like God in that we are created in the image of God. We proceed from God as creatures from a perfect Creator, and we represent God in our tendency toward creaturely perfection (I 35.2 *ad* 3). Bond interprets Thomas as saying that humans represent God most fully in our tending toward intellectual perfection.[17] I would argue that, for Thomas, humans represent God most fully in our tending toward moral, as well as intellectual, perfection. We are in the image of God in that we are created to find our complete repose in knowing and loving God and all that is God's (I 19.1 passim and *ad* 2; 19.2).

Second, persons are like God in that our creaturely intellects and wills are conformed to the reality of God in the act of knowing and loving God. Our intellects are conformed to the reality of God insofar as God becomes for us an intentional object—an object that is "intentionally present in the intellect in such a·way that the intellect in act *is* the thing known in act."[18] According to our natural human powers, we cannot have as an intentional object God as God is in Godself, for the Uncreated cannot be made an object of creaturely intention without being made into something other than what it is. We can, however, have as an object of our intention God as God is for us—e.g., God as First Cause abstracted from the creative effects of that Cause.

> The form of God with which [the human being] thus becomes in-
> tentionally identified, though it does not represent the intrinsic
> nature of God, is, nevertheless, a true form, representing God as per-
> fectly as [God] can be represented in the merely natural order, and
> the assimilation or conformity to God which [the human being]
> thus achieves is the closest assimilation to God which is attainable
> by the purely natural powers of the human intellect.[19]

Similarly, our wills are conformed to God insofar as the finite image of God-for-us becomes something in which we become complacent—insofar as our finite human knowledge of God elicits in us an initial sense of kinship with God.[20] This sense of kinship makes us like God in that it constitutes a partial impression upon our appetites of the presence of God. Impressed with God's presence, we are assimilated to God in that we are made fit to long for the increased fullness of God's presence. We are made fit to tend toward our own goodness in God with an intensity that exceeds our comprehension. According to Thomas's epistemology, "Knowledge is perfected by the thing known being united, through its likeness [i.e. through an image], to the knower. But the effect of love is that *the thing itself* which is loved, is, in a way, united to the lover. . . . Consequently the union caused by love is closer than that which is caused by knowledge" (I–II 28.1 *ad* 3, my emphasis).

Third, and more significantly, similitude is achieved beyond the natural realm through the supernatural elevation of our natural human capacities. As Bond notes, "it is by reason of [the human being's] natural ability to become assimilated to God through knowledge and love, that he is capable of being elevated to a state of supernatural knowledge, love, and similarity by grace."[21] With the infusion of grace in the form of the theological virtues, the infused virtues, and the gifts, human beings are assimilated to God in that they are made capable of knowing and loving as participants in the very knowing and loving of God.

For example, with the infusion of faith, it becomes possible for human beings to know God as more than God-for-us. It becomes possible for us to form a representation of God that more closely approximates the nature of God as God is in Godself.

> While by natural knowledge the intellect knows God under the limitations of an object proportioned to its own mode of being and knowing, in supernatural knowledge through faith, the intellect is elevated to know God as [God] is in [Godself], not clearly and perfectly as in the beatific vision, but in an obscure and veiled manner, by adhering to the divine truth on the authority of God.[22]

With the infused capacity to assent to the revealed truths of religion, it becomes possible for the human intellect to have as its object "that which is also the proper object of the divine intellect, though it knows that object in a mode different and far inferior to the mode in which God" knows it.[23] Persons of faith are like God, partly in that their infused habit of knowing God constitutes a preliminary participation in God's own knowing of Godself.

Through charity, an even fuller assimilation becomes possible, according to Thomas. As we have seen, Thomas holds that,

> whereas the intellect is assimilated to an object by drawing it, as it were, into itself, the will becomes assimilated to an object by going out to that object as it is in itself. The intellect is assimilated to its object only as it is represented within itself, while the will, though it depends upon and presupposes the representation of the object

in the intellect, is not limited to that representation, but its act terminates directly at the object itself.[24]

In charity, our appetites are impressed by and conformed to God as God is in Godself. They are made fit to "go out to" and become united in the act of loving with a God whose very essence is love, but whose mode of loving cannot be comprehended fully by the intellect, even in faith. Persons of charity are like God partly in that their infused habit of loving God constitutes a preliminary participation in God's own loving of Godself.

In light of our earlier treatment of the theological virtues, the infused virtues, and the gifts, we can gather that, for Thomas, all of these habits taken together dispose us to be like God. They dispose us to be like God, not only in that they orient us to love God as God is in Godself, but also in that they orient us to love all created beings as God's. They dispose us to desire and to enjoy *with* God the good of all that we know in faith to be God's. As knowers and lovers who are caught up in God's own knowing and loving of what is God's, "we are said to be good with the goodness which is God, and wise with the wisdom which is God (since the goodness whereby we are formally good is a participation of Divine goodness, and the wisdom whereby we are formally wise, is a share of Divine wisdom)" (II–II 23.2 *ad* 1).

Finally, let us recall the perspective of Johann. The human self is like God in that its knowing and loving of God and God's creatures, especially as this knowing and loving are elevated by God into a more than humanly perfect participation of God's own knowing and loving, is the same knowing and loving by which the self properly knows and loves itself. In each case, the object of the knowing and the loving is, at root, the same. For what the self knows and loves in itself is that which makes it distinctly and irreplaceably who it is, but that which makes the self uniquely who it is, is that which unites the self to God (and through God to other selves), i.e., *this* self's subjectivity *qua* grounded in the Absolute. Loving the self as embodied subject, says Johann, "I give and devote myself explicitly to the full unfolding in being of this . . . unique subjectivity to which I am present in myself, and which as in me is myself."[25] And yet devoting myself to the unfolding of this subjectivity amounts to devoting myself to the unfolding of Absolute Subjectivity itself, in its myriad concrete manifestations, for "What indeed do I love in myself but a value that transcends me on every side?"[26]

[T]he most profound and original orientation of our spirit is, not toward the self confined within the limits of our proper nature, but towards a *Thou*. That is why a [person] becomes himself only in existing more intensely, only in suspending his life from values that surpass the narrow limits of his own existence—and this does not mean the effacement of the *I* before an impersonal ideal, but on the contrary an adhesion that is eminently personal to the Source of all personality.[27]

The self is like God, then, in that the very act in which the self properly knows and loves itself as this particular subject is a participation in the Act in which God knows and loves Godself as Subject—the Subject in which all created subjects have their being.[28]

In the Company of God

Once again, if similitude is to yield something more than parallel sameness and unfold into the intimate sharing of a life and even a self, there must be a deliberate exchange of thought and feeling between the friends over time. Is this sort of exchange possible between human beings and God? Bond frames the question a bit differently. Taking for granted that the exchange of thought and feeling requires mutual knowledge, he asks: "How then, are God and [a human being] to know one another?"[29] Bond recalls that, for Thomas, "God is in all things by [God's] power, inasmuch as all things are subject to [God's] power; [God] is by [God's] presence in all things, as all things are bare and open to [God's] eyes; [God] is in all things by [God's] essence, inasmuch as [God] is present to all as the cause of their being" (I 8.3). On account of the fact that God is "in" a human being in these ways, says Bond, it is plain that "God knows [a human being] far more intimately than [the human being] knows himself. [God] knows [a human being's] every thought, his every desire, his every motion."[30] Hence, there is nothing that a human being can say to God, even in prayer, that God does not already know. God's knowledge of human beings is thus sufficient to serve as a partial ground of friendship.

With respect to a human being's knowledge of God, Thomas says that, "there is a communication between [human beings] and God, inasmuch as [God] communicates [God's] happiness to us" (II–II 23.1). Paul Wadell explains that, in Thomas's scheme, the happiness of God is the

activity that God performs eternally in accordance with God's proper
function, which is "the friendship love between Father and Son that is
Spirit." God's happiness is the "everlasting community of friendship love
we call Trinity, where love offered is love wholly received and wholly re-
turned, where the perfect mutuality of love between Father and Son is
the Spirit of Love."[31]

As we have seen, God communicates God's happiness to us by cre-
ating us with natural powers sufficient to "acquire at least an indirect
knowledge of the nature of God by reason of the natural law which was
impressed upon [us] in creation."[32] God communicates God's happiness
to us by elevating and conforming our minds and our hearts in a more
perfect way to God's goodness through the infusion of supernatural
habits. God communicates God's goodness to us also by means of revelation as recorded in Christian scripture. In Thomas's view, "All the
knowledge that it was necessary for [us] to have about God in order to
make friendship with God possible in this life was communicated by
Christ to His Apostles and through them to all [humankind]."[33]

The knowledge that God has of us and the knowledge that we have
of God is, for Thomas, a necessary basis for friendship. The *communicatio*
of which Thomas speaks, however, includes more than mutual knowledge per se. It includes "a certain familiar colloquy" between humans
and God—an intimate fellowship in which the lives of humans and God
are intricately intertwined (I–II 65.5). Keeping our extended analysis of
friendship between humans in mind, a relationship with God that is
modeled on human friendship will have to include something like a
weaving together of perceptions, beliefs, and desires through the deliberate sharing of conversation and activity over time.

Something like this occurs, according to Thomas, when God communicates Godself to us and we assent to being ordered by God's communication. To be sure, it would be a mistake in Thomas's view to say
(even analogically) that God's perceptions, beliefs, and desires are shaped
through God's encounter with us, as Thomas's God is ultimately immutable.[34] It would not be a mistake, however, to say that the perceptions, beliefs, and desires of human beings are formed and continually
reformed in our encounter with God, such that we come into our own
precisely by being drawn more and more fully into God or by allowing
God to become more and more present within us. The more we engage
in the loving contemplation and the active embodiment of the divine

Truth and Goodness—the more this Truth and Goodness become our own—the more capable we become of receiving and responding to all things through the eyes of God.[35]

According to Bond's analysis, similitude and communication are prerequisite to friendship, but they do not constitute its essence. With reference to Thomas's commentary on Aristotle's *Nicomachean Ethics*, Bond defines the essence of friendship as "mutual benevolence, mutually known, and based on an honest good,"[36] where mutual benevolence is taken to be habitual and efficacious, such that we are "always prepared actually to do what is in [our] power to promote the welfare of the other," and "honest good" refers to the good of virtue, which is desired for the other, for her own sake.[37] This definition is limited in that it does not take explicit account of the mutual affection that binds friend to friend. One could argue, in Bond's terms, that a discussion of similitude and communication is sufficient to account for the element of mutual affection, but then mutual affection comes off as a mere prerequisite to Thomistic friendship, which is wrong (II–II 27.2). We would do best, I think, to stick to our working definition of friendship, according to which friendship is a relationship of mutually known and reciprocal affection in which friends wish and do good to each other for each other's own sakes. This definition is the same as Bond's, except for the explicit addition of the element of mutual affection.

Affection

We have seen that, for Thomas, friendship "denotes a certain union of affections between the lover and the beloved, in as much as the lover deems the beloved as somewhat united to him, or belonging to him, and so tends towards him" (II–II 27.2). In charity, human friends are attracted to each other as unique and irreplaceable (albeit imperfect) embodiments of divine goodness. They take complacency in each other's goodness, and they desire to embrace and delight in this goodness more and more through time.

Thomas maintains that the best sort of love between friends is an intellective love in which friends rest in each other's elevated capacities for rational excellence and seek mutually the perfect exercise of these capacities.[38] Yet he recognizes that human friends are embodied creatures who encounter each other as such. They are beings who gain knowledge of each other's goodness partly by means of sense apprehension, and they are beings whose apprehensions of sensible goods elicit movements of the sense appetite, i.e., passions. It would seem, then, that even the most intellective of human friendships will include a kind of affection that is appropriately characterized as passionate. Despite comments to the contrary,[39] Thomas seems to hold that friends with bodies remain bound to each other, even in charity, by at least some of the "eagerness" of sense desire (II–II 27.2). They continue to feel in each other's presence an "intense" sense of intimacy and connectedness (II–II 26.7).

Regarding the mutual affection that binds human beings together with God, Thomas holds that God desires in God's own fullness and perfection to spread abroad God's goodness to God's creatures (I 19.2). God is not drawn to us out of lack or need, according to Thomas, but out of a desire to infuse God's created goodness into us and enjoy it with us (I 20.2, I–II 65.5). Human beings are drawn toward God in God's goodness. Unlike God, however, we are drawn toward God not simply in the desire to celebrate God's or our own abundance, but partly in the desire to meet our needs. We are attracted to God as to our highest good, the possession and enjoyment of which completes us as persons in relation to God (I–II 3.8).

For Thomas, that which binds God and humans together is the reciprocal movement of intellective, rather than sense appetite. God is without passible bodily organs and therefore has no sense appetite; movements of the sense appetite are "properly to be found where there is corporeal transmutation" (I–II 22.3). And human beings, although they have sense appetites, do not undergo movements of this appetite directly toward God because God is not a sensible object; movements of the sense appetite are elicited by apprehensions of sense (I 80.2).

Much to the chagrin of those who wish to avoid dualistic construals of the self and its operations, Thomas says that the "rational mind" is the subject of charity (II–II 25.12 *ad* 2). The "soul alone" is the seat of affection for God (I 77.5). We have seen that, according to Thomas, the "soul-body composite" (rather than the "soul alone") is the subject of passion, but it looks as though the affection that binds human beings to God does not, in the final analysis, count as a passion. It may elicit a bodily resonance that feels like a passion (II–II 25.12; 25.5 *ad* 2). But, then again, it may not: "By *suffering* Divine things is meant being well affected towards them, and united to them by love: and this takes place without any alteration in the body" (I-II 22.3 *ad* 1).

We have already discussed the tension in Thomas's thought regarding the contribution that bodily-based appetites can and should make to the love of God.[40] Recall that Thomas says,

> Accordingly just as it is better that [a person] should both will good and do it in his external act; so also does it belong to the perfection of moral good, that [a person] should be moved unto good, not only in respect of his will, but also in respect of his sensitive appetite; according to Ps. lxxxiii. 3: *My heart and my flesh have rejoiced in the living God:* where by *heart* we are to understand the intellectual appetite, and by *flesh* the sensitive appetite (I–II 24.3).

In this passage, Thomas points to the possibility that the body can and should be affected by God, not simply by suffering a resonance from an intellective appetitive movement, but also by undergoing its own proper movement toward God.

I want to suggest that this position is truest to Thomas's best insights, as these receive expression in his theory of the passions. As I have argued, this theory presupposes a continuum with respect to the human appetites, beginning on the one end with appetites that arise with the apprehension of sensibles and extending toward the other end into appetites that arise with the reapprehension of these sensibles in terms of increasingly explicit judgments of value.[41] Consistent with this perspective is the view that a person can arrive at affection for God in and through affection for sensibles. When a person is drawn, say, in affection for a friend toward the ground of her friend's being (without thereby losing sight of her friend as a sensible particular), her affection issues forth in an affection for God the Friend. Insofar as this affection for God remains at least in part an affection for God *as* manifest in *this* person, it will retain certain sense appetitive features.

Granted, there is no reason why affection for God cannot arise principally via intellectual contemplation. A highly intellectual affection can remain to a large degree dissociated in experience from bodily-based passion. It can also elicit passion in such a way that this passion feels like nothing more than a secondary resonance. By the same token, however, there is no reason why affection for God cannot arise via encounters with created particulars, in such a way that emerging intellectual aspects of these encounters remain grounded in passion.[42] The latter possibility is pointed to by our treatment of Johann. As we have seen, Johann argues that it is partly by loving our own and each other's embodied selves, and by learning over time how to love them rightly, that we encounter the abyss of human subjectivity. Stepping up to this abyss, we confront the Power of Being itself, such that our affection for particular beings becomes partly affection for them *qua* unique manifestations of Power. Affection of this kind easily gives rise to affection for God *qua* manifest in the concrete.[43]

Along similar lines, it may be worthwhile to image God as being in some sense bodily so that God's affection for human beings can be experienced readily by human beings as having a depth and intensity that is difficult for us to attribute to a disembodied love. The experience of many human beings is that the finest of our loves—including such seemingly disembodied loves as a love of philosophy—are loves that comprise powerful bodily yearnings and pleasures. It may be difficult for us to appreciate fully the transformative power of God's affection for us without imagining that God, too, has some manner of a body, such that God is bound to us partly out of bodily longing and delight.

Contemporary believers could benefit by imaging God as a friend who is capable of experiencing *in* God's affection for us excruciating bodily pain, as well as pleasure—a friend who aches over our pain as profoundly as the physical Christ ached over the nails that were driven through his hands and feet, and over his abandonment by his friends.[44] Permitting ourselves to envisage and engage God as one who is capable, say, through the person of Christ, of feeling a powerful sense of bodily connectedness toward all bodily beings could give us a more acute sense than we are otherwise likely to have that God is indeed God-with-us who suffers with physically charged affection for those whose body-selves are in pain.[45]

To develop the theological implications of these suggestions would take us well off course. Suffice it to say for present purposes that, for Thomas, the affection that binds human beings and God together in charity is constituted, at least in part, by reciprocal movements of intellective appetite. This affection tends, at least in humans, to causes rich bodily reverberations.

Benevolence

To continue our analysis, friendship includes more than mutual affection. It also includes the wishing and doing of good to each other for each other's own sakes. We have seen that, for Thomas, the best of friends wish for and do what contributes to each other's flourishing. They wish for and do what is likely to promote each other's excellence as a moral agent who exercises her agency within an intricate relational matrix. The best of friends contribute to each other's excellence for each other's own sake, even if they know that they, and others to whom they and their friends are bound, will be benefited in the process. They benefit each other simply because it is good that each of them should be well and do well.

Clearly, Thomas believes that God wishes and does what contributes to the flourishing of God's human friends. God is perfectly good and powerful; hence, it would be out of character for God to do otherwise than to promote the excellence that is allotted to each of us.[46] God wishes and does good to us for our own sakes, even though God loves in us a participation of God's own goodness: God wishes and does good to particular manifestations of God's goodness, simply because it is good that God's goodness should be manifest in particular ways.

How can persons, in turn, wish and do good to God, given that God is already perfect and has no need of our help in this or any other regard? Bond suggests that persons can exercise efficacious benevolence toward God by rejoicing in God's infinite goodness and by

> desiring and striving to promote the external glory of God, which, though it does not pertain to [God's] own intrinsic welfare, pertains, nevertheless, to the welfare of God considered exteriorly on the part of creatures inasmuch as it is a manifestation by creatures of their appreciation and love of the intrinsic goodness of God. By striving to promote the appreciation and love of God both in themselves and in others, creatures are in a sense giving to God things which [God Godself] does not possess, for the appreciation and love of [God's] goodness by creatures is something which only creatures can give.[47]

In charity, persons promote the revelation and glorification of God's goodness. We do so partly because God's goodness constitutes our highest end and we naturally seek happiness in everything that we do, but we do so principally for God's own sake, because God's goodness is "infinitely lovable in itself."[48]

Finally, friendship's mutual affection and benevolence must be mutually known. In friendship with God, God knows the affection and the benevolence that humans have toward God, as God knows the whole of our embodied hearts and minds. And humans know the affection and the benevolence that God has toward us insofar as we undergo the faithful appropriation of revealed truths and we experience in charity an intimacy with God that exceeds even the grasp of faith. Taking the sum of these ideas together, it does seem possible to speak meaningfully and truthfully, albeit analogically, about friendship with God and of God and humans as "other selves" relative to each other. For each of us is bound to the other with tender affection in the shared pursuit of making Truth and Goodness visible and effective in the course of human history.[49]

CHOOSING TO LOVE THE NEIGHBOR AS GOD'S

Thomas says that, in charity, we will regard as friends, not only those with whom we choose to share a life, but also those with whom we share little more than our humanity. In charity, we will extend our love of ourselves to all of our neighbors, loving even strangers and enemies, to some degree, as "other ourselves." The degree to which we regard each other as such may be minimal in many cases, but it is nevertheless substantial, and it is for that reason of considerable moral significance.

Thomas explains that a person extends her love of herself to someone else in two ways:

> first in respect of [the other], and in this way friendship never extends but to one's friends: secondly, it extends to someone in respect of another, as, when a man has friendship for a certain person, for his sake he loves all belonging to him, be they children, servants, or connected with him in any way. Indeed, so much do we love our friends, that for their sake we love all who belong to them, even if they hurt or hate us; so that, in this way, the friendship of charity extends even to our enemies, whom we love out of charity in relation to God, to Whom the friendship of charity is chiefly directed (II–II 23.1).

A person extends her love of herself to another in charity on the principle that the other—every single other—is created by God to participate with us in "the fellowship of everlasting happiness" (II–II 23.5). Every human being is oriented by God toward God as the source of her highest bliss. Every human being is invited to taste something of this bliss here and now by participating in the dynamic life of God.

This may not seem like very much to have in common. It does not come close to the sharing of visions, interests, deliberations, choices, pleasures, and pains that takes place between the closest of friends and binds them together into a single, extended self. It is impossible to share visions, interests, and the like, with people whom we do not even know. It is impossible to share these things with people who explicitly disavow our deepest loves and commitments and seek deliberately to undermine us at every turn. Yet the fact that we are all created by God to find our bliss in God is, in Thomas's view, a sufficient likeness between us to ground a kind of friendship. It is a likeness that is sufficient to give us the sense that the "familiar colloquy" that we share with God is an open, expansive colloquy capable of including any and all others who wish to participate. From the point of view of this colloquy, all human beings seem familiar to us. Their needs, their longings, their habits, their shortcomings, their joys, etc., all strike us as so familiar that they could just as easily be our own. All human beings seem like us and even "one" with us in our common struggle to achieve meaning and value in our lives.

Thomas says that, in charity, a person will extend her love of herself even to her enemies. She will love her enemies, as she loves all human beings, on account of the fact that they, too, are created like her with the destiny to enjoy their highest good in intimate friendship with God. Despite her revulsion over what she regards as her enemies' wickedness, the friend of God will love her enemies, "as to their nature, but in general: and in this sense charity requires that we should love our enemies, namely, that in loving God and our neighbor, we should not exclude our enemies from the love given to our neighbor in general" (II–II 25.8). The friend of God will also show to her enemies the "effects and signs of love" that she shows to the rest of her neighbors, "as when we pray for all the faithful, or for a whole people, or when anyone bestows a favor on a whole community" (II–II 25.9).

These passages suggest that charity for enemies and for the rest of our neighbors, all of whom participate with us to some degree in the nature of God, amounts to a general benevolence, i.e., a tendency to recognize other humans as being like us in their humanness and to experience toward them a weak, but dependable sense of affection and good will. Actually, Thomas indicates that in charity a person is "prepared in mind" to love enemies individually and in their particularity, "if the necessity were to occur." To love enemies personally, "without it being necessary . . . to do so belongs to the perfection of charity," and is thus supererogatory (II–II 25.8, 9). To commit acts of beneficence that express personal love is also supererogatory, "for then we not only beware of being drawn into hatred on account of the hurt done to us, but purpose to induce our enemy to love us on account of our kindness" (II–II 25.9). Nevertheless, charity appears to require that we choose to allow ourselves, now and then, to be captivated by and inclined toward at least some enemies with a genuine love of friendship.

Pressing Thomas here, charity would seem to require that as friends of God we choose to exercise our imaginations in such a way that valued commonalities between ourselves and at least some of the neighbors (including the strangers and the enemies) with whom we come into contact day by day come to our attention and elicit individualized, particularized affection on our parts. As Thomas recognizes, we cannot in the fullest sense befriend every person in the world. Even if we could become acquainted with every person in the world, we are not capable of loving all of them with the "intensity and desire" that is integral to complete friendship. Still, charity would seem to require of us that we choose to engage other human beings, as often as we reasonably can, not simply as generic human beings, but as particular persons who are apportioned to us and embedded in us in their particularity.

Why? Because, when we engage our neighbors in the way that we engage our closest friends, as persons who captivate our passionate interest partly on account of characteristics that are unique to them, we are more likely to have an ineluctable sense that the predicament in which they are caught is our predicament as well, that their weal and woe matters to us personally. This means, as I shall argue in Part III, that we will be more likely to feel and to act toward them with compassion. Of course, for how much of our time, with what intensity, and for how long we ought to regard *which* strange and even repulsive neighbors as we regard our friends is a judgment regarding the mean. We shall pursue the mean of compassion subsequently.

Finally, friends of God are called and empowered in charity to love all human beings, including the closest of our friends, as friends of God. But Thomas does not for a moment suppose that neighbor-love levels all existing relationships—as if our most intimate and treasured friendships will simply be subsumed into a watered-down general benevolence. Neighbor-love alters existing friendships in that it gives friends a "higher" vision of their own and each other's good; it provides them with an "elevated" love of that highest good; it alters the way in which they exercise their moral agencies in the cradle of that love. Still, the special affection that is sparked by other character similarities and is cultivated in the deliberate sharing of the friends' lives remains in Christian friendship, such that our love for a neighbor who happens also to be a dear friend will be more intense than our love for a neighbor who is not a dear friend. A believer will wish and do what is likely to benefit all friends of God, in general, but she will naturally and appropriately focus a proportionately large amount of time, energy and other resources on benefitting those who are united to her most closely in affection and in blood.[50]

Thomas says that we have more reasons for loving persons close to us and that we have more ways of loving them:

> For, towards those who are not connected with us we have no other
> friendship than charity, whereas for those who are connected with
> us, we have certain other friendships, according to the way in which
> they are connected. Now since the good on which every other
> friendship of the virtuous is based, is directed as to its end, to the
> good on which charity is based, it follows that charity commands
> each act of another friendship, even as the art which is about the
> end commands the art which is about the means. Consequently this
> very act of loving someone because he is akin or connected with us,
> or because he is a fellow-countryman or for any like reason that is
> referable to the end of charity, can be commanded by charity, so
> that, out of charity both eliciting and commanding, we love in more
> ways those who are more nearly connected with us (II–II 26.7).

Loving our closest friends in more ways, we love them more intensely. Thomas says that, in charity, we love most those who are closest to God, in that we wish for them the greatest good in accordance with divine justice (II–II 26.7), but he weighs the value of our affection for persons who are close to us more heavily than the value of our affection for objectively good persons to whom we are not particularly attached. He thus makes a strong statement with respect to the trustworthiness and the value of our deepest feelings of connectedness (II–II 26.7).

As a friend of God, the charitable person will love most intensely and seek most intently to benefit other friends of God to whom she is specially attached—friends with whom she shares a divinely-inspired life—because it is particularly in the faces of intimate friends that the divine Face is freely and generously revealed. It is particularly in the vulnerability and the trust of mutual influence and commitment that the divine life is engaged and co-participated. The person of charity will not, however, allow her intimate friendships to inhibit her wider fellow feeling. Just as the believer who loves herself discovers that the self she loves is a relational self whose good includes the good of others, the believer who is specially attached to a certain few friends discovers in these friendships an openness toward other selves, a divine presence yearning to be embraced and celebrated by more and larger circles of participants.[51]

To conclude, we have examined throughout this part of the project the nature of our interrelationality as human beings and as friends. We have appealed to Aristotle in order to explicate some of the ways in which as persons in relation we can be said to share our lives and aspects of our moral agencies with "other ourselves." We have appealed to Thomas in order to explicate some of the ways in which, even prior to spending our days with our friends in richly communicative activities, we can be said to recognize and experience our friends as "other ourselves." Thomas allows us to expand our discussion of friendship to consider friendship with God. He allows us to say that in relationship with God the Friend a believer is able to recognize and experience fellow human beings to whom she is not already attached as "other selves" relative to her, albeit in a weaker sense than she considers her most intimate friends to be her "other selves."

In Thomas's view, friendship with God gives a believer a new orientation toward a new end, and it gives her special resources to pursue her new end in intimate relationship with others—others who have their goodness in their own irreplaceably unique pursuits of the same end. Friendship with God pursued in friendship with others gives a believer the unforgettable impression that all human beings have a share in the divine Life, that all human beings by virtue of our participation in the same Life are embedded in each other's lives, that the genuine good of each of us includes inescapably the good of every other, and that finally we will flourish—or wither—together.

Eight

Compassion's Complacency

In Part I we examined the nature of character virtue. We reconstructed and extended the insights of Aristotle and Thomas Aquinas, each of whom holds that acquired virtue is a habitual disposition concerned with choosing both to act and to feel in accordance with the mean of practical rationality. In Part II we examined the nature of friendship. Once again, we reconstructed and extended the insights of Aristotle and Thomas, each of whom attends to some of the senses in which friends engage each other as "other themselves." Our final task is to integrate and develop further certain insights at which we have arrived in order to disclose the way in which character-friends exercise virtue *as* friends. Our more specific task is to reveal what it is for friends to exercise the virtue of compassion toward those whom they regard as "other themselves" as well as toward those whom they would not ordinarily regard as such. Our task is also to reveal the intrinsic and instrumental value of compassion for friends.

Aristotle and Thomas have little to say about compassion; hence, it will not be helpful to begin with their accounts. We will begin, instead, by constructing our own account, building on the foundation that Aristotle and Thomas have helped us lay. We will construct our account with reference to some contemporary scholarship on compassion and the related phenomenon of caring. Two accounts of compassion or caring are of special significance to this project. The first is Nel Noddings's *Caring*.[1] Noddings's approach differs in important respects from the approach that we will take. It also suffers from some serious weaknesses. It is, however, more helpful than other contemporary approaches in eliciting a discussion of the ethical issues that bear on the construction of a broadly Aristotelian account of compassion. It is particularly helpful in provoking a discussion of the interplay between passional receptivity and instrumental rationality, which takes place during deliberations about whether and in what way to show compassion.

The second account that is of special significance for this project is Donald McNeill, Douglas Morrison, and Henri Nouwen's *Compassion*.[2] Their approach, too, differs considerably from the one that we will take. Moreover, it does not attempt the kind of in-depth ethical analysis that we shall pursue. Still, it is more helpful than other contemporary texts at raising a range of theological ethical issues that must be confronted if we are to make sense of our broadly Aristotelian account of compassion in terms of a Christian worldview. *Compassion* is particularly helpful for our purposes in that it calls to mind perennial issues regarding the meaning of Christian love. Yet it does so with an uncommonly sharp focus on the form that Christian love takes in the face of human suffering. It is thus of more value to us than accounts of *agape* per se.

To proceed, we have defined virtue as a habitual disposition concerned with choosing both to act and to feel in accordance with a mean. But what does this definition tell us about the nature of compassion in particular? We have said that our friends are persons to whom we stand as to "other ourselves." But what does this entail about the way in which we stand, as compassionate persons, to "other ourselves" who are in pain? The next three chapters will focus on three issues that come to the fore when we attempt to bring our general accounts of virtue and friendship to bear on the specific case of compassion for friends.

The first issue concerns the relationship between compassion and Thomistic *complacentia* or complacency: What is it to suffer with our "other selves?" What is it habitually to take in, or to be taken in by, the pain of our friends, such that we become accustomed to suffering their pain as partly our own?[3] The second issue concerns the relationship between compassion and choice: What is it to suffer with our "other selves" without losing ourselves in others? What is it habitually to remain separate enough from our friends that we are able to seek the alleviation of their pain from a perspective that is uniquely our own? The third issue also concerns the relationship between compassion and choice. What is it deliberately to choose to show compassion for our "other selves?" What is it habitually to choose to do this in the right way?

All three of these issues are raised well by Nel Noddings's analysis of caring.[4] Hence I begin here and there, in this and the following two chapters, with parts of Noddings's analysis. These parts serve, in effect, to illuminate a backdrop against which my own analysis of compassion can come into relief. To put it another way, I begin repeatedly with what I take to be some common (albeit largely implicit) beliefs about caring as a way of standing in relation to persons in pain. I then subject these beliefs to scrutiny in order to reveal some of their conceptual and ethical strengths and weaknesses. Finally, I bring forward some beliefs about compassion that I think are truest to what an experienced and good person would likely judge, upon reflection, to be a good way of being human in the presence of those who suffer.[5]

CARING

Noddings argues that caring consists, to begin with, in "see[ing] the other's reality as a possibility for my own,"[6] which seems to involve a double movement of sorts. On the one hand, seeing the other's reality as a possibility for my own involves becoming "engrossed" in this reality and undergoing a "motivational displacement" in its direction, such that I am impelled "to act as though in my own behalf, but in behalf of the other."[7] In caring, I experience the feeling that "I must" do something to protect and enhance the well-being of the other.[8] On the other hand, seeing the other's reality as a possibility for my own involves seeing the other's predicament as a possible occasion for the exercise of my own virtue and being impelled to act on her behalf out of an interest in my "ethical self."[9] In caring, I also experience an "I must" that is directed toward my own protection and enhancement as one-caring, i.e, toward the fulfillment of my "ethical ideal."[10]

Caring, then, involves feeling that "I must" help the other for the other's own sake and, at the same time, that "I must" help the other for my own sake.[11] When the former feeling (which we shall, for the sake of clarity label the "I must$_1$") conflicts with present desires—when I feel the "I must$_1$" only weakly or not at all—then the latter feeling (which we shall label the "I must$_2$") has to pick up the slack if caring is to occur.[12]

The implicit logic of Noddings's account seems to proceed as follows:[13] I believe that my response in a given situation will either enhance or diminish me morally (i.e., it will either help or hinder me in being "the way I want to be"),[14] and I want to be enhanced morally. I believe that responding in a caring manner will enhance me morally, and thus I want to respond in a caring manner. That is to say, I feel the "I must$_2$," and choose to act accordingly. At the same time, however, I believe that a caring response that does not include the "I must$_1$," will not enhance me as one-caring to the degree that a response that includes the "I must$_1$," will. Hence, I want very much to feel the "I must$_1$." I believe that "I must$_2$," feel the "I must$_1$," if I am to care well, both for myself and for the other,[15] so I "accept" whatever "I must$_1$," I already feel and I try to "fetch . . . out of recalcitrant slumber" any "I must$_1$," that remains latent.[16]

Our immediate concern is with the "I must$_1$," as an analogue to what we shall refer to as compassion's complacency. The more deliberate "I must$_2$," will be of concern to us in the following chapters as we hone in on the issue of choice. What, according to Noddings, is the nature of the "I must$_1$," and how is it that I stand in relation to someone for whom I feel that "I must$_1$," do something? Noddings says that feeling the "I must$_1$," is a matter of feeling "engrossed" with someone and undergoing a "motivational displacement" in his regard.[17] Feeling "engrossed" is a matter of "Apprehending the other's reality, feeling what he feels as nearly as possible."[18] "Feeling what another feels" is a matter of feeling "invaded,"[19] "captured,"[20] and "totally with the other," such that (in Martin Buber's words) the other "fills the firmament."[21] When we are "totally with the other," we are in a "mode of consciousness" that Noddings describes as "subjective-receptive," "receptive-intuitive," "receptive or relational."[22] We are in a "precreative mode characterized by outer quietude and inner voices and images, by absorption and sensory concentration. The one so engrossed is listening, looking, feeling."[23]

Feeling the "I must$_1$," involves "feeling what [another] feels as nearly as possible," but it also involves "feeling that I must act accordingly."[24] That is to say, it involves undergoing a "motivational displacement" in the other's regard. When I am "invaded" by the other, says Noddings, "My motive energy flows toward the other and perhaps, although not necessarily, toward his ends. I do not relinquish myself; I cannot excuse myself for what I do. But I allow my motive energy to be shared; I put it at the service of the other."[25] At the other's disposal, I feel "regard, desire for the other's well-being;"[26] I feel "impelled to act as though in my own behalf, but in behalf of the other."[27]

Pressing further into the nature of the "I must₁," and asking what the possibility of feeling the "I must₁" indicates about the way in which we stand in relation to each other in our caring, Noddings reflects: "As I think about how I feel when I care, about what my frame of mind is, I see that my caring is always characterized by a move away from self."[28] "When I look at and think about how I am when I care, I realize that there is invariably this displacement of interest from my own reality to the reality of the other."[29] "Caring involves stepping out of one's own personal frame of reference into the other's."[30]

In these passages, Noddings seems to suggest that the caring self temporarily leaves itself behind in order to become another, separate self. There is little indication that the caring self's own interests and perspectives are retained, deliberately brought to bear on, or altered in the self's encounter with the interests and the perspectives of the other.

Elsewhere, Noddings suggests that the caring self remains partly itself, but takes the other into itself, such that it becomes in relation to the other a "duality." In caring, she says, "I receive the other into myself, and I see and feel with the other. . . . The seeing and feeling are mine, but only partly and temporarily mine, as on loan to me."[31] "It is as though [the other's] eyes and mine have combined to look at the scene he describes. . . . I feel what he says he felt."[32]

Elsewhere yet, Noddings suggests that the caring self retains its own interests and perspectives in the caring moment, but that it assumes the interests and perspectives of the other as well, such that it is able to alternate back and forth between separate points of view. Describing a caring parent, Noddings says that, "The one-caring receives the child and views his world through both sets of eyes. . . . The one-caring assumes a dual perspective and can see things from both her own pole and that of the cared-for."[33]

Noddings intimates in these scattered passages that, in the caring moment, there are respects in which the one-caring and the cared-for become one and the same relative to each other, and yet there are respects in which they remain separate and different. What *are* these respects? Specific to our purposes, how can the self be sufficiently one with its "other self" that it is able to feel something of the same pain and the same desire to alleviate that pain, and yet also sufficiently separate from its "other self" that it is able to choose whether, in what manner, and to what degree such sharing is desirable and morally fine? What is it, in the first place, to feel with "another oneself" the same pain that she feels, and what is it to allow this sort of co-suffering habitually to condition one's deliberations?

In the rest of this chapter we will explore at least some of the senses in which the compassionate self feels the "same" pain with respect to its "other self." We have gained from Noddings an initial, intuitive sense of what is to "feel what another is feeling as nearly as possible," so that we feel compelled "to act as though in [our] own behalf, but in behalf of the other." But we need to press beyond this sense and into a detailed discussion of what it is to "feel what another is feeling" when the other is feeling *pain*. Only then can we hope to grasp what it is, and how it is possible, to feel something of the same pain that is felt by someone else. Compassion is more than a disposition to co–suffer the same pain as another;[34] still, this disposition is a basic component of compassion, and it is with this component that our analysis must begin.

SHARING PAIN WITH ANOTHER ONESELF

We have to know what it is for a person to feel pain before we can know what it is for one person to feel the same pain as another person. Suppose, for example, that my exhausted friend trips over a tree root and badly sprains her ankle before we are able to complete a difficult wilderness trek. If I feel compassion for her, does that mean that I, too, will feel in my ankle the sensation of a sprain? Is it expected that I will feel any physical sensation at all? Is this all that I will feel? What if my friend begins to curse? What if she begins to cry? Does my friend's behavioral reaction tell me anything about the kind of pain that she is feeling? Will it make a difference to what I feel in response? Would it make a difference to my friend's experience of pain that she deemed finishing this trek to be important to the rebuilding of her diminished self-esteem? Would my knowledge that finishing the trek was important to my friend for this reason make a difference to what I feel with her?

PAIN

Questions like these begin to make manifest that even the pain associated with a sprained ankle can be more complex than we might initially imagine. Let us begin with a look at some of the psycho-physical constituents of physical pain. We shall turn to passional (i.e., emotional) pain subsequently. It seems clear that, in order for a particular physical sensation to count as one of pain, the sensation must be disagreeable or distressing, which is to say that we must dislike the sensation.[35] But what is it to dislike a physical sensation?

On the one hand, disliking a sensation seems to involve wanting it to cease. Part of what we feel in feeling physical pain is a desire that a particular disagreeable sensation stop. Part of what we experience is a head-on confrontation with the sensation (manifest, for example, in tensing our muscles and shouting expletives) in which we muster our resolve not to bend under the weight of the sensation. Anger, hatred, courage, and other passions are likely to be ingredient in this aspect of our pain.

On the other hand, disliking a sensation seems to involve feeling an aversion to something that we take to be inhibiting our good, where "aversion" signifies "flight" more than "fight." Part of what we experience in feeling physical pain is a desire to run away and hide from the sensation (manifest, for example, in curling up in a ball and crying). Part of what we experience is a desire to recede and cease to feel, period; we experience a weakening or a squelching of the wanting that constitutes the self's natural dynamism.[36] What we feel in wanting to turn away from the disagreeable sensation is still a wanting, but it is a diminished wanting. Fear, sorrow, despair, and other passions are likely to be ingredient in this aspect of our pain.

Accompanying the frustration of our desire in any case is a physical sensation of tension or agitation beyond the original sensation itself. We naturally want goods that are productive of our flourishing. When our wanting is frustrated—especially when our wanting to overcome or to escape the frustration of our wanting is itself frustrated—then the physical-emotional energy associated with our wanting accumulates within our bodies and makes its unsettling presence felt.

What this means, in short, is that when we feel physical pain, an initial physical sensation becomes the object of a passion or a set of related passions, and it is this sensation *with* this passion (and its related bodily reverberations), that together constitute the pain that we feel. Physical pain thus includes a felt physical sensation, a dislike of that sensation (which includes an evaluation that this sensation is frustrating or injuring our good), an intentional desire that the pain stop (or that we stop feeling it), and a sensation of bodily agitation in addition to the original sensation. We can also surmise that pain frequently includes imaginings about the original sensation and its larger significance, where these imaginings, too, elicit passional and physical effects.[37]

This may seem like too much to be happening in an experience of physical pain, even if we suppose that most of it remains implicit. Elaine Scarry, for example, argues in her book, *The Body in Pain*, that "physical pain—unlike any other state of consciousness—has no referential content. It is not of or for anything. It is precisely because it takes no object that it, more than any other phenomenon, resists objectification in language."[38] Pressing further, Scarry argues that in pain, "in the most literal way possible, the created world of thought and feeling, all the psychological and mental content that constitutes both one's self and one's world, and that gives rise to and is in turn made possible by language, ceases to exist."[39]

Scarry seems to me to overstate her point here. I imagine to the contrary that, at least most of the time when we feel even intense physical pain, we loathe the sensation that we suffer and we long for it to cease, and this loathing and longing constitute part of the pain experience.[40] Even if we are unable to give clear expression to the sensation that we suffer, we are able to give some expression to it, to our loathing of it, and to our longing for its cessation in our moaning, groaning, screaming, or wailing.

Scarry says that "Physical pain does not simply resist language but actively destroys it, bringing about an immediate reversion to a state anterior to language, to the sounds and cries a human being makes before language is learned."[41] But even if we sound like infants in our whining and crying, it is not necessarily the case that our state of consciousness in pain is itself infantile. Our whining and our crying, our moaning and our groaning, are expressions, not of an emptying of consciousness, but rather of our loathing and our longing, and we can get some idea of just what another is feeling by attending to these particular expressions.

We can discern, for example, something of the kind of pain that an actively birthing woman is experiencing by attending to the sounds that she is making in her pain. If she is launching high-pitched screams, we can usually gather that part of her pain experience consists in panicking and feeling out of control. If she is moaning or roaring deeply, then we can usually gather that part of her pain experience consists in attending to and working in coordination with her painful bodily sensations. It is not simply the quantity of pain that differs in the different cases. It is the quality of pain that differs as well. Pain experienced as panic feels very different from pain experienced as power.

It is significant that pain expressions can themselves be learned, and that deliberately changing our pain expressions can, in turn, change our pain experiences: shifting with another's help from a scream to a growl can give a birthing woman a renewed sense of self-initiative. In any case, even though we may seem in extreme physical pain to lose touch with everything outside of pain's immediacy, that pain must include at least some passional content in order to qualify *as* pain, rather than, say, a state of unconsciousness. This passional content may, however, remain largely implicit.

Passional (or emotional) pain is similar to physical pain in many respects. The biggest difference between the two lies in the object that each takes. Physical pain takes as its object a particular, occurrent bodily sensation (and secondarily, the imagined significance of that sensation). Emotional pain takes as its object some occurrence or circumstance in the larger world of personal experience.[42] Obviously, passional pain has passional content: it is commonly constituted by a belief or a perception that some circumstance obtains, and by a dislike of that circumstance—a dislike that comprises both a wanting for the circumstance not to obtain and a wanting to escape from a circumstance that nevertheless does obtain (whether in fact or in imagination). Like all passion, passional pain includes physical agitation as well, agitation that will vary in felt quality, depending upon the persons involved and how they are put together physically, and depending upon the other passions that happen to contribute to the pain experience.

SHARING PAIN

This brief overview of pain's content begins to bring to light some of the ways in which the sharing of pain might be possible between separate selves, especially between friends who regard each other as "other themselves." Let us consider what it is to become "engrossed" or "complacent" in a friend who suffers physical pain. What is it in particular to take in, or to be taken in by, a friend's original physical sensation, her dislike of that sensation, her wanting that sensation to cease, and her accompanying agitation, such that we can be said to feel one and the same pain?

Sharing Original Sensations

It is rare that we experience in our own bodies the same original physical component of our friends' pain, where "same" refers to qualitative or descriptive sameness.[43] That is to say, it is rare in our compassion for friends that we experience in our own bodies a physical sensation that we would describe in exactly the same way that our friends would describe their own sensation.[44] Most of the time when we co-feel bodily pain with our friends, we seem to co-feel some of the physical agitation that is part and parcel of the passional component of their pain—an agitation that tends to be much less intense, localized, and focused than the original sensation. But it does sometimes happen, I think, that we experience with our "other selves," if only in a flash, something of the original physical component of their pain.

For example, when I see my toddler daughter Hannah run, trip, tumble, and badly skin her knees on the sidewalk, I sometimes feel in compassion's complacency that my own knees hurt, at first with the sharp sensation of skinning, and then with a dull ache. Part of what I feel in my knees might result from a spontaneous recalling of an earlier experience of skinning my own knees, a recalling that brings to mind and to knees a memory of felt sensation. Part of what I feel might be more directly a result of imagining my present self to be skinning my own knees alongside of Hannah, an imagining that elicits a corresponding sensation. Part of what I feel might be a result of imagining vividly what Hannah is feeling in her knees and finding that my imagining causes pain in my knees, just as the actual skinning causes pain in Hannah's knees.

There is, however, something of the experience that these probable explanations do not seem to capture. When I see Hannah fall and skin her knees, my experience is not that I am a separate person who uses my imagination to bridge the gap between my own and another separate person's experience. My experience is that we are one extended self, skinning our knees together. Actually, we are one sharply contracted self, skinning our knees together. There is no distance between us to overcome, no chasm to bridge, only the immediate, shared sensation of knees scraping pavement: my knees, her knees, where these seem for the moment to be the same.

Hannah and I are one, rather extended self prior to the fall: I am enjoying my own, separate interests and activities, even as I am mindful (and bodyful) of Hannah's. I am snapping beans up on the porch, even as I feel strangely that I am Hannah running on the sidewalk. But when I see my girl fall and skid, I feel as though I am myself slammed abruptly into the pavement. I feel that I am slammed from this pole of our extended body, the pole that is up here on the porch, to that pole of our body which is sprawled out over the sidewalk. Our usually rather extended body has contracted and the sensation of skidding has become the center of our most immediate, shared experience.

I am not pressing, here, for a causal explanation of the ache in my knees that somehow circumvents visual perception and the workings of imagination. We can only receive what we first perceive, and our perceptions are always already structured by habits of imagination. Instead, I am pressing for a description of our interbodied connectedness that makes it possible for us to capture vividly the experience of sharing another's sensation in compassion's complacency. I am pressing for a construal of our interextensionality that enables us to experience our physical, as well as our emotional, boundaries as much more flexible and expansive than we might previously have thought them to be. We have discussed what it is to share our lives with others. Have we appreciated fully that the lives we share are embodied? When we share our selves with friends, we share perceptions, desires, visions, pleasures and pains, and so on. But each of these is inescapably an embodied activity. It seems appropriate, then, to say that, in sharing these activities with our "other selves," we share with our "other selves" a body of sorts—a single, more or less extended body of experience.[45]

The metaphor of shared body can be helpful in capturing a physical component of some rather common experiences. Perhaps most of us can recall, for example, trying to part with intimate friends whom we did not expect to see again for a long time and feeling, as we sought gently to extricate ourselves from their embrace, that flesh was being pulled away from our bone. Such a feeling is not simply one of brokenheartedness; it is much more one of having our flesh clutched and stretched (even though it is *not* being clutched or stretched). And when we miss these distant friends most intensely, we do so with a painful, fleshly longing, as though our flesh is aching for an easing of the extension that continues to pull us apart. The notion is that we share with these friends a single, extensible body, but a body that can tolerate only so much actual extension—a body that tends characteristically toward the enjoyment of a more contracted intercorporeality.

Shifting to an experience of friends' bodies in proximity, some of us may have had the experience of sitting up late with a distraught friend and finding that, as our friend began to tense up her forehead and this tension began to spread down her neck and into her back and arms, the tension seemed to flow through her limbs and into our own, making the two of us singularly rigid. We may recall similarly that, as our friend began to relax her muscles and sink heavily into the couch, a feeling of heaviness flowed gently and freely into this pole of our body as well, so that the whole of our shared body collapsed limply into a single center.

Examples like these are not intended to suggest that fleshly interconnectedness can be understood adequately apart from the dynamics of passional interconnectedness. Clearly, it cannot. The point is simply that when we come to share a single, extended self with a friend, our experience is often that we share with her a single *body* of experience—a flexible, extensible bodily frame that is capable of supporting a certain degree of polarity (before it utterly splits in two) and a certain degree of coincidence (before it loses extensity altogether). When we feel compassion for a friend with whom we share an extensible body, we "rest" with familiarity in her embodied presence, which means that we sometimes "rest" in a presently embodied experience that strikes us as distinctively hers—located over *there* relative to where we experience ourselves to be enfleshed, yet partly ours—located over *here* in part of a body that extends from over *there* to over *here*. Actually, the sensation seems to remain located over there; it's just that we (who were, up to now, over here) have been propelled over there, such that we experience something of the same sensation with our friend who is over there.

We could say that the sensation is the "same" in that it is descriptively much the same. If Hannah were to describe the sensation in her knees, for example, she might (if she were well beyond her years!) describe it as "a stinging and a burning that comes and goes in waves." And if I were to describe the pain in my knees, I might describe it in the same terms. Yet the sameness that characterizes my experience and Hannah's is more than a parallel sameness between separate selves. It is a sameness that is constituted when I am thrown into Hannah's experience of her own bodily state. If I were to describe in more detail the pain that I feel in this thrownness, I would say that, "the stinging and the burning that I feel in my knees seems like a stinging and a burning that Hannah feels in her knees—as if my knees were somehow coincident with hers—especially in that the feeling in my knees draws my attention more to her knees than it does to my own." The sensation of stinging is the same in that it seems to approach numerical sameness within Hannah's own body.

It is going too far, however, to say that the pain in our knees is numerically the same. For that to be the case, our bodies would have to be numerically the same, such that whatever happens to Hannah's body automatically registers in my own, whether I am paying attention to Hannah or not.[46] But our bodies are not numerically the same. Rather, Hannah and I share a body in the sense that my own bodily states are, as a matter of habit, intimately attuned to Hannah's bodily states. Over the years, countless numbers of Hannah's changing bodily states (and the conditions under which they arise and cease) have come to my attention. I have become so familiar with her habits of bodily reception and response—habits that are being formed partly under my influence—that sometimes I spontaneously receive and respond to stimuli as Hannah does, as my trained bodily awareness of Hannah's bodily states allows me to do.

The sensation that I experience with respect to Hannah's sensation is descriptively much the same, then, but it is much the same in that it is partly constituted by shared habits of physical awareness, sensitivity, and responsiveness—habits that we have, in effect, cultivated *with* each other and *in* each other over the years, such that the (partial) interweaving of our moral agencies has resulted in a (partial) interweaving of our bodily dispositions. We could say that the sensation that I experience with respect to Hannah's sensation is "constitutively much the same," in that it is constituted *with* Hannah's experience partly on the basis of complex interactions between our agencies that have formed our bodily attunements and sensitivities in tandem. Our sensation is the "same" in that it makes us "one" with each other, i.e., more than merely "like" each other, but less than "identical."

Sharing Dislike

In the end, the experience of single-bodiedness and the sharing of bodily pain cannot be well conceived without reference to the experience of sharing moral agencies. Physical pain never occurs apart from perception, and perception always includes passionate reception and some interpretation, elements of moral engagement that are formed and re-formed through extended interactions with our friends. Consider, then, what it is for one self to share with "another oneself" other aspects of the pain experience. Consider, first, what it is for one self to take in, or to be taken in by, another's dislike of a physical sensation, such that the one self suffers something of the same dislike as the other.

I have indicated that, when we undergo compassion's complacency in relation to another self who is suffering physical pain, we sometimes experience in our own bodies something of the same original physical sensation that the other experiences, even though we may experience it only briefly or sporadically. To the extent that we experience the same sensation as another, we are likely to experience something of the same dislike of that sensation. That is to say, we are likely to experience something of the same desire that *that* sensation stop. It is not simply that we will dislike the portion of the sensation that occurs at *this* pole of the body that we share with the other, i.e., the weaker and more transient portion that is located in the flesh that we take to be most intimately ours. Rather, our dislike will be focused mainly on the sensation that is located at *that* pole of the body that we share with the other (the pole toward which we feel ourselves propelled), i.e., the sensation that the other experiences as continuous with her own self-awareness.

To the extent that we experience something of the same physical sensation that the other experiences, such that part of our awareness is propelled into the immediacy of the other's own experience, it makes sense to say that we experience a dislike of the sensation that is descriptively much the same as the other's dislike. If the other were to describe her dislike, she might say, for example, that the object of her dislike is the insistent obtrusiveness of the sensation—the way in which it forces itself upon her consciousness without reprieve and thus disables her over long periods of time from thinking about anything else. And if we were to describe our own dislike of the same sensation, we might say that we, too, find disagreeable the way in which that sensation continually insinuates itself into the other's-our own consciousness. True enough, the dislike that we feel toward this aspect of the sensation is likely to differ from the dislike that the other feels in that we only glimpse sporadically what the other cannot but stare in the face, namely, the feeling of being completely absorbed here and now with *this* bodily sensation. Still, the glimpse makes it possible for us to construe the object of our dislike in much the same way that the other construes the object of her dislike, which is likely to elicit descriptively much the same desire in us.

When we are not caught up in something of the same physical sensation that is experienced by the other (which is, I suspect, most often the case), it is more difficult to speak about having the same dislike of that sensation, but it is not impossible. We can take as an object of our dislike an imaginative *idea* of the other's sensation, insofar as the other is willing and able to communicate to us the particular nature of her sensation. To the extent that the other's communication is adequate and our understanding of it is sound, our dislike will be descriptively much the same as the dislike that the other feels, in that both of us will desire "that *this* physical sensation of [the other] stop." Of course, these dislikes will also be descriptively different in that the desire that [the other]'s sensation stop has a distinctive quality when the [the other] is "me."

We can also take as an object of our dislike the simple notion that the other is undergoing and disliking some loss to her bodily good (where the nature of this loss is presently unknown to us). To the extent that we take the other's good to be ingredient in our own good, any perception that the other is suffering a loss is, in and of itself, sufficient to elicit within us an immediate sense of dislike. It is not simply that we dislike the loss that *we* suffer at the included other's loss. The dislike that we experience may be as yet open-ended and undefined (on account of our ignorance), but it is nevertheless focused clearly on the other and on whatever it is that might be causing her such distress. In such a case, the dislike that we feel is descriptively much the same as the dislike felt by the other in that we and the other both desire "whatever is causing [the other] distress to stop." To the extent that we are oblivious to the physical locus of [the other]'s distress, however, our desire is bound to differ significantly from hers.

Whether we are or are not caught up in another's original physical sensation, it does seem possible to feel descriptively something of the same dislike of that sensation, even if the content of that sensation remains obscure. But feeling the same desire involves more than feeling a desire that has much the same intentional content as the desire of another. It also involves being captivated by and caught up in the dynamism of the other's desire, such that we find ourselves spontaneously wanting *with* the other something of what the other wants, even though we may be unable at the moment to grasp the object or the nature of that wanting. It involves being captured and made a participant in the basic thrust of the other's desiderative experience.

The seduction that draws us, if only for a moment, into the immediacy of another's desire is difficult to account for, but we can begin by recalling some of the ways in which the moral agencies of separate selves interpenetrate within the context of character-friendship. Just as it happens that, after years of physical presence and contact, we and our friends become attuned to and are (probably to a small degree) formed by each other's characteristic bodily sensitivities and dispositions, so it happens that, after years of conversation and other character-building activities, we and our friends become attuned to and are formed (to a much greater degree) by each other's habitual patterns of perceiving, desiring, thinking, feeling, deliberating, choosing, and acting.

To the extent that we have undergone and continue to undergo this attunement, formation, and re-formation in relation to our friends, we will be disposed to conceive particular objects of bodily sensation and perception in somewhat the same terms as our friends, taking certain aspects of an object to be central and other aspects to be peripheral. We will be disposed to see as our friends see because part of what binds us together as friends is the mutual desire to see the world of experience from a combined, enlarged perspective. Taking the same object under much the same description to be the object of dislike, we will be disposed to desire with our friends, with much the same intensity, the destruction or avoidance of the object so conceived. We will want the same thing with regard to the object of dislike because we and our friends have cultivated with and in each other much the same vision of the good and much the same love of the good so envisioned. Part of what binds us together is the mutual desire to love what each other loves.

The "sameness" of our dislike and our friends' dislike is thus a "constitutive sameness" in that we and our friends both constitute our dislike out of patterns of reception and response that we have cultivated in concert. Each of us has had a hand in teaching the other which bodily sensations are to be cried over, and which are to be borne with a stiff upper lip. Each of us has had a hand in helping the other articulate sensations that would otherwise have remained opaque to both of us. Each of us has had a hand in leading the other toward or away from reflections regarding the larger significance of our disagreeable sensations. In short, each of us has had a hand in making the other the sort of person that she is, and the sorts of person that we are has everything to do with the sorts of things that cause us dislike and the sorts of dislike that these things cause.

In the case of passional pain over some situation or occurrence, the sharing of much the same pain is easier to account for. If, in sharing a life with another, we share (in the sense of co-construct) with him a vision of the good, perceptions of particular happenings, consequent evaluations, deliberations, and desires, then we will tend to share in his dislike of certain situations. If we are together when a particular situation comes about, it is likely that we will see what happens at the same time and from much the same angle. We will likely pick out the same features as noteworthy, reach the same judgment regarding agent intentionality and culpability, wrestle with the same ambiguities, with much the same sensitivity, and want the same things in response.

Once again, it is not simply that we who are very much like the other will receive and respond to a particular situation in a manner that happens to parallel the reception and the response of the other. What we see, we will see with the other's seeing in mind; we will see what we see from over *here*, but we will see it in light of what we anticipate, from years of shared experience, that the other sees from over *there*. We will evaluate what we see in light of what we and the other have persuaded each other over the years to understand and to value as the most precious of our shared goods. We will loathe whatever injures our good, and we will ache as one flesh in our loathing.

If we are not with the other when an injurious situation occurs, then it might take some time for us to figure out what the other is undergoing passionally in response to that situation. But it will not ordinarily take long, and we will already be sharing his dislike, even as we try to discern the nature of the dislike into which we have been drawn. It will not take long because we know the sorts of things that bother our friend and why. We know his deepest fears and vulnerabilities. We know the loves and the commitments that drive him to do whatever he does. We know what he has been up to today and who he has been with. Often a single sentence of explanation is enough to bring the dislike that we already feel at the sight of our friend into full synchronicity: "Bobby was on my case again today." We are already familiar with the dynamic between our friend and his condescending boss, and this is all we need to hear in order to place what our friend is feeling, such that we can place and give more definitive shape to what we are already feeling *with* him. Notice that, in compassion's complacency itself, it does not yet matter to us exactly what our friend is disliking and whether or not he is justified in disliking in this way. It only matters that he dislikes. We may find his boss pathetic and innocuous, but he does not, and it is his dislike that we feel as our own.

A Closer Look

Let us look more closely at this dislike. Recall that a dislike of a sensation, occurrence, or situation that we take to be injurious to our good is basically a desire that whatever is injuring us cease to do so. Recall, too, that dislike can and usually does take both a positive and a negative form. In its positive form, it is a desire to resist or do away with a present evil. In its negative form, it is a desire to escape or avoid a present evil. Accordingly, if the dislike of "another myself" is in part a desire to fight and in part a desire to flee in fright, then the dislike that I share with him in compassion's complacency will be a desire to fight and to flee as well. Here we discover a fascinating difficulty internal to complacency.

First, consider the desire to fight. In his pain, my friend will likely hate whatever injures him, but in hating what injures him, he might end up hating something that has already become a part of his identity. He might end up hating the self that gives life to the hateful injury. Hating a physical injury, the friend might end up hating his own flesh, wanting desperately to command it, manipulate it, and refashion it into something that is not so corruptible. He might end up wanting to construct a formidable wall of defense against an enemy that has already penetrated his borders. Hating a passional injury, the friend might end up wanting to unmake or to destroy, not only the situation that presently injures him, but also his own injured and injurable self, e.g., the vulnerability and the powerlessness that make such injury possible and, perhaps, inevitable.

Consequently, if I am complacent in my friend's wanting, I will likely want to dig my heels in beside my friend to repel an evil that threatens to destroy both of us. At the same time, however, I will likely feel repelled by my friend. I will feel repelled by the vulnerability and the powerlessness, the painful experiences of which have become partly constitutive of his own sense of identity. I will want to be *with* him in common struggle against an impinging evil and yet, at the same time, I will want to struggle *against* the one in whom that evil is contained. Part of me will want to control and manipulate my friend in order to make the evil that he embodies go away. Part of me will want to make *him* go away.

Usually, we think of this desire to control the other or his predicament as an external constraint on our capacity to co-feel and, indeed, it often is. But here we see that it can sometimes be ingredient in compassion's complacency itself, with the result that, instead of feeling close to our friend, we feel ambivalent and antagonistic toward him. Sometimes this dynamism surfaces as an irritability with our suffering friend, an unrealistic blaming of him for succumbing to a present evil. Even in our wanting that our friend "shape up," however, there can be an unrecognized synchronicity. We chastise ourselves for feeling animosity when, some of the time, what has happened is that we have been captured by our friend's own desire to shape himself up and out of his intolerable predicament.

The same sort of dynamic can occur with respect to the shared desire to flee an evil in fright. Wanting to flee an injury that has already become a part of his identity, our friend might end up wanting to flee from himself. Repelled and repulsed by a physical injury, he might end up wanting to escape, not only the constraints of that particular injury, but the constraints of his very embodiment. Repelled and repulsed by a passional injury, our friend might end up wanting to flee, not only the situation that presently injures him, but also the self who participates in the injury by being and remaining injured. Maybe the friend brought the injury on himself; maybe he was a victim of circumstance. In any case, it might seem to him that he has *become* the injury that he suffers, and when he turns away in aversion from the injury, he inadvertently turns away from himself.

Accordingly, if I become complacent in my friend's wanting, I will likely want to withdraw *with* him to a place where we can hide from what injures us both. At the same time, however, I will likely want to withdraw *from* him. I will want to withdraw from the one who experiences his injurability and injuredness to be central aspects of his present identity. The fear of vulnerability and of pain can and often does inhibit compassion's complacency, but we can see that such fear can also be part and parcel *of* complacency. When we take in, or allow ourselves to be taken in by, someone whose experience consists chiefly in a fear of his pain/himself, we are likely to experience this fright as partly our own.

Sometimes, then, when we expect in compassion to feel a straight-forward love and tenderness toward our friends, we are caught off guard with a desire to blame or to turn away. Note, however, that even these desires can be consonant with what our friends are feeling; even these desires can be ingredient in our feeling of the "same." Of course, complacency in these sorts of desires can propel us right out of complacency. My irritability and my blaming can inflate like a balloon, forcing my friend/his pain into the far corner of our shared self, forcing him/his pain right out of the boundaries of "my" extended self and into the realm of the "other" toward whom I feel no particular attachment. My turning away in fear can expand into an out-and-out avoidance, a burying of myself in one distraction after another, such that I am no longer able to hear my friend's petitions.

The difference between wanting to fight and to flee *within* complacency and wanting to do so *outside of* complacency is partly that *within* complacency I experience conflict and tension between my desire to fight and to flee *with* my friend whatever threatens to overcome us both and my desire to fight *against* and flee *from* what seems to have become him-apart-from-me. Wanting to fight and to flee *outside of* complacency is not similarly conflicted: the tension has snapped and what is now "other" ceases to exert a pull. Unfortunately, there is no discreet line of demarcation that we know ourselves to be crossing from wanting in complacency to wanting irrespective of the other's wanting.

What I am suggesting, then, is that compassion is not a simple loving of a person who happens to be in pain. It is not a simple wanting with another that the other's pain be alleviated. It is, in part, a co-wanting in which we experience, not only the other's desire for his own, distinctive flourishing, but also the other's hatred, rage, terror, and horror at what injures him and makes him so prone to being injured. Once we examine critically the wanting that we experience in a given moment of complacency, we might decide that it is distorted, distorting, irrational, contradictory, or whatever, and we might want deliberately to alter it or to ignore it. But in the immediacy of complacency itself, what we often feel is an awful mess.

A Case in Point

Let me make my point more explicit by means of an example. Early one morning a friend of mine appeared at the door in tears. Spying Jane through the window, I felt a heavy panic and a loathing in my flesh. I had no idea what was amiss, but I was immediately caught up in her apparent distress. After I hurriedly opened the door and drew Jane into the house, she told me that she had just been raped.

What I remember most about my reception of and response to Jane's unfolding story is how torn and conflicted I felt, tossed to and fro by one passion after another. I wanted to be *with* Jane in such a way that I could provide for her a secure resting place in my coincident and thus confirming desire, but my desires were manifold and scattered. I wanted to humiliate, castrate, and finally annihilate the man who raped her, as if in doing so, I could willfully unmake her injury. I also wanted to withdraw Jane into a location in our experience in which her rapist had no power. I ached in utter frustration of both desires. In a way, I felt that I was aching *with* Jane over the frustration of our shared desire, but at the same time, I had the impression that I was not. I knew that she raged. I knew that she feared. I knew that she loathed. And yet she seemed to be raging, fearing, and loathing over *there*, at *that* pole of our extended self, while I raged, feared, and loathed over *here*. What was keeping us apart?

Part of me wanted desperately to manipulate a reality that I could see from Jane's body had already become part of her. The smell, the taste, the feel of his flesh, the feel of that cold knife pressed against her belly—all of this had permeated her flesh in a way that no amount of wishing or washing could erase. Wanting to control Jane's injury, I set myself up in opposition to Jane. Indeed, she inadvertently set me up to oppose her by opposing herself—the self in whom I was complacent. Another part of me wanted to run and hide, not simply from "the rape," but from "Jane who was raped." Wanting to flee Jane's injury in a panic, I turned away from Jane. Again, she inadvertently set me up to turn away from her by turning away from the self in whom I was complacent. I wanted more than anything to approach Jane with a reassuring intimacy, but I kept feeling that I was being shut out and flung back upon myself.

Being the particular person that she was and is, Jane could not help but loathe herself, rage at her own flesh, fear her own reflection in the mirror. And as I rested complacently in her wanting, I felt similarly compelled. Of course, outside of the immediacy of my complacency, my own, separate wanting for her to flourish was stronger than ever, and this wanting dominated my other impulses. But the point I wish to make is that what we feel in compassion's complacency itself is dependent upon what our friend is feeling in her pain. If our friend perceives herself to be in part or in whole identified with the evil that she dislikes in her pain—if she turns her disliking back upon herself—then we are likely spontaneously to do the same.

Sharing Subsequent Sensations

To round off our discussion of compassion's complacency we should make explicit that all of this wanting, the frustration of wanting, the conflict between opposed wantings, and so forth, is ordinarily accompanied by perceptible physical agitation. All human wanting is embodied wanting and, as such, it includes component physiological changes that tend to elicit corresponding sensations. If we share with a friend a passionate perception of a particular occurrence, an evaluation of that occurrence as evil, a desire to fight or to flee the evil that is already wreaking havoc on both of us, then we will likely share with her a corresponding physical reaction to the evil in question. Granted, even persons who have had a hand in shaping each other's bodily sensitivities and temperaments over time will likely experience a given passion's enfleshment somewhat differently. We, for example, may experience sorrow chiefly as a tightening in the chest and stomach; our friend may experience sorrow chiefly as a heaviness and a numbness in the shoulders and arms. Perhaps it is sufficient to say that we share with our friend the same sensation in our sorrow, but that, at *this* pole of our extended body, the sensation is more focused in the chest and stomach, whereas at *that* pole, it is more focused in the shoulders and the arms.

Then again, if we are genuinely complacent in another's sorrow, if we are complacent in the whole of the one who sorrows, it seems that we are likely to be taken captive by the peculiar fleshly reverberations that are part and parcel of that sorrow. If we notice, for example, that our friend is hunched over in his sorrow, clutching at his gut, and that his breathing is becoming increasingly heavy and labored, then we are likely to discover that we, too, have some tension in our gut and chest. Our tension will undoubtedly be less intense, and it is likely to come and go in a way that our friend's tension does not, but our tension will nevertheless be descriptively much the same as our friend's. More than this, the sensation that we and our friend experience will be "constituted" much the same on account of the attunement to and the affection for each other that have allowed our embodied moral agencies, over the years, to interweave.

Putting the present inquiry into perspective, we began the chapter with an introduction to the "engrossment" and the "motivational displacement" that seem to many of us to take place in caring. This led us to pursue some of the senses in which a compassionate person could meaningfully be said to feel something of the "same" thing that is felt by a person in pain. We have covered only a short distance in this pursuit, but we are in a position to say that, at least within the context of character-friendship, two selves can be so intimately acquainted with and accustomed to each other, and they can have such a hand in the construction of each other's beliefs, perceptions, evaluations, and desires, that their sensations and their passions will sometimes be "constitutively the same." The sensations and the intentional, embodied desires that they undergo in each other's company, particularly with respect to pain, will not only be descriptively much the same (some of the time), but they will also be constitutively much the same (some of the time) in that they will be formed (deliberately and/or spontaneously) out of some of the same, basic building blocks of experience—building blocks that are, to some degree, accessible to both of them and employed interchangeably.

There is, as we have noted, much more going on in compassion than compassion's complacency. What we have tried to do in this chapter is to shed some light on a mere sliver of a larger phenomenon. It should be evident, however, that I take this sliver to be a significant part of the whole. Compassion's complacency is the reconfiguration of desire that gives us the uncanny, but powerful impression that those who suffer in our midst matter to us personally. It is the "glue" that keeps our affection and attention focused just as carefully on the good of those who suffer as it is focused on our own good. It is the basis of the appetitive pull that keeps us from being able to look away from the suffering—the poor, the sick, the hungry, the depressed, the wounded, and the wicked—without giving them a second thought. In short, it is that which constitutes us enough the "same" relative to "others" that we feel compelled to extend toward them the love with which we already love ourselves. Proper self-love can be a powerful source of moral motivation.

Nine

Compassion and Choice (1)

Compassion is more than a disposition to be caught up in the immediacy of other people's pain. Compassionate people are not simply sponges who are accustomed to absorbing other people's pain, such that they have to struggle continuously to keep from drowning in the "same." Compassion is a disposition concerned with choosing both to act and to feel in a manner that we lovingly believe and perceive is most likely to alleviate pain that remains, in significant respects, other than our own. Although compassionate people exercise their moral agencies within the context of extended selves, they do so as irreducibly distinct and therefore separate contributors to these selves.

In this and the following chapter, we will explore the way in which the compassionate self experiences something separate and different from its "other selves," even as it experiences something one and the same. We will focus, in particular, on the way in which the complacent self keeps or draws a part of itself back from the immediacy of the other's pain, such that it is able to deliberate and decide, partly on the basis of its own distinctive desires, beliefs, and perceptions, what it ought to do relative to the other. In other words, we will focus on the deliberative process that is central to the effective exercise of compassion.

Recall that, from an Aristotelian perspective, the process of deliberative choice making can be represented in the form of a practical syllogism, where the major premise represents a desire for a particular end, the minor premise represents a belief or a perception regarding what in the present situation is most likely to contribute to the desired end, and the conclusion represents an action or an intention to act in the way that we believe or perceive is most likely to contribute to that end. We would do well, in my view, to organize our discussion of compassion and choice in terms of this representation,[1] focusing in the present chapter on compassion's desire and the way in which this desire conditions compassion's belief and perception, and saving a consideration of compassion's choice, proper, for the chapter that follows.

COMPASSION'S DESIRE

Implicitly, the major premise of the practical syllogism represents different layers of desire. Although in any given process of decision making, we begin our deliberations with a desire for a good that is specific to the circumstance at hand, such a desire cannot be separated completely from more general desires regarding the kinds of people we want to be and the kind of world we want to inhabit. Our general desires to live good lives dispose us to perceive and to construe the world in a particular way, making it likely that we will notice and focus attention on certain things in that world (according to certain descriptions) more than others. This, in turn, causes certain desires rather than others to be elicited in given predicaments (i.e., desires whose intentional content is partly constituted by the descriptions that we give to the particulars that we notice). At the same time, desires for particular goods can indicate to us, partly through the confirmation of value that we experience in our wanting, what makes our lives worth living. Hence, they can serve to re-orient or re-constitute our desire for *eudaimonia*.

Keeping this layering and mutual conditioning in mind, let us begin our discussion of compassion's desire with a focus on compassion's more general desires, i.e., desires that are not specific to a particular circumstance, but nevertheless frame the way in which a compassionate person "sees" any circumstance. Let us examine the abiding desires for the good that appear to be part and parcel of compassion itself. Nel Noddings's analysis of caring gives us a place to start and an immediate sense for what is at issue.

DESIRES FOR CONTEXT-UNSPECIFIC GENERAL GOODS

For Noddings, caring is a matter of "seeing another's reality as a possibility for my own,"[2] which includes "feeling what he feels as nearly as possible"[3] and, at the same time, seeing in his predicament an opportunity for enhancing my own "ethicality."[4] "The source of ethical behavior," she says, lies "in twin sentiments—one that feels directly for the other and one that feels for and with [my own] best self."[5] The first sentiment, which is the sentiment of "natural caring," is the feeling that "I must$_1$," do something to assist the other. The second sentiment, which is the sentiment of "ethical caring," is the feeling that "I must$_2$," do something to assist the other, even if I do not feel that "I must$_1$." "Ethical caring" arises when we see a person in need of assistance, when we recall "our own best moments of caring and being cared for," and when we long "to maintain, recapture, or enhance" those moments here and now by acting in accordance with what we take to be ethically ideal.[6]

For Noddings, "ethical caring" is partly constituted by the desire to realize a *particular* "ethical ideal."[7] Noddings characterizes the content of this ideal as a "realistic picture of [myself] as one-caring, that guides [me] as [I] strive to meet the other morally."[8] It is a "vision of what I might be" if I manage "to struggle toward the other through clouds of doubt, aversion, and apathy."[9] As such, the "ethical ideal" appears to be an image that the self has of itself as one who excels at caring. Elsewhere, Noddings specifies that it is an image that the self has of itself as one who excels at caring *and* at being cared for, where the "virtue" of caring consists in being disposed to give, as well as to receive, appropriate care.[10] What drives me to care when caring does not come naturally is thus a vision of my own excellence and a desire to promote my excellence through the exercise of my capacity to give and to receive care: "In response to the question why I should behave morally toward one about whom I do not care, we shall see that interest in, caring for, my ethical self induces the characteristic 'I must.'"[11] Whereas "caring arises naturally in the inner circles of human intercourse . . . it must be summoned by a concern for the ethical self in situations where it does not arise naturally."[12]

When Noddings moves away from an explicit consideration of the "ethical ideal," however, she says something different about the good at which "ethical caring" aims. She indicates that what I tend toward in caring for others whom I do not naturally find "engrossing" is not so much the good of myself as one-caring and cared-for, but rather the good of caring itself as it exists in and through interactions between members of a caring community. In "striving to meet the other morally," she says, my efforts are "directed to the maintenance of conditions which will permit caring to flourish."[13] As a person who values "the relatedness of caring" itself, I want through my own efforts to "increase . . . the likelihood of genuine caring" taking place, now and in the future.[14] What I seek as an individual is my "completion in the other—the sense of being cared-for and, I hope, the renewed commitment of the cared-for to turn about and act as one-caring in the circles and chains within which he is defined."[15]

What, then, is the object of "ethical caring?" I propose that we sharpen Noddings's analysis and distinguish between three general goods that we typically aim at as "ethically ideal." What drives us to care when caring does not come naturally is, first, a desire for our own *eudaimonia*: we want to care and to be cared for partly because it is precisely in doing so that we flourish. As relational human beings, we are constituted in such a way that the consistent giving and receiving of care is *constitutive* of our "living well and doing well in action."[16] Of course, in order to become proficient at caring and being cared for, we need others: we need them to serve as objects of our care, and we need them to make us objects of their care. The desire for our own *eudaimonia* thus drives us to promote in others, as well as in ourselves, excellence at caring and being cared for.

At the same time, what drives us to care when caring does not come naturally is, second, a desire for the *eudaimonia* of other human beings. We want in our "ethical caring" to promote the excellence of others,[17] partly with respect to the giving and the receiving of care, regardless of the personal affection that we may or may not feel toward them. Why? Because we want other human beings to excel at being human. Insofar as we are persons of fine character, we want to promote fine character in others. It brings us satisfaction to assist others in the acquisition of virtue, but we do not aim at this acquisition simply for the sake of our own satisfaction. We aim at it because the acquisition of virtue, wherever it occurs, has intrinsic value.

Thirdly, what drives us to care when caring does not come naturally is a desire to contribute, partly through our own exercise of the virtue of caring and being cared for, to the formation and the maintenance of a flourishing human community. We want to contribute to a community whose members share with us a love of human excellence and a commitment to its cultivation. We want this partly because it is instrumentally valuable to us, as parts of the whole, but also because a community that is bound together by a shared commitment to goodness has intrinsic value. We want to promote this value. As Aristotle puts it,

> though admittedly the good is the same for a city as for an individual, still the good of the city is apparently a greater and more complete good to acquire and preserve. For while it is satisfactory to acquire and preserve the good even for an individual, it is finer and more divine to acquire and preserve it for a people and for cities.[18]

Once we begin to make distinctions between the various aspects of what we take to be "ideal," we can see that what drives us to care when we do not care naturally is typically a desire to flourish, to promote the flourishing of others, and to contribute to the flourishing of the human community. Notice that we want in our "ethical caring" both private and shared goods. On the one hand, we want our own good, the good of other human beings, and the good of the community as a whole, whether or not particular others want these goods *with* us. We want these goods because they are good and because we want to want what is good. On the other hand, we want our own good, the good of others, and the good of the community as a whole, partly because those in the community who are good have taught us to want what is good, and we want to want *with* them what both of us take to be good. We want to be more than personally satisfied and independently good in our wanting; we want also to feel connected to others through a shared love of the good.

In sum, we may wish to say with Noddings that what drives a person to care for someone when she does not care naturally is "a picture of myself . . . [as] the way I want to be," but if we make this move, we will have to be careful not to give the impression that this picture is simply an individual's image of her own perfection. We can see that it is on account of a broader array of desires for basic moral goods that a caring person feels the "I must$_2$," even when she does not spontaneously feel the "I must$_1$."

To put the matter in terms of the practical syllogism, it is on account of her love of the good and its component parts that the caring person is disposed to notice and to take advantage of opportunities for promoting what she takes to be good. It is on account of her longing for intimate human community, for example, that she is disposed, as a matter of habit, to "see" various circumstances *as* chances to promote intimate human community, and it is because she "sees" present circumstances in these terms that the desire to show *this* person the value of such intimacy, here and now, is likely to arise and continue to exert its pull. It is the desire to care for *this* person in *this* way for *this* reason and to *this* end (represented by the major premise) that gives impetus and direction to the deliberative process.

DESIRES FOR CONTEXT-SPECIFIC PARTICULAR GOODS

Noddings indicates that what we want in caring for a particular person is "to act so that the happiness and pleasure of the cared-for will be enhanced."[19] We want "not to achieve for ourselves a commendation but to protect or enhance the welfare of the cared-for. . . . [W]e wish to please him for his sake and not for the promise of his grateful response to our generosity."[20] Noddings says that we see the cared-for as he is and as he might become, and we want in our caring to assist him in becoming his own "best self."[21]

To expand a bit on Noddings's suggestions, there are any number of things that we might want for the other in our caring. That is to say, there are many ways in which the intentional content of our desire to benefit the other might be specified. We might want for the other a physical good, a psychological good, a spiritual good, a moral good, or some combination of these. We might want for him a private good whose attraction we cannot understand or appreciate, but whose pursuit we can nevertheless respect. We might want for him certain shared goods that the two of us will be able to enjoy together. We might want goods that are necessary to the well-being of *any* human being. We might want goods that are necessary only to the well-being of *this* human being. We might want what we regard as bare necessities, and we might balk when the other seems to be in need of what we regard as mere luxuries. The distinctions and qualifications that come to mind in trying to specify what we typically desire in wanting to benefit the particular other seem endless.

When we tend toward this or that good in our caring, some of us will presuppose a rather thin understanding of the good,[22] i.e., we will presuppose that the principal values at stake with respect to the well-being of the other are few, say, liberty, autonomy, and self-respect. We might want for the other what *she* regards as a benefit, on the presumption that (because she is a rational moral agent) she is the person who is best qualified to specify her own needs. Others of us will presuppose a much thicker understanding of the good, i.e., we will presuppose that a substantial set of personal and communal excellences are at stake. We might want for the other what the moral exemplars of our community deem best (or would deem best if they could make their wishes known), taking into account but not privileging the perspective of the cared-for.

The context-specific goods that we desire for the particular other will depend on the other and on the sorts of persons that we are as ones-caring. In general, however, it seems safe to say that what most of us want in our caring is partly to benefit the other in accordance with our own understanding of the good, and from our own, distinctive perspective on the other's predicament, where our perspective is informed, but only partly formed, by our awareness of the other's perspective. Yet, what most of us want in our caring is, at the same time, partly to benefit the other as the other himself wants to be benefitted, in accordance with his understanding and love of the good as this comes into focus for him within the framework of his unique predicament. What most of us want is to benefit the other from what we take to be the best of both perspectives, in light of both sets of loves. Of course, when our respective perspectives and loves differ, the conflict is not always easy to adjudicate.

Noddings intimates that we can only be good at making these adjudications if we are, indeed, attuned to what the other is wanting. That is to say, our own wanting to benefit the other can only be constituted virtuously if we are, to some degree, informed by the wanting of the other.[23] Our wanting becomes informed through "engrossment, commitment, [and] displacement of motivation."[24] I suggest that our wanting becomes informed by allowing ourselves to take in, or be taken in by, the wanting of the other, such that we find ourselves wanting something of what the other is wanting. It is when the other's wanting becomes partly our own that we are most likely to have the other's interests, rather than our mere projections of his interests, at heart in our deliberations. Granted, we can sometimes know better than another that the other is in need of benefit and that he is in need of *this* sort of benefit, such that our intentional desire for his benefit is more "on the mark" than his own desire. Nevertheless, we are most likely to be well informed regarding what is at stake for *this* person if we remain open and attentive to *his* desire.

In terms of the practical syllogism, our caring is partly constituted by a set of related desires to benefit one or more persons in some way (represented by the major premise). We might not, in our desire, have a clear sense for what constitutes a benefit in this case, and we might not, in our desire, have a clear sense for how to accomplish what we take to be a benefit. The work of discernment begins with the feeling of caring's desire, but it can proceed only with the introduction of other, more explicitly cognitive elements—elements whose introduction contributes to the further specification of desire. With the feeling of caring's particular desires in place, however, we do feel a sense of attachment to a particular object or set of objects whose well-being now concerns us personally, and it is this sense of attachment that drives and orients our choice-making efforts.

Wanting With and Wanting For

Before we proceed to a discussion of the beliefs and perceptions that contribute to the decision to care, I want to consider more closely the way in which the varied desires that orient our deliberations (and thus evoke certain beliefs and perceptions rather than others) orient us as persons in relation to the objects of our care. Focusing, more specifically, on the compassion that we exercise toward friends, I want to consider the way in which we are, in our compassionate wanting, one and the same with respect to our friends and yet, at the same time, separate and different. Such a consideration should clarify how it is that our wanting draws us into the thick of compassion and establishes a desiderative framework within which to engage relevant particulars.

As we have already discussed, a friend is someone much like us with whom we have come to share a life through the sharing of conversation and other activities over time. A friend is someone with whom we have come to share visions, interests, perceptions, deliberations, pleasures, pains, and so on, such that our unique and separate selves have been knit together into a single, extended self. It is within the context of this single, extended self that oneness, separateness, and the relationship between them must be considered. Oneness must not be construed as a fusion in which it becomes impossible for self or other to bring their own, unique interests to bear on the exercise of an extended moral agency. And separateness must not be construed as an alienation in which it becomes possible for self or other to pursue their own interests completely irrespective of the interests of the other.

What is it, then, that a compassionate person wants in her compassion, and what does her wanting signify about the way in which she stands in relation to her friend? Imagine, if you will, that "you" and "I" are friends.[25] In my compassion for you, I want a number of different things. I want certain things *for* you. I want them for *you* who seem to be over *there*, at *that* pole of our extended self. Insofar as I want something for you that you do not appear to want for yourself, I experience myself to be separate from you in my wanting. Insofar as I want something for you that you appear to want for yourself, but I want it for my own reasons and on account of my own loves, I still experience myself to be separate from you in my wanting.

In my compassion for you, I also want certain things *with* you. I want them from *that* pole of our extended self, but where *this* pole has been propelled into *that* pole, making it possible for my wanting to be to some extent coincident with yours. Insofar as I want something with you that I would not want, but for the fact that you want it, I experience myself to be one with you in my wanting. Insofar as I want something with you that I would want anyway, but I want it for reasons and on account of loves that you and I share, I still experience myself to be one with you in my wanting.

In my compassion for you, I experience myself as becoming who I am, moment by moment, along a continuum between me at *this* pole and you at *that* pole. I experience myself as me-you, and I experience the center of my self to be moving back and forth between me and you, such that what I am aware of in my reflective self-consciousness is something that is sometimes closer to the me-pole and sometimes closer to the you-pole.[26] I experience my self to be at one point in the continuum with respect to certain thoughts, perceptions, desires, pleasures, or pains, and at other points in the continuum with respect to other thoughts, perceptions, desires, pleasures, or pains. Sometimes a desire to be as close to you as you are to yourself comes to the fore and I am drawn into the immediacy of your experience. But then a desire to escape the suffocation of singularity comes to the fore and I am pushed back out of your experience. Sometimes the desire that comes into prominence seems to be distinctively mine-apart-from-yours. Sometimes it seems to be yours-become-mine. It moves this self along the continuum in either case.

Sometimes I slide more toward *that* pole out of a sense of lack. Sometimes I do so out of a sense of abundance. Sometimes I slide more toward *this* pole out of a sense of fear. Sometimes I do so out of a self-loving passion to pursue a private good of my own. Sometimes I am conflicted in my-your wanting and I want both to approach you and to withdraw from you at the same time. Sometimes I move back and forth in my-your wanting from moment to moment, maintaining a loose sense of equilibrium. Sometimes I remain very steadily at one point of balance or imbalance. In any case, my concern here is not to construct an entire theory of the self *qua* extended, but rather to communicate an impression of the fluidity that can exist within and between selves who are friends, especially in the sometimes separate, sometimes shared wantings that are ingredient in compassion for friends.[27]

When I speak of what I want in compassion, then, I mean to call attention to what I-you want, i.e., what I want over *here* apart from you, what I want over *there* along with you (such that *there* becomes *here*). Sometimes my wanting occurs in distinction or contradiction to your wanting, sometimes it occurs in synchronicity, and sometimes in both (but with respect to different desires), all depending upon what *you* want, i.e., where *you* are in the continuum vis-à-vis me, and thus where we are able and willing to meet as one and, at the same time, separate.

A Closer Look

Let us consider more closely some of the wantings that contribute to the decision to exercise compassion. Obviously, different people want different things in relation to different persons who are in different predicaments, but we can indicate some of the possibilities that are consistent with the preceding analysis. We have already explored what one self wants *with* "another itself" in compassion's complacency. Part of what I want with you who are in pain is to fend off, to avoid, or to escape a disagreeable sensation or situation. In *your* pain, the focus of attention and affection is on the sensation or the situation itself and on the (often frustrated) desire to fight and/or to flee the sensation or situation; other aspects of your experience are forced into the periphery. Being *with* you in your pain, I share your (frustrated) desire to fight and/or to flee *this* sensation or situation, which means that I am captivated by what has become nearly the sole content of your experience. In compassion's complacency, we become one self wanting much the same relief.[28]

But then there is more to compassion than complacency. In addition to wanting certain things *with* you from over *there* (such that what was once *there* now seems to be *here*), I want certain things *for* you from over *here* (such that I experience myself to be separate from you in my wanting). I want to reach out to you, to comfort you, and to protect you from further harm. I want to lift you up and out of the constraints of your immediacy and into the possibility of a broader perspective on a broader range of experience. I want to make available to you resources that are mine, partly by virtue of the fact that I am not you. I realize that I am free to transcend your-my pain in a way that you are not and that this makes your-my pain "yours" in a way that it is not "mine." I want to use this difference to your advantage.

Part of what I want *for* you is to use my leverage to alter the sensation or the situation that is presently eliciting your desire to fight and/or to flee. I want to effect a change in your desire by altering the causes of that desire, whatever those causes might be. Part of what I want *for* you is to approach you "from the outside" in a way that restructures what is happening "on the inside" and thereby draws you "out from the inside." That is, I want to effect a change in your desire by changing its intentional content and its intensity—perhaps by providing new information and by inspiring other, competing desires, like the desires that are partly constitutive of hope. Part of what I want *for* you is to hand you the goods that are presently out of your reach. I want to effect a change in your desire by meeting what desires I can, even if the only desire I can meet is your desire not to be utterly alone in your pain.

In addition to wanting certain things with and for *you*, it is important to note that I also want certain things for *me*. In my compassion for you, I want certain things for me insofar as I stand in relation to you. Part of what I want for me is to fight and/or to flee, not only the conditions that drive you-me or you-apart-from-me to fight and/or to flee, but also the condition of you wanting to fight and/or to flee (and being frustrated in your wanting). That is to say, sometimes I experience pain at or about your pain, and I want to alleviate my pain by overcoming or avoiding your pain. Part of what I want in my compassion for you is to alleviate my pain by alleviating yours.

But if my concern is partly to alleviate my pain at or about your pain, then why do I not simply turn my back on you and your pain, alleviating my pain by running away from you and your pain altogether?[29] For one thing, insofar as I share a self with you, I *cannot* disregard completely your wanting and its frustration without engaging in self-forgetfulness and self-deception with regard to the relational nature of this self. More than this, I *do not* run from your pain (or, even as I run, I also turn toward your pain) because part of me *wants* to suffer for and with you in your pain.

Part of me *wants* to suffer *for* you, as one who is able, at any moment, to choose how to suffer or not to suffer at all, because I believe that wanting painfully in response to other people's painful wanting is ingredient in living a full human life. It constitutes a bond between me and others, the frequent experiencing of which is part and parcel of my flourishing as a relational moral agent and friend. It also contributes to the good of others and to the formation of compassionate community, both of which are intrinsically valuable and both of which are likely to be of direct benefit to me (or to persons who are part of me) in the future.

Part of me *wants* to suffer *with* you, as one who is deeply vulnerable to being taken in by your painful wanting, because in being taken in, I discover things about you that I cannot discover in any other way. I discover things that are so threatening and so frightening to you that you ordinarily hide them, not only from me, but also from yourself. I can discover, for example, the terrifying depth of your sense of vulnerability and powerlessness, and I can discover this sense in a full-bodied way, with a vividness and a completeness that is impossible from an emotional distance. For I can experience your vulnerability and powerlessness as partly my own.

This is not simply to say that, in perceiving your weakness I am reminded of my own weakness, such that I really suffer my own, separate sense of vulnerability and powerlessness alongside of you. This may be part of what happens. But it also happens that I experience *your* sense of vulnerability and powerlessness insofar as I am one with you. I share your perception of the situation at hand, your evaluation of it, and your desires in its regard. As I try to place what you and I are feeling, the focus of my attention and energy is on your experience into which I have been propelled. (In other words, the focus is on my experience insofar as I have become you). I might experience in your presence a queasiness in my stomach, a heavy paralysis in my limbs, a panicking, or a loathing, but it does not strike me that these feelings are distinctly my own. They do not seem to me to be component parts of my passional reaction to your experience as I imagine it from over *here*. Rather, they seem to be parts of your passional experience that have spread from *that* pole of our extended flesh to *this* pole, just as tension in the forehead spreads to the neck and down the back.

But why do I *want* to know you in this way? Why do I want to gain access to the deepest recesses of your embodied experience, especially when that experience is so painful to both of us? One answer is that, in sharing your feelings of vulnerability and powerlessness, there is the chance that these feelings will be transformed, largely on account of a change wrought in your own self-understanding and experience. There is the chance that these feelings will cease to be the lonely, desperate feelings of a solitary individual and they will become, instead, possibilities for the creation, sustenance, and enhancement of intimate human fellowship. Shared with me, your vulnerability may become (in some measure) the need and the willingness to trust. Shared with me, your powerlessness may become (to some extent) power for relation and power in relation.

We might say that, at bottom, what I want in compassion is to "save" you, but I want to save you in the sense of empowering you by means of enlarging and expanding you, by means of adding myself—my presence and my power—to you and thus eliciting within you an uncanny sense that this life of yours, which might seem to you in your pain to be so puny and insignificant, so expendable, is actually a component part of something larger. It is at minimum a part of my life.[30] In short, the sharing of pain is power active in the creation of humanly good meaning and value, and this is a power in whose participation I flourish. As we have seen, human flourishing is not simply a matter of avoiding pain in order to maximize the enjoyment of simple pleasures; it is a matter of enjoying the alluring, promising complexity and richness of a morally active life.

If I feel compassion for you, then what I want is to save you from your-my pain, both for your sake and for my own, but where our respective sakes are, in the immediacy of co-suffering, hardly distinguishable to me. I am compelled to aid you in the same way that I am compelled to aid myself: I just do it, for I can do no other. True enough, I may have the sense that, if you were to drown in your pain, I would likely go down with you, but I do not reach out to save you because I judge that it is in my own interest to do so, as if saving myself is the real object of my desire. I just reach out to save you as I reach out to save myself, for you are part of the self within whose parameters I locate "me."

And yet, at the same time, despite the goods that I am able to enjoy in co-suffering, part of me fears this painful intimacy or values it less than I value other goods whose pursuit requires the maintenance of considerably more separateness. Part of me does not acknowledge or is willing to relinquish the promise of co-suffering—bittersweet and ambiguous as its satisfactions are. Part of me wants to keep my life less complicated—less complete, perhaps, but more straightforward and manageable. Hence, I want to save you in a way that saves me from having to become you.

It seems evident that some of us are, as a matter of habit, more intimately related to our friends. Some of us are prone to go beyond intimacy and to "lose ourselves" in (so-called) service to our friends such that we seem unable to perceive, to think, and to want for ourselves. Some of us are habitually more removed from our friends. We can hardly remember the last time that we were caught up in our friends' pain. We do want different things out of life and are therefore differently motivated. These sample specifications of compassion's desire are intended mainly to spark imagination with regard to what is possible for human beings who share their lives with "other themselves."

COMPASSION'S BELIEF AND PERCEPTION

We have discussed some of the many desires that contribute to the decision to exercise compassion. Consider next some of the many beliefs and perceptions that combine with our desires to yield compassion's choice. Let us focus, in particular, on what we commonly take to be the more cognitive aspects of the deliberative process—those aspects in which we discern or figure out the best ways to further specify and to realize the objects of our desire. Again, using Noddings's analysis as a point of reference will enable us to cut to the heart of the matter.

A MODEL OF THE DELIBERATIVE PROCESS

Noddings holds that the process of moral decision making has traditionally been "discussed in the language of the father."[31] The process has been construed as being "governed by the logical necessity characteristic of geometry." It has been construed as having mostly to do with "the establishment of principles and that which can be logically derived from them."[32] In Noddings's view, the deductive approach of the "father" stands in stark contrast to "the approach of the mother," which she takes to be "feminine in the deep classical sense—rooted in receptivity, relatedness, and responsiveness."[33]

It is not that women or men who are "feminine in the deep classical sense" are unable to "arrange principles hierarchically and derive conclusions logically," says Noddings. It is that "feminine" persons tend to "see this process as peripheral to, or even alien to, many problems of moral action."

> Faced with a hypothetical moral dilemma, women often ask for more information. We want to know more, I think, in order to form a picture more nearly resembling real moral situations. Ideally, we need to talk to the participants, to see their eyes and facial expressions, to receive what they are feeling. Moral decisions are, after all, made in real situations; they are qualitatively different from the solution of geometry problems. Women can and do give reasons for their acts, but the reasons often point to feelings, needs, impressions, and a sense of personal ideal rather than to universal principles and their application.[34]

Rather than perceiving a situation of moral import in terms of the possible application of this or that predetermined rule, such that we "abstract away from the concrete situation [only] those elements that allow a formulation of deductive argument,"[35] women tend to perceive a given situation with focused attention to its particulars. We tend to wade through the "complicating factors of particular persons, places, and circumstances" in such a way that we become engrossed in and "modified by the introduction of facts, the feelings of others, and personal histories."[36]

Obviously, perceiving particulars in a way that leaves us affectively altered by them does not in itself suffice to inform us practically of what counts as the best possible response to the situation at hand. Noddings says that deciding what to do requires shifting from a "feminine mode" that is "subjective-receptive" and "essentially nonrational,"[37] to a "masculine mode" that is "rational-objective," abstract, impersonal, logical, and instrumental.[38] It requires stripping the other's predicament of its "complex and bothersome qualities, in order to think it." It requires analyzing, studying, and interpreting this predicament, however, in a way that remains "tied to a relational stake at the heart of caring."[39]

> If rational-objective thinking is to be put in the service of caring, we must at the right moments turn it away from the abstract toward which it tends and back to the concrete. At times we must suspend it in favor of subjective thinking and reflection, allowing time and space for seeing and feeling. The rational-objective mode must continually be re-established and re-directed from a fresh base of commitment. Otherwise we find ourselves deeply, perhaps inextricably, enmeshed in procedures that somehow serve only themselves; our thoughts are separated, completely detached, from the original objects of caring.[40]

Effective deliberation, says Noddings, requires the recognition and the observation of "turning points" in our feeling and our thinking.

A Critique of the Model

Noddings is right, I think, to suggest that the passionate perception of particulars and rational reflection upon these particulars are central to the deliberative process, but there are problems with the way in which she frames this suggestion. First, while it is true that academic moral philosophy has been and is pursued mostly by males in a way that is inescapably, to some degree, reproductive of patriarchal values, "traditional" thinking with regard to the deliberative process is too complex and varied to be classified as straightforwardly universalistic, abstract, and rationalistic. As we have seen throughout this project, Aristotle and Thomas Aquinas are moral philosophers who emphasize the crucial role that practical reasoning plays in the decision-making process, where practical reasoning is construed as being deeply attentive to particulars and to the way in which these particulars affect us passionally. Even if Aristotle and Thomas remain, in certain respects *overly* rationalistic, it is inappropriate implicitly to dismiss them as just two more figures in a homogeneous "masculine" tradition. Instead of invoking and solidifying oversimplified categories of "masculine" and "feminine" moral philosophy, let us focus on constructing models of moral deliberation that speak powerfully to women and men who regard currently "dominant" models as insufficiently illuminative of their experience.[41]

Second, Noddings's model of the decision-making process is problematic in that it misconstrues the nature of our feeling and our thinking and the relationship between the two. As we have seen, Noddings holds that a person who deliberates well exercises two distinct "modes" of moral passivity and activity: a "subjective-receptive mode," which is characterized by "[the] sharing [of] a feeling"[42] and a "rational-objective mode," which is characterized by "[the] formulating or [the] solving [of] a problem."[43] A human being who deliberates well moves back and forth between these static modes in "alternating phases" of deliberative activity. First she undergoes an "essentially nonrational . . . engrossment and displacement of motivation";[44] then she engages in a process of abstraction in which she "converts what [she has received] from the other into a problem, something to be solved."[45] Next, she turns her attention back to "the concrete and the personal"[46] in order to renew her commitment to the particular other; then she transforms the other's reality, once again, into "data, stuff to be analyzed, studied, interpreted."[47] According to this model, "What seems to be crucial is that we retain the ability to move back and forth and to invest the appropriate mode with dominance."[48]

Noddings's model is helpful in that it calls attention to the fact that one cannot arrive at sound solutions to actual persons' moral problems without making some passional investment in their lives. It is also helpful in that it makes plain that passional investment is not in itself sufficient to determine a practically wise response. But the model comes up short in that it presupposes that there are two distinct "modes" of human consciousness—a "feeling mode" and a "thinking mode"—where "feeling" is construed as "essentially nonrational," and "thinking" is construed, to the contrary, as "instrumental . . . rationality (in its objective form)."[49] Noddings's model fails to capture the way in which feeling and thinking function together to constitute a single process of reasonably empassioned reflection.

For example, Noddings draws a sharp contrast between "judgment (in the impersonal, logical sense)," on the one hand, and "faith and commitment," on the other, without clarifying that "judgment (in some other sense)" is part and parcel *of* faith and commitment.[50] She contrasts "instrumental thinking" about "what to do once I have committed myself to doing something" with the commitment that gives rise to such thinking, without clarifying that caring commitment remains passionate *and* reasonable at the same time.[51] She says that there is a "danger in failing to think objectively and well in caring situations," without clarifying that "thinking well" involves more than "thinking objectively," if it involves the latter at all.[52]

I have sought to make manifest throughout this project that all of our feeling has *some* cognitive content (otherwise we could not refer to it meaningfully as *this* or *that* feeling), and all of our thinking is driven to *some* degree by desire (even if it is only the desire to remain free of passional attachment). Our best feeling is thoughtful feeling (i.e., passion that has been educated over time to arise and to persist "in the right way"),[53] and our best thinking is feeling-full thinking (i.e., thinking that takes place fundamentally in the service of love). Rather than imaging the deliberative process as a movement back and forth between "[caring] enough . . . [to] do something wild and desperate," on the one hand, and "climb[ing] into clouds of abstraction," on the other,[54] it would be more cogent to construe it as a movement of passionate, practical rationality that integrates effectively the best of our feeling and the best of our thinking, at the same time.

There might be good motives and reasons for continuing to feel and to think about our feeling and our thinking as being basically different in kind. It might be impossible to discuss the various aspects of our moral agencies without making some such distinctions. But there are no good motives or reasons for bifurcating their respective natures as sharply or as completely as Noddings does. Emphasizing their "qualitative difference"[55] can only serve to reinvigorate age-old habits of "dualistic thinking."[56]

AN ALTERNATIVE MODEL

We have pointed repeatedly in this project to the ways in which desire, belief, and perception interact and interpenetrate to constitute the deliberative activity of the practically wise person—e.g., the way in which desire "selects" what we "see" and how we "see" it, and the way in which what and how we "see," in turn, becomes ingredient in what and how we desire. We can therefore anticipate what a passionate, practical rationality will look like. The following reflections introduce integrated passional-cognitive features of the decision to exercise compassion, particularly compassion for friends. Our reflections on compassion and choice will continue into the next chapter.

As we have seen, we typically want a number of different things in the compassion that we exercise toward our friends. We want certain things *with* our friends. We want certain things *for* our friends. We also want certain things for ourselves insofar as we stand in relation to our friends. It is because (and only because) we feel bound by this bundle of desires that we are moved to initiate a deliberative process aimed at assisting our "other selves" in their painful predicaments. Central to the deliberative process is the discernment of what is at issue in *this* predicament and what counts as the most appropriate response to *this* predicament. As Aristotle says, and as Thomas confirms, discernment with respect to particulars depends upon perception. Let us consider the way in which perception contributes to the decision to show compassion.

Again, imagine that "you" and "I" are friends, that you are in pain, and that I feel some stirrings of compassion for you. Imagine that, in my compassion for you, I want *with* you to withdraw in fear from the pain that I experience to be yours-mine. I want *with* you to become oblivious to the sensations that are imposing themselves upon your-my consciousness. At the same time, I want *for* you to pay close attention to the kind, the location, the intensity, and the duration of the sensations that I experience to be mostly yours-apart-from-mine. I want *for* you to discern what it would take for me to make your sensations cease. I also want for myself to be at your side when you suffer the realization that there is relatively little that can be done to make your sensations cease. I want for myself to be the one who helps you to bear up under the weight of this realization.

From the way in which I have specified the objects of my desire, it is evident that some distinctive perceptions have already conditioned my desire and have, indeed, become ingredient in it. I have, for example, seen you curled up on the bed in tears; I have heard you tell me that you have the flu; I have witnessed the terror in your eyes, and it has reminded me of the time you told me that you fear having the flu because it makes you feel so fragile; I have heard you ask for my company; I have recalled the times that you accompanied me through similar terrors; I have perceived with bittersweet satisfaction how closely we are bound together in our shared commitment to suffer the constraints of our human condition with honesty and tenderness.

Had I come into the room and perceived you hunched over the dresser, pounding your fists and cursing the heavens for your pain—had I recalled from experience that you hate the flu, that you become belligerent every time that you are forced to submit to the dictates of bad fortune, that you like to be left alone and to remain hidden from view in your humiliation—then I would likely have wanted with you, for you, and for me, very different things. For example, I would have wanted *with* you to struggle against, rather than to withdraw from, the sensations of nausea, cramping, and feverishness; I would have wanted *for* you to figure out how to alleviate your symptoms while promoting the impression that you are the one who is in control of your destiny; I would have wanted for myself to assist you in a way that reaffirmed our shared commitment to respect for privacy.

Accordingly, what I want, on account of my initial way of perceiving you and your predicament, conditions further what I perceive: it becomes ingredient in my passionate perception of what counts as meeting effectively the exigencies of *this* predicament. For example, wanting *with* you to withdraw from your-my pain, I perceive you-me as being rather like a frightened child whose immediate need is to be reassured and treated gently. Wanting *for* you that you be reassured, I perceive that I can assist you most effectively by offering you a pain reliever, a cool compress, ice chips, the television remote control, and whatever else your verbal expressions and body language indicate to be appropriate. Wanting for myself to be with you when you are most vulnerable, I perceive that your needs and at least certain of mine can best be met by canceling my plans to attend an evening lecture.

As simple examples like these make manifest, a great deal of our deliberative activity concerning what is going on, what is at stake, whether and how it matters, and whether and how we are able and willing to assist our friends, is accomplished in our integrative wanting, perceiving, and believing. It is a mistake to suggest that I can or should put my feeling and my perceiving on hold in order to reason "objectively" about what is *really* going on. What is really going on is that I am deeply attached to your well-being, I am intensely desirous of meeting your immediate needs, I am afraid that I might not be able to meet some of these needs, and I want to meet whatever needs I can in a way that has a positive and lasting impact on our friendship.

What is really going on is that these desires are making it possible for me to notice things about you that I would not otherwise be inclined to notice (it is only because I *treasure* you that I notice just how helpless you are). They are making it possible for me to attend to what I notice much more carefully than I would otherwise be inclined to do (it is only because I *treasure* you that I wrestle with the question of how I can assist you without inadvertently making you feel more helpless than you already feel). They are providing a passional intensity to my wrestling that I would otherwise not be inclined to experience (it is only because I *treasure* you that the alleviation of your helplessness seems to me to bear directly on your good, my good, *and* the good of our friendship). Hence, to put my desires on hold would be to disable, rather than to enable, my passional-perceptual discernment.

Of course, my desires can be conflicted, and they can yield conflicted perceptions. I might be so terrified of seeing you in such a fragile state, I might be so concerned about what people will say when they see that I have missed the evening lecture, I might be so angry with you for allowing yourself to get sick at such a bad time that these desires overpower my other desires and lead me to perceive wrongly that you wouldn't mind if I left the house for a few hours, and that what you really want and need is a little peace and quiet. My desires can also become conflicted with yours, leaving us conflicted in our perceptions. You might want to ingest some solid food, and you might perceive that it is now appropriate to do so; I might want to keep you from becoming nauseous, and I might perceive that the best way to do so is to insist that you wait until your stomach is more settled. You might perceive my insistence as s/mothering; I might perceive it as an exercise of prudence

The way to adjudicate these conflicts, however—the way to insure the appropriateness of the overall structure of our own desire and the appropriateness of our consequent perceptions—is not to try to extricate ourselves from the pull of desire (which is impossible). Rather, the thing to do is to *feel* the range of our desires and to reflect upon them honestly in light of a well-deliberated vision of the good and an abiding desire for its realization. We ought to engage in empassioned reflection, privately, in conversation with our friend, and in conversation with other friends who are adept at exposing our base selfishness and the self-deceptions that we employ to keep our selfishness from being exposed. Of course, lack of time and other constraints can make such conversations impossible. This is one reason why sharing our lives with friends who share with us a commitment to the long-term moral education of our desire is so crucial. When actual conversations are impossible, past or imagined conversations function to bring to the fore our dominant loves, and to raise critical questions in light of these loves.

I believe that the more we seek to clarify the relationship between our desiring, our perceiving, and our thinking, as these combine to contribute to the decision to exercise compassion, the more these aspects of our moral agencies will seem to us to be inextricably intertwined. The more we reflect upon our desiring, the clearer it will become to us that it is always an intentional desiring that is set up, partly constituted, and reconstituted by our changing beliefs and perceptions. The more we reflect upon our thinking, the more convinced we will become that it is always an embodied thinking that is initiated, directed, sustained, and enjoyed *in* desire (and the more concerned we will become to educate our desires well).

In any case, our desiring, our perceiving, and our thinking function together to constitute a unified process of discerning what is most likely in this situation to contribute to the end desired. Notice that, at the same time that we take in, or are taken in by, our friend's own wanting, such that our perceptions of him and his predicament are conditioned by *that* wanting, we are and remain separate from our friend in our own wanting, such that our perceptions are also conditioned by *this* wanting. Part of the work of discernment consists in teasing apart the sometimes tangled web of our wanting and our friend's wanting, such that we are in a good position to distinguish between several different perspectives on a given predicament, and we are able to "see" from those different perspectives at the same time, assessing with well-ordered passion what we "see."

The idea is not to squelch our self-regarding desire (which is, in the end, impossible), but rather to arrive through shared and private reflection at a configuration of self-regarding and other-regarding desire that is appropriate to the circumstance. The idea is to insure, as far as possible, that our perceptions of a given predicament (and our perceptions of our involvement in it) are guided by a well-reflected configuration of desire. Our perceptions will be guided by some set of desires in any case. But how is it that the appropriateness of our desiderative orientation can be determined and insured? I pursue this thorny question in what follows, under the rubric of discerning compassion's mean.

Ten

Compassion and Choice (2)

Paying particular attention to compassion for friends, we have discussed the nature of compassion's complacency. We have also discussed the way in which a more inclusive set of desires, perceptions, and beliefs comes into play with compassion's complacency to constitute the act of becoming aware of and passionally attached to friends in pain, such that we are moved to reflect upon and to determine the best possible response to their predicaments. Our task in the present chapter is to discuss in more detail the way in which compassion's discernment takes place, and the way in which this discernment issues forth in the act of compassion, proper, i.e., the act of feeling-acting in the way that we discern to be best.

In terms of the practical syllogism, we have explored the content of the major premise (representing compassion's desire), and we have begun to explore the content of the minor premise (representing compassion's belief and perception). We have also explored the way in which compassion's complacency conditions the formulation of the major and minor premises by contributing the element of wanting *with* to the passional-cognitive mix. In this chapter, we will focus principally on the conclusion of the syllogism (representing compassion's act or intention to act), i.e., the way in which the (already conditioned) major and minor premises combine to issue forth in a choice to exercise the virtue of compassion.

Qua virtue, compassion is a habitual disposition concerned with choosing both to act and to feel (passion) in the way that we deem to be best on the basis of our deliberations. It is a habitual disposition concerned with choosing both to act and to feel in accordance with the mean, where the mean just *is* the best action-passion possible (i.e., the "right" action-passion) in a given circumstance. To limit the scope of our inquiry, we will focus mainly on the *choosing to feel* that constitutes a significant (though not sufficient) part of compassion's "act." We will examine, in particular, what it is to choose to feel compassion well, i.e., "in the right way." It is one thing to desire the alleviation of another person's pain, such that we are moved to figure out how best to accomplish that alleviation. It is another thing to carry out our desiderative-perceptual discernments "in the right way." The *virtue* of compassion requires the latter.

CHOOSING TO FEEL COMPASSION'S COMPLACENCY

Nel Noddings maintains that the impulse of "natural caring," i.e., the feeling that "I must₁" do something on behalf of the particular other who confronts me in his or her need, is "innate, [lying] latent in each of us, awaiting gradual development in a succession of caring relations."[1] This does not mean, however, that every time the feeling that "I must₁" do something arises within us, we are compelled either to keep feeling it or to act on what we feel. In both cases we have a choice.

Regarding our initial "engrossment," Noddings claims that (normally) "our apprehension of happiness or misery in others, comes through immediately," but once we "receive" what the other is "feeling," we have a choice: "we may accept what we feel, or we may reject it."[2] We may choose either "to proceed in a state of trust or to deny what [we] have received and talk [ourselves] into feeling comfortable with the denial."[3] Regarding subsequent feelings of "motivational displacement," Noddings says that here, too, we have a choice:

> I may reject [the "I must,"] instantaneously by shifting from "I must do something" to "Something must be done," and removing myself from the set of possible agents through whom the action should be accomplished. I may reject it because I feel that there is nothing I can do. If I do either of these things without reflection upon what I might do in behalf of the cared-for, then I do not care. Caring requires me to respond to the initial impulse with an act of commitment: I commit myself either to overt action on behalf of the

cared-for (I pick up my crying infant) or I commit myself to think-ing about what I might do.[4]

What if I do not feel an initial "I must₁"? Even if the impulse to care is "natural," it is not natural to feel it in every circumstance of human need with which we are confronted. Can we *choose* to care, even in cir-cumstances where the impulse to care does not arise spontaneously? I am asking two different questions, really. First, can we choose to become en-grossed in someone whom we do not naturally find engrossing? And second, can we choose to care even if we are unable to become en-grossed? Noddings's answer to the second question is that, in cases where we do not feel engrossed in the other, we can at least act *as though* we care. We can benefit the other out of concern for our own ethicality, leav-ing open the possibility that we might in time become engrossed. Apart from feeling engrossed, however, we cannot really be said to care for the other.[5]

Noddings's answer to the first question is unclear. Asking whether or not there can be a moral "demand" to care, Noddings replies that "There can be, surely, no demand for the initial impulse that arises as a feeling, an inner voice saying 'I must do something,' in response to the need of the cared-for."[6] The reason seems to be because we have no access to the impulse to care when the impulse fails to arise spontaneously. Elsewhere, however, Noddings says that "I am obliged, then, to accept the initial 'I must' when it occurs and even *to fetch it out of recalcitrant slumber when it fails to awake spontaneously*,"[7] which implies that we *do* have access to the impulse to care when it fails to arise spontaneously.

THE ISSUE OF ACCESS

The issue of access is an important one. If engrossment is essential to caring and we have no access to the impulse toward engrossment, then we cannot be morally obligated to care: "ought implies can." Similarly, with respect to compassion for friends, some measure of complacency is essential to the exercise of compassion. Apart from it, we are not re-oriented by others passionally to experience the initial sense of familiarity with and attunement to their suffering that enables us to seek the al-leviation of their suffering as we seek the alleviation of our own. But if complacency is essential to compassion, then we are bound to ask: What access do we have to complacency? Can we *choose* to feel compassion's complacency in cases where it does not arise spontaneously?

Suppose that my friend is in pain, that I want to alleviate her pain, and that I also want to alleviate my pain at her pain. Suppose that I want to alleviate our pain from a desiderative-cognitive location in our extended self that is far removed from the desiderative-cognitive location in which my friend experiences the constituents of her pain. And suppose that, for one reason or another, I regret this remove, and I wish that I could take my friend in, or be taken in by her, in such a way that it becomes possible to experience her pain constituents as partly my own, if only briefly. Perhaps I want to become a more compassionate person and I see this as an opportunity to cultivate the openness and the vulnerability that are basic to compassion. Perhaps I want to experience in compassion's complacency an intimacy in which the moral significance of my life is confirmed. Perhaps I want to be in the best position possible to discern what it is that my friend is suffering so that I can aid her effectively in that suffering. In any case, how can I choose to become spontaneously captivated by another's experience of pain?

Putting the question this way sounds paradoxical. Most of us are accustomed to thinking of choice as an intention to act that is brought about by force of intellect and will. We neglect to consider passion's contribution to the deliberative process, and we neglect to consider the access that we have to our choice-constituting passions. Moreover, we are accustomed to thinking of choice as an intention to act that can only be well made after substantial deliberation has taken place, and we forget that it is possible to choose, over time and with a lot of practice, to become the sorts of persons who are disposed to make certain snap decisions well. It is possible repeatedly to entertain the sorts of beliefs, perceptions, and desires that will dispose us to take in, or to be taken in by, the suffering of our friends. Still, there does seem to be something odd about the notion of choosing complacency, for complacency is a matter of being passively moved by someone, and we cannot simply choose that someone move us. Or can we? Is there anything that we can do to contribute to our complacency in someone's experience of pain?

In *Friendship, Altruism, and Morality*, Lawrence Blum considers three different views regarding the kind of access that we have to what he calls our "altruistic emotions" (i.e. emotions that take as their objects other persons in light of their weal and woe).[8] Let us take a brief look at these views and at Blum's responses to them. According to the first view, which Blum finds in Henry Sidgwick and Immanuel Kant,[9] "it is possible for us to bring it about that we have a greater amount of altruistic feeling than we might otherwise have, by placing ourselves in circumstances which we know to be causally related to producing altruistic feelings in ourselves."[10] For example, if visiting hospitals tends to elicit compassion in us, then we can become more compassionate people by volunteering to work in a hospital on a regular basis. In Blum's view, this sort of tactic is likely to meet with success in only certain sorts of people. Placing ourselves in direct contact with suffering, he argues, is likely to elicit altruistic emotion (as opposed to feelings like disgust and contempt) only if we are already "open to feeling the full human force of the circumstances in question," and only if we have already removed "various obstacles within [ourselves] which would block such an effect."[11] In other words, this technique will only work if we are the sorts of people who really *want* it to work, and a change in circumstance alone is not sufficient to elicit a change in our wanting. It is not sufficient to elicit a change in what Blum calls our "being-towards-others," i.e., "those aspects of our attitudes, emotions, sentiments, ways of treating and regarding, patterns of behavior, feelings, emotional responses, values, and moral beliefs which have to do with the weal and woe of other persons."[12]

The second view, which Blum finds in Philip Mercer,[13] is that it is sometimes possible to summon up altruistic emotions directly by attending deliberately to certain features of a given situation more than others. For example, it is possible to summon up compassion for a person in pain when compassion does not arise spontaneously by focusing on the ways in which the person is like us, rather than the ways in which he or she is unlike us. Blum thinks that this ploy will work for some people, but certainly not for everyone. He argues that, "the will can operate to bring about altruistic feelings only in people (or people in certain situations) who are already normally prone to that altruistic feeling" and are simply struggling with something like a bad mood that can willfully be dismissed.[14] Again, the question is: what can we do to make ourselves more prone to altruistic feeling in the first place?

The third view, which Blum identifies with theorists like Anthony Kenny and Stuart Hampshire,[15] is that, because altruistic emotions are partly constituted by cognitions, we can rid ourselves of inappropriate emotions and acquire appropriate ones by altering the beliefs and judgments that are currently holding our attention. For example, suppose that the fear of becoming infected with the AIDS virus is blocking our attempt to show compassion toward a particular persons with AIDS. We might be able to rid ourselves of this fear (and thus to unblock our compassion) by becoming convinced that the virus is not spread through "casual contact." Blum is sympathetic to this view, but argues that, while it is often possible to talk ourselves *out of* emotions by determining that we were previously mistaken in certain of our beliefs or judgments, it is much more difficult to talk ourselves *into* altruistic emotions: "For we can come to be convinced of the facts on which it is appropriate to feel certain emotions, and yet nevertheless not come to feel them."[16]

> Thus there seems to be a gap between acknowledging something as an appropriate object of an altruistic emotion, and coming to have that emotion. Other elements in our attitudes, feelings (towards particular people or towards people in general), or general being-towards-others can prevent the connection from being made. Thus, though assessing objects and beliefs can play some role in moral change regarding our altruistic emotions, there are distinct limits to that role.[17]

In sum, Blum argues that each of these views tells us something about the access that we have to our altruistic emotions, but each of them is incomplete: "not only does each view give us only some of the ways that we are able to change morally; but in addition, they all fail to portray adequately what is involved in the processes of moral change which they do articulate. What all fail to bring out is that our being-towards-others is fundamental to moral change."[18] What sort of access, then, do we have to our "being-towards-others"? How can *it* be changed? It is beyond the scope of Blum's project to pursue this question.

Blum's criticisms are, in my judgment, convincing. Looking specifically at compassion's complacency (the disposition toward which is an aspect of our "being-towards-others"), it looks like none of the views considered by Blum will, taken in isolation, suffice to settle the question of access for us, either. But suppose that we were to combine these views, fill them out, and give them a fleshly focus in an imaginative, practical activity. If our "being-towards-others" is indeed a totality of "interconnected and interpenetrating . . . beliefs, attitudes, and emotions regarding the weal and woe of others,"[19] then perhaps we can change our "being-towards-others" by making and repeatedly remaking substantial, integrated, and well-focused changes in our "beliefs, attitudes, and emotions" vis-à-vis persons in pain.

STRATEGIES FOR GAINING ACCESS

Along these lines, let me suggest some of the things that a person can do to summon up complacency toward "another himself" or "another herself" when complacency does not arise spontaneously. I make these suggestions in light of all that has been said up to this point about the nature of character virtue and the way in which virtue is exercised within the context of character-friendship. I can contribute to my own complacency in my friend's wanting *if I want to*[20] by doing two principal things. First, I can invite the other to reveal something of his experience to me. To this end, I can assure him of my trustworthiness. I can tell him that I *want* to suffer with him and that he would be promoting my good, as well as his own, by allowing me to do so. I can tell him that I will be in a better position to help him if he communicates to me what he is experiencing. I can tell him that, even if it turns out that I cannot do anything to alleviate certain aspects of his pain, communicating his experience to me is likely to make him feel less isolated in the pain that he continues to feel.

If I find a good that is tempting enough to elicit the other's self-revelation, then I will gain some information about what it is that the other finds so distressing, how distressing he finds it, how it is that he wants to be helped, what he envisions my role in that process to be, and so on. At the same time, I will initiate a process of shared deliberation in which patterns of desiderative-cognitive movement that my friend and I have cultivated over the years are likely to regain a place of prominence in my perspective. These patterns will provide me with a horizon of shared meaning against which the communicated desires, perceptions, and beliefs of the other become more and more familiar to me, to the point that the "voice" of the other becomes, again, one of the "voices" within myself with which I tell myself what is going on, what is at issue with respect to what is going on, and how much it matters.

What happens if I ask excellent questions and get excellent answers, but still feel passionally numb or distant? A second thing that I can do is to try to dispel certain of the desires, perceptions, and beliefs that appear to be working together to inhibit my complacency. I do not construe this as a process in which "reason" grabs hold of "passion" in order to steer it and, if necessary, whip it into shape. Rather, I construe this as a process in which we, as well-integrated thinkers and feelers, seek to gain or to regain a kind of "reflective equilibrium" with respect to the full range of intentional desires that currently condition our affective awareness.[21] We gain or regain this equilibrium by feeling thoughtfully and reflecting passionately upon our current desires for context-specific goods in light of our abiding desire for *eudaimonia* and its constitutive components, where our desire for the good life has been shaped and reshaped over the years in conversation with friends who are committed to exposing our vicious self-deceptions and the related perversions of our loves.

Suppose I discover through feeling and reflecting that the passion of anger is presently inhibiting my complacency. Because I am angry with my friend, I perceive her and her predicament in light of a desire to punish her, such that her suffering actually pleases me to some degree, rather than wholly displeasing me. If I want to become complacent in the other's wanting to be free of her pain, then I will have to dispel my anger. I can sometimes do this by "talking myself out of" the anger, e.g., by reasoning that what I took to be a slight was not in fact a slight, that the other did not slight me deliberately, or that she has already suffered enough for what she did. But I will only be motivated to engage in such "talk," and I will only find it convincing, to the extent that my deepest loves are engaged. I will have to recall and re-feel that I love being a compassionate healer more than I love being an administrator of just vengeance. I will have to recall and re-feel that I love to treasure my friend in her vulnerability more than I love to be in a position of control. If my rational reflection does not succeed in seducing desires like these to the fore of my perspective or, to put it another way, if desires like these do not take an interest in my reflection, then I will not be persuaded to be compassionate.

Suppose I discover through reflecting and feeling that what is presently inhibiting my complacency is a simple desire to have a "good time." Because I am interested in having a "good time," I perceive my friend as being a "drag," which in turn makes me want to ignore him. If I want to become complacent, then I will have to bring into affective perspective a broader range of desires. I will have to bring into focus my desire to be a good person who is unable easily to turn away from those who suffer, my desire to be a good friend who sacrifices immediate pleasures for the sake of my friend's well-being, my desire to have a friend who will do the same for me, my desire to enjoy the bitter, but sweet satisfactions of intimacy in pain, and so on. To the extent that I succeed in reordering and re-feeling my desires in light of a well-deliberated vision and love of the good, I will succeed in displacing my desire for immediate pleasure to the periphery of my passional awareness.

These kinds of maneuverings can be ineffectual in bringing about the desired complacency, even if we are people who value complacency greatly. The reason, I think, is often because we try to alter our passional orientations irrespective of our embodiment. We figure that if we think about it hard enough and exert our will with sufficient intelligence, the complacency that we desire will be forthcoming. But sometimes our bodies seem to have "minds" and "hearts" of their own. They seem to "insist" upon a feeling of paralysis, a heaviness, a tension in the muscles, or a feeling of pressure building under the skin. These feelings are usually the bodily aspects of passions that continue to inhibit our complacency. Sometimes, changing these passions requires putting our feeling and reflecting into a practice that embodies the change desired. How can this be accomplished?

First, we need a reasonably concrete vision of the end to be achieved. Wanting to feel more connected to my friend in her pain, I might imagine that she and I really do share a single, extended self. She and I remain separate from each other in that we embody from moment to moment numerically different configurations of desire, perception, and belief that can only to a limited degree be constituted the same. And yet she and I remain one with each other in that the habits of desire, perception, and belief that partly constitute our respective orientations are jointly constructed and reconstructed through the sharing of conversation and other activities over time.

Accordingly, I might envision myself being drawn into the depths of my friend's painful experience, not in order to be "lost" therein, but in order to "relocate" my experience relative to hers. I might seek to "find" myself constituted partly by the experience of my "other self" so that I will be in a better-informed position to contribute to the alleviation or the reconstruction of her-my experience. I might envision my self-constituting movements of desire, perception, and thought to be emanating from that pole of our extended flesh, so that what I ordinarily regard as *this* body seems to become coincident with *that* body, and the bodily sensations that my friend experiences as uniquely hers seem to become partly mine.

We are most likely to be effective in accomplishing what we imagine ourselves to be accomplishing if we attempt to embody our imaginings in act. What we need, second, is a physical activity that enables us to "body forth" imagined changes in our desire, perception, and belief. For example, wanting to bring about a contraction of the extended flesh that I have come to share with my friend, I might engage in an imaginative breathing exercise in her presence. Suppose that my friend is lying on a bed in pain. I might bring myself to curl up behind her, feeling at first that my embrace is forced or otherwise awkward, but gradually feeling more relaxed and "at home" as I begin to focus on her breathing. Listening to her breathe and feeling my hand rise with the expansion of her rib cage, I might begin to breathe *with* my friend, imagining that I am breathing in through *my* mouth and out through *hers*, or that I am breathing in through *her* mouth and out through the locus of *her* pain, wherever she indicates that locus to be.

What this does is to relax me and give me an imaginative, physical sensation of passing right through the visible (skin) boundaries that seem ordinarily to separate our respective bodies. It gives me a sense of actually embodying the desires, beliefs, and perceptions that I imagine myself to be sharing with my friend. The pleasure of warm flesh against flesh (ambiguous though it is when that flesh is aching) yields to the bittersweet pleasure of "touching" another's bodily experience, which in turn yields to the suffering of her-my pain.

Breathing in unison also provides me with information regarding what the other is feeling. I recall, for example, breathing in synchronicity with a friend while he was suffering acute abdominal pain and realizing only in our quick, shallow, irregular breathing that he was utterly terrified. I could see that he was in pain, and I suffered pain *at* his pain, but it was not until my body was caught up in his body's basic movement that I discerned the particular nature of his pain as terror and felt this terror *with* him. Breathing with this friend, I became momentarily paralyzed by a fear that was distinctly his, but had become partly mine, as I had become partly him.

It makes sense to say that, once I experienced my friend's breathing pattern, I recognized it to be a pattern indicative of fear, such that the

belief that my friend felt fear caused and partly constituted my own, responsive fear. What paralyzed me, then, was not the same object that
paralyzed my friend, but rather my perception of my fearful friend. But
this sensible explanation fails to capture the experience well: the experience was that, while I was breathing with my friend, I was invaded by a
foreign terror. I was invaded by a sensation in my flesh that seemed to me
to originate in the flesh of another, and it was only after being physically
taken with this sensation that I judged it to be a physical component of
my friend's-my terror. The implication is that I shared part of the physical component of my friend's terror before I came to share (more fully)
the cognitive component. It might be the case that, when we feel (mostly)
resistant to the possibility of sharing intentional desire, our (relatively
weak) desire to share desire anyhow can be strengthened relative to other,
competing desires by seeking to share physical sensation.

By employing these and other, related strategies we *can* choose to
feel (where "choosing" is construed broadly as an intelligent-empassioned
act of both doing and letting happen). We can choose to feel compassion's
complacency, in particular, by engaging in well-conceived activities that
are intended to bring about the experienced dissolution of what we ordinarily take to be boundaries between separate selves and the shared
embodiment of occurrent beliefs, perceptions, and desires. Pursuing
such activities includes focusing on certain aspects of a situation more
than others, e.g., construing our friends as "other ourselves" with whom
we share our lives and with whom we continue to co-constitute our
moral agencies. It also includes assessing some of the beliefs and judgments that are ingredient in our passions (where "assessing" is construed
as taking place partly through the feeling of our desires for various
goods), e.g., reflecting upon and feeling into focus our abiding desires to
promote the good of our "other selves," to strengthen the bonds of our
friendships, and to cultivate our own excellence, such that conflicting desires get displaced to the periphery of our awareness.

Choosing to feel involves more, however, than choosing here and
now to entertain and to privilege beliefs, perceptions, and desires that are
productive of a particular passion. It also involves choosing to become,
over time, the sorts of persons who are disposed as a matter of habit to
be passionally moveable. Choosing to feel compassion's complacency, in
particular, involves choosing repeatedly, inside and outside of situations
in which we are actually confronted with those who suffer, to be and to

become the sorts of people who are characteristically attuned to what other people are going through, ready and even eager to take in, or to be taken in by, their experiences. It requires anticipating and eventually becoming wholeheartedly convinced that this is the best way to be. And it requires the coordinated cultivation of a host of interrelated excellences, like courage, honesty, humility, attentiveness, self-confidence, generosity, and practical wisdom.[22]

Unfortunately, it is no easier to specify how *these* virtues are acquired than it is to specify how the virtue of compassion is acquired. It should be evident from what has already been said, however, that the acquisition of moral excellence requires the continual refinement of our loves and our ways of seeing within the context of various character-friendships. This formation and re-formation takes place as we make one decision after another, as we feel, reflect, and converse about whether the decisions that we have already made have been productive of *eudaimonia*, and as we feel, reflect, and converse about how we can make our future decisions more productive. The moral significance of having friends, from the earliest years on, who are good, good for us, and pleasant to be with—friends who share with us a desire to live well and to discern what counts as a life lived well—is hard to overstate.

CHOOSING THE MEAN OF COMPASSION

As we ponder some of the ways in which we might choose to feel with someone a passion that we do not feel spontaneously, many of us are likely to think-feel something along these lines: "There are often good reasons why I do not undergo complacency relative to a particular friend's frustrated wantings. True enough, complacent co-wanting can and usually does empower and enrich my life in morally significant ways. It can and usually does enable me to help my friend more effectively. But it does all of this at a high price. Sometimes I am unable or unwilling to pay that price. I am committed to my friend's well-being, but I also have commitments to myself and to other people in my life. Sometimes it seems best not to take on any more pain than I am utterly constrained to take on."

As reflections like these make manifest, individuals who are compassionate by disposition are often in the position of having to make difficult decisions about whether and how to exercise the compassion toward which we are disposed. We cannot exercise compassion toward every person who confronts us with his or her pain. We cannot even exercise compassion toward every one of our friends every time that they are in need. The needs of the world are virtually infinite, and we are finite creatures who must set limits to where and how we expend our precious moral resources. How do we go about setting these limits well?

What is the mean of compassion? Recall that hitting the mean (i.e., the bull's-eye) is a matter of steering a course between the extremes of excess and deficiency. It is a matter of acting and feeling "at the right times, with reference to the right objects, toward the right people, with the right motive, and in the right way."[23] Hitting the mean of compassion, in particular, will be a matter of choosing rightly what manner of compassion to have for whom, in what circumstances, to what end, and with what motive. Clearly, choosing what is intermediate and best with respect to compassion will require the exercise of practical wisdom. It will require choosing what to feel and how to act in light of our abiding visions and values, with empassioned attunement to perceived particulars. We cannot, therefore, expect to come up with principles whose application to particular cases will yield up ready and easy answers. What we can do, however, is to begin asking pertinent questions about what is at issue in exercising compassion well. As Nel Noddings puts it, we can try to discern, apart from our engagement in any particular predicament, "the kinds of things I must think about when I am in a conflict of caring."[24]

Let us consider, then, some of what is at issue with respect to the proper exercise of compassion, focusing on the following questions: (1) What is at issue in feeling compassion for the right end? How can we effect the right relationship among the various ends at which we aim in our compassion? (2) What is at issue in feeling compassion in the right manner? How can we effect the right balance between our wanting *with* others and our wanting *for* them? (3) What is at issue in feeling compassion for the right persons? How can we effect the right measure in feeling compassion for some persons but not for others? Questions like these are more than academic. It is in shaping our intentional desires, our passionate perceptions, and our careful reflections, particularly in conversation with our "other selves," that our characters are formed and re-formed. It is in embodying our character-shaping feeling and reflecting through repeated acts of compassion that the virtue of compassion is acquired.

CHOOSING TO FEEL COMPASSION FOR THE RIGHT END

We have already discussed some of the goods at which we typically aim as we deliberate about whether and how to feel compassion. We have discussed these in terms of compassion's desire. Let us consider, however, what is at issue in shaping *well* the intentional content of our compassion-constituting desires. Let us begin with a look at the end/s of caring.

The End/s of Caring

Recall that there are a number of ends at which we aim in "ethical caring." First, we aim at our own perfection: "The very goodness I seek," says Noddings, is "the perfection of ethical self."[25] The ethical self is defined in terms of the capacity to give and to receive care. Hence, the perfection of the ethical self amounts to the perfection of its capacity to care and to be cared for.[26] The end at which we aim in our caring is thus our own perfection as sources and recipients of care, and the "joy" that accompanies this perfection.[27]

Second, we aim in our caring at "the welfare, protection, or enhancement" of the other, for the other's own sake.[28] Because the other, too, is defined in terms of caring, this means that we aim in our caring at the enhancement of the other's capacity to give and to receive care with joy. As Noddings puts it, we "see the cared-for as he is and as he might be," and we work to help him actualize his "best self."[29] We work to effect in him the "renewed commitment . . . to turn about and act as one-caring in the circles and chains within which he is defined."[30]

Third, we aim in our caring at the good of caring relation itself.[31] That is, we aim generally to increase "the likelihood of genuine caring" taking place between the members of our community.[32] We increase the likelihood of caring taking place when we aim at the maintenance and the enhancement of our own and each other's personal ethical ideals: "Since we are dependent upon the strength and sensitivity of the ethical ideal—both our own and that of others—we must nurture the ideal in all of our educational encounters. . . . The primary aim of all education must be nurturance of the ethical ideal."[33]

It is appropriate, in Noddings's view, to aim at all three of these goods in our caring. But what is the relationship between these goods? How are they to be ordered relative to each other? Noddings does not pursue this question. She does say, however, that "Caring preserves both the group and the individual. . . . I must meet [the] other . . . as one-caring so long as caring itself is not endangered by my doing so,"[34] which suggests that the end at which we ought chiefly to aim in our caring is the promotion of caring relations—including those in which we are not direct participants. Of course, we promote caring relations partly by caring for others.[35] And prerequisite to caring for others is caring for ourselves. "The one-caring . . . needs no special justification to care for herself for, if she is not supported and cared-for, she may be entirely lost as one-caring. If caring is to be maintained, clearly, the one-caring must be maintained."[36]

What happens when we find ourselves in conflicts of caring? What happens, for example, when aiming at another's perfection as one-caring and cared-for requires diminishing our own perfection as ones-caring and cared-for? Noddings seems at times to imply that conflicts between caring for self and caring for others do not arise. "Since I am defined in relation," she says, "I do not sacrifice myself when I move toward the other as one-caring."[37] Rather, I benefit myself by "act[ing] in accordance with that which is good in my deepest nature."[38] Elsewhere, however, Noddings acknowledges that the one-caring can sometimes find herself in situations in which she is "overwhelmed by cares and burdens." In such situations, "The ethical responsibility of the one-caring is to look clear-eyed on what is happening to her ideal and how well she is meeting it."[39] The responsibility of the one-caring is to preserve herself *as* one-caring, for the sake of others and, ultimately, for the sake of caring itself.

Ordering the End/s of Compassion

Noddings is right to insist that it is appropriate to aim in our caring, not simply at the good of particular others, but also at the good of ourselves and at the good of the community as a whole. But I think that she construes these goods too narrowly and, as a result, does not capture much of what is at issue for the person who wishes to care for the right end/s. It is, indeed, appropriate that we aim partly at our own good in caring for others. But aiming at our own good involves much more than aiming at an increase in our capacities to care and to receive care from others. It involves much more than aiming at the joy that accompanies the exercise of these capacities. Aiming at our own good involves aiming at a whole range of character and intellectual virtues, and at the material and social conditions that make the cultivation of these virtues both possible and enjoyable. It includes aiming at the *eudaimonia* that accompanies the life of complete virtue (and good fortune).

Similarly, it is appropriate that we aim in our caring for others, not simply at the promotion of the joy that they will experience in exercising their capacities to give and to receive care, but also at the promotion of the *eudaimonia* that they will experience in exercising courage, honesty, generosity, patience, perseverance, practical wisdom, and other virtues, too, under conditions that are conducive to the enjoyment of their exercise. It is appropriate that we aim in our caring for others also at the good of the community as a whole. Promoting the good of the whole is no simple matter, but it involves working to establish the conditions under which as many human beings as possible are likely to do as well as possible. Human beings are likely to do well under conditions of caring and cooperation, but they are also likely to do well under conditions of justice, respect for human rights, jurisprudence, and certain forms of competition.

Once we acknowledge that many more goods are at stake in our caring than the promotion of joy in caring relation, it becomes more difficult to sort through what is at issue in choosing *well* what to aim at in our caring. Suppose we take the flourishing of ourselves and every other human being to be of equal moral value, and that we are inclined to aim in our caring at the promotion of as many relevant private and shared goods as possible, with the good of the community as our ultimate, but distant aim. How do we order the various goods that we take to be constitutive of our own flourishing as individuals? (Do we value the cultivation of our excellence in alleviating pain more than the cultivation of our excellence in helping people to face the painful truths of human existence? If we do so with good reason and passion, does this entail that it is ordinarily best for us to aim in our caring at the alleviation of pain, even when this requires feeding people's self-deceptions?) How do we order the various goods that we take to be constitutive of the flourishing of others? (Does the other value in herself the good of being honest with herself more than the good of being free of pain? If she does so with good reason and passion, does this entail that it is ordinarily best for us to aim in our caring for her at telling her the truth, even though doing so will cause her pain?)

How do we adjudicate conflicts between our own (ordered) goods and the (ordered) goods of others? (What if telling the other the painful truth not only causes *her* pain, but causes *us* pain as well? How do we weigh the moral significance of her-our pain against the loss of good that the other would suffer by being deceived? What if we can deceive the other without her knowing it?) And how do we make these adjudications in the interest of the larger community? (Is it better to constitute ourselves as a community of pain-relievers, as a community of truth-tellers, or as a community of persons who rank these and other goods differently? How much tolerance with respect to differences in vision and value is compatible with the kind of social order that we value most?)

Sharpening our focus a bit, let us consider some of the questions that typically come to the fore as we seek to form rightly our intentions to exhibit compassion toward "other ourselves." First, is it best to aim in my compassion for a friend of good character at what *she* perceives to be productive of her good or at what *I* perceive to be productive of her good? Because my friend and I are in the habit of forming and reforming our visions and loves of the good conjointly, our visions and loves are likely to be constituted to a certain degree "the same." True enough, my friend is likely to value certain things that I would not ordinarily value, but the very fact that someone so valuable to me values these things is likely to have an impact on my affection and attention. It is likely to leave me open to the possibility of discovering for myself the basis for my friend's valuation. Where this basis remains opaque to me, I am likely to be interested in making some "connections" between our differences, partly by recollecting deeper structures of commonality in valuing. In short, I am likely to construct my own passionate, perceptive "take" on the present predicament in light of the passionate, perceptive "take" of my friend, settling at any given moment for the "angle" that strikes me as clearest and most compelling, all relevant "angles" being considered.

We can see, then, that the question we have asked does not reflect the relational reality in which the compassionate person typically locates "herself." Feeling compassion for the right end/s is not simply a matter of choosing between two essentially separate perspectives on the end/s. It is a matter of cultivating an affective awareness of the many goods that are at stake for me, for my friend, and for other of the participants in the present predicament. It is a matter of allowing my empassioned attention to be captivated by the different ways in which the different participants construe these goods. And it is a matter of weighing possible responses to the predicament as one who is *gripped* by this array of perspectives. At some point, "I" am the one who must decide, on the basis of a perspective that "I" regard with good reason and passion to be most adequate to the circumstances, which of the goods at stake are the most pressing, which of them can be coordinated and thus aimed at together, which of them can be put off until later, and which of them can or must be sacrificed altogether. "I" am the one who must constitute my own conception of and passion for the end/s on the basis of my own vision and love of the good. Still, my compassion is best constituted when "I" allow "myself" to be constituted partly by the moral experience of "the other." My intention is best formed when I take a personal interest in the interests of my friend.

Second, is it best to aim in our compassion at our own good or at the good of our friend when we cannot aim at both at the same time? Because my friend and I share a life, I am disposed in friendship to take a personal interest in the interests of my friend. I am disposed to share certain of her interests, and I am disposed to respect those interests in private goods that I am unable to share. At the same time, I am disposed in friendship to have my own interests, some of which are shared by my friend, and some of which are not. As I seek to decide which end/s to aim at in my compassion, I will feel the tug and the pull of all relevant (and even some irrelevant) interests. Feeling this tug and pull, I will be inclined to seek as a benefit what I think-feel will promote as many of these interests as possible.

How can I weigh these sometimes competing interests well? How can I constitute the end/s of my compassion in light of an appropriate configuration of interests? A lot depends on the nature of these interests and the persons who have them. I can, however, begin to reflect-feel about the relationship between my good and my friend's good, considering, for example, that a loss of my good will likely count as a loss to my friend's good, insofar as my friend includes my good in his own. Even though my friend will likely gain certain goods on account of the sacrifice that I make on his behalf, he will at the same time lose certain goods. Similarly, I can consider that my sacrifice will count, in certain respects, as a loss to my good, but it will count in other respects as a gain, insofar as I include my friend's good in my own. I will therefore do best to weigh, not simply my loss against his gain, but my losses and gains in relation to his losses and gains, seeking to maximize the gains that my friend and I have come to regard as most integral to our separate and shared pursuits of *eudaimonia*, seeking to minimize what we have come to regard as the most serious losses, and seeking to do all of this in light of the good of others/the larger whole.

In the end, the decision rests with perception. It rests with the passionate perception of the various private and shared goods that are at stake in the situation at hand. Becoming well disposed toward the passionate perception of particulars requires years and years of reflection and conversation about what is of how much value in human life. It requires years of attention to the moral dimensions of human experience, to the ways in which human beings differ in their experiences of goodness, and to the ways in which these differences can and cannot be "bridged." It requires making decision after decision in light of the best vision and love of goodness that we have conceived to date, with the expectation that this vision and love will undergo change as we assess the consequences of our decisions, and as we continue to engage in character-forming activities with our friends.

CHOOSING TO FEEL COMPASSION IN THE RIGHT MANNER

To continue our inquiry into compassion's mean, what is at issue in choosing to feel compassion in the right manner? This question is closely related to the question just considered. Let us sharpen our focus: What is it to attain deliberately the right relation between the many desires that contribute to the feeling of compassion? Specifically, what is it to balance and to integrate well our wanting *with* another in compassion and our wanting *for* him?

In her analysis of caring, Noddings does not distinguish between wanting *with* another in our caring and wanting *for* him, where wanting *with* involves participating in "constitutively the same" wanting, and wanting *for* involves participating in a wider range of wantings, most of which are inaccessible to one who is immersed in the immediacy of his pain. Noddings argues that caring well requires becoming "engrossed" in the cared-for's "feelings," which may or may not involve wanting *with* him something of what he is wanting,[40] but she does not argue that caring well also requires remaining separate relative to the feelings of the cared-for by affirming a different set of wantings. Noddings implies that separateness can be important to good caring, but this is a separateness that is achieved through "instrumental thinking," rather than through extended wanting. Hence, we do not get the sense from Noddings of our care-constituting wanting expanding and contracting in scope along with the expansion and contraction of our critical and creative perspective. Instead, we get the sense of our wanting being put on hold momentarily in order that we might achieve some "distance" via our thinking.

In my view, feeling compassion in the right manner requires recognizing that our best wanting in compassion is well-reasoned wanting, and our best thinking in compassion is well-empassioned thinking.[41] As I draw back from the immediacy of my friend's experience in order to gain needed perspective on her painful predicament, I do so not by reasoning that I must set certain of my desires aside in order to "think objectively" about what to do. Rather, I do so by conceiving and feeling a widening range of desires for particular ends that I perceive will likely effect my friend's relief. Drawing back, I do think critically, carefully, and constructively about what actions and passions on my part are likely to have what kinds of immediate and long-range effects on which persons. But my thinking is largely an act of perceiving passionately what is possible and paying attention as my strong, but as yet rather undefined, desire to benefit my friend "tries" various possibilities "on for size," looking and feeling for the best "fit." If my desire "tries on" a possibility that really "rubs me the wrong way" in that it conflicts with certain other of my desires, then I look and feel for other possibilities, wanting to bring about as many significant shared and private goods as I can.

As I slip back into the immediacy of my friend's suffering in order to test the adequacy of what I now desire *for* her, I do so with a marked narrowing in my passionate awareness. I allow a certain few of her-my beliefs, perceptions, and desires to become the most prominent constituents of my experience. And yet I bring *to* my friend's experience a deliberative desire for what I have discerned from a larger perspective to be the action-passion most likely to promote her good. If my wanting *for* her seems in connection with my wanting *with* her to be most adequate to my friend's predicament, then I act and feel accordingly. If my chosen action-passion alleviates my friend's pain, then she and I will be pleasantly enlarged and enhanced together; we will move through and beyond the particular constraints of her pain into a broadening horizon of possibility. If my action-passion does not alleviate her pain, then I will draw back again in my wanting *for* her to reconsider and re-feel the remaining options.

Regaining a greater reflective and desiderative perspective, I might perceive that what my friend wants for herself is something that she ought not to have. I might discern this precisely in feeling the full range of my considered passions for the good—passions that have been shaped over the years in conversation with my friend. I might choose, accordingly, to let my wanting *for* to retain a position of prominence in my affective awareness, and I might assist my friend by contributing to the reconfiguring of her desire, bound by what my wanting *for* continues to mark out as best. Then again, I might perceive that what I have been wanting *for* my friend is not, in fact, what is best for her, but is rather what I imagine would be best for me if I were in her situation. I might discern this in recollecting and being moved by my friend's own passion for the good, particularly by aspects of this passion that I have never been able to share, but that I have nevertheless been inclined to respect. Accordingly, I might choose to let my wanting *with* assume a more prominent position in my perspective, and I might assist my friend by first reshaping my wanting *for* her so that it will be less likely in the future to distort my discernment of what is best.

Choosing to feel compassion in the right manner is thus a matter of listening carefully, yet critically to the intentional desires that draw us in and out of other persons' experiences. It is a matter of working with and on these desires in order to conceive and commit ourselves to a well-considered set of ends. It requires, on the one hand, becoming pliable and manipulable enough to be drawn into a very small "space" in the constricted center of another's experience. It requires being conformed, to a limited degree, to another's dynamism such that her experience becomes partly our own. And yet it requires, on the other hand, wanting always to retain our autonomy, i.e. our deliberateness about whether, for how long, in what manner, and to what end, we will be so conformed. It requires wanting confidently to enjoy an array of goods that we take to be distinctively "our own," so that the desire to co-feel does not draw the whole of ourselves into pain's suffocating embrace.

Again, feeling compassion in the right manner requires expanding our desiderative awareness in order to gain a better sense of the goods at stake and a clearer grasp of whether and how these goods could be coordinated and pursued together. It requires widening and deepening our perspective by entertaining beliefs, perceptions, and desires that could not be entertained by someone who is immersed in pain. And yet, at the same time, it requires enlarging our perspective without thereby becoming distracted from and oblivious to the experience of the concrete other. It requires wanting to bring our enlarged perspective to bear on a particular person's painful predicament.

In the end, feeling compassion in the right manner requires wanting to alleviate someone else's pain in and through the act of constituting our own experience partly the same as hers, yet partly different. How much sameness ought to be combined in what manner with how much difference will depend upon the particulars of a given situation, and upon the ways in which the persons involved choose justifiably to rank various goods like intimacy and privacy, vulnerability and self-command, interdependence and independence. Becoming persons who are well disposed as a matter of habit to feel compassion in the right manner requires choosing to cultivate desires for *all* such goods, so that each of these desires will be likely to exert its influence when we are in a situation of choosing to feel. Fine-tuning the relative strengths and intentional contents of these desires, and learning to "listen" to them in "noisy" situations, is a matter for long-term moral education, particularly within the context of character-friendships.

CHOOSING TO FEEL COMPASSION FOR THE RIGHT PERSONS

Let us consider finally some of what is at issue in feeling compassion for some persons but not for others. We cannot extend compassion toward every person in the world who is in pain. How, then, can we choose well among the potential recipients of our care? Most of us enjoy special attachments to certain friends, and we do not want to weaken these attachments by spreading our affection, our attention, and our other resources too thin. Yet most of us want to live in a community whose members are inclined to extend their compassion beyond the narrow bounds of the "private sphere." Granted that we need to set some limits on the extension of our compassion, how do we set these limits well?

Caring for Some but Not for Others

Noddings's arguments on this score are provocative. She says that, "We find ourselves at the center of concentric circles of caring."[42] In the innermost circle, "we care because we love." As we move out from the innermost circle, we care because we have a "personal regard" that is weaker than love, but is still strong enough to elicit caring in compliance with basic social rules.

> Beyond the circles of proximate others are those I have not yet encountered. Some of these are linked to the inner circle by personal or formal relations. Out there is a young man who will be my daughter's husband; I am prepared to acknowledge the transitivity of my love. He enters my life with potential love. Out there, also, are future students; they are linked formally to those I already care for and they, too, enter my life potentially cared-for. Chains of caring are established, some forming whole new circles of potential caring. I am "prepared to care" through recognition of these chains.[43]

We are obligated to remain "prepared to care," but prepared to care for whom? Noddings says that, "practically, if we are meeting those in our inner circles adequately as ones-caring and receiving those linked to our inner circles by formal chains of relation, we shall limit the calls upon our obligation quite naturally."[44]

What, exactly, does this entail about our obligation to care for strangers? Noddings argues that our caring for strangers and familiars alike should be guided by two criteria: "the existence of or potential for present relation, and the dynamic potential for growth in relation, including the potential for increased reciprocity and, perhaps, mutuality."[45] According to the first criterion,

> If the other toward whom we shall act is capable of responding as cared-for and there are no objective conditions that prevent our receiving this response—if, that is, our caring can be completed in the other—then we must meet that other as one-caring. If we do not care naturally, we must call upon our capacity for ethical caring. When we are in relation or the other has addressed us, we must respond as one-caring. The imperative in relation is categorical.[46]

According to the second criterion, however, we must discern the appropriate *extent* of our caring commitment to a particular other by looking "at the nature of potential relation and, especially, at the capacity of the cared-for to respond" to our caring.[47] "If the possibility is dynamic—if the relation may clearly grow with respect to reciprocity—then the possibility and degree of my obligation also grows. . . . [T]he second criterion binds us in proportion to the probability of increased response and to the imminence of that response."[48]

Noddings argues that we are only obligated to care when our caring is likely to be "completed" by the cared-for in a way that is readily visible to us. This entails that I am not obligated to care for the *distant* stranger: "I am not obliged to care for starving children in Africa, because there is no way for this caring to be completed in the other unless I abandon the caring to which I am [already] obligated."[49] The *proximate* stranger, by contrast, is harder to dismiss. Whether it be "the stray cat . . . at the back door—or the stray teenager at the front," the proximate stranger is capable of "completing" our caring by "growing" and "glowing" in our presence.[50] Hence, "if either presents himself, he must be received not by formula but as individual."[51] The priority with which I "receive" the cat or the teenager will depend upon how quickly and how extensively I expect each of them to bear the fruit of my efforts.

Preconditions for the Extension of Care?

Noddings's argument that we are only obligated to care when it appears to us that the potential cared-for will "complete" our caring is not a compelling one, in my view. It is, indeed, good to see someone flourish under the influence of our caring, particularly when her flourishing consists in an eagerness to give to others what she has received from us. It is good to see our caring reciprocated, although I believe that it is often best that the cared-for reciprocate our caring by caring for someone other than us—someone who needs the care of that cared-for even more than we do. To say that "completed" caring is good is not, however, to say that "uncompleted" caring is without substantial moral value. It is also good, I submit, to care for someone when we know that we will remain anonymous in our caring, and when we know that the results of our caring will remain hidden from our view.

First, acts of "uncompletable" caring are good because they are likely to issue forth in benefit to particular others. It is good for others to be benefited whether or not this benefit is observed by us. It is also good for others to be benefited whether or not our beneficence is observed by them. Granted, it is sometimes best that others observe that *we* are the ones who benefit them, particularly when the benefit that we seek to bestow upon them includes the reassurance that *we* care for them. At other times, however, it is best that others be benefited anonymously, particularly when we seek to benefit already overburdened others by in-suring that they not feel bound to return our care, or when we seek to benefit overly dependent others by helping them to stand on their own two feet.[52]

Second, acts of "uncompletable" caring are good because they are likely to strengthen the bonds of human community, according to which each of us trusts that everyone will take at least some interest in the well-being of everyone else, simply because each of us is a human being. To be sure, if our interests in each other were always hidden from view, then we would not have much of a sense of community. But the fact that our in-terests in each other are sometimes hidden from view (i.e., the fact that we sometimes benefit each other and are benefited anonymously) is provocative of a sense of community in which we feel free to trust that someone will care for us even when it looks as though we have been abandoned. This "sense" is good because it promotes beneficence and in-hibits maleficence, and because it is a component part of our flourishing as relational creatures.[53]

Third, acts of "uncompletable" caring are good because they disci-pline us to care without being too attached to the consequences of our caring. That is to say, they discipline us to keep on caring, even when our caring seems repeatedly to meet with unreceptive hearts. Granted, it is critical that we not become exhausted and bitter in caring for those who repeatedly respond poorly to our care, but the upbuilding that is required to keep us strong in our caring need not be provided by the cared-for himself or herself. It can be and regularly is provided by friends (both human and divine) with whom we share our lives—friends who care for us and who care to encourage us to keep on caring.

To say that "uncompletable" caring is good for these and for other reasons does not settle the question of what sort of caring is, in a given situation, best. But it creates a presumption in favor of not limiting our caring, in principle, to those who are likely to "complete" it. It creates a presumption in favor of acknowledging and weighing in the balance a number of benefits other than or in addition to "completion" that might be achieved by caring without making probable "completion" a precon-dition.

Let us explore further some of the problems associated with making probable "completion" a precondition of our caring. As we have seen, Noddings argues that "I am not obligated to care for starving children in

Africa, because there is no way for this caring to be completed in the other unless I abandon the caring to which I am [already] obligated."[54] The suggestion here seems to be that, because caring requires visible "completion," caring for starving children in Africa requires that we who live outside of Africa put ourselves in a position both to benefit these children and to "receive" their being-benefited in return. It requires that we do something like join the Peace Corps and go to Africa ourselves. But doing this would require abandoning caring relations to which we are already committed, and these relations are too valuable to abandon.

There is something to be said for focusing our limited resources on benefiting those who are closest to us in spacial location, given that spacial intimacy puts us in a good position to monitor the effectiveness of our passion-action and thus to adjust our approach as necessary. But the idea that we ought to exclude from our affective awareness those with whom we are not in direct contact is morally unacceptable, in my view. The notion that privileged persons could see children who are starving to death on the television or elsewhere in the media (i.e., in situations where "completion" of our caring would be impossible), feel *nothing* for those children, and feel morally *justified* in feeling nothing is unconscionable.

We are not obligated to become engrossed with every starving child that we see or about whom we hear, for (depending upon the intensity of our engrossment) this could leave us incapacitated and ineffectual. But we are obligated to become engrossed with at least some of these children some of the time, such that we are *struck hard* by the horror of their situation, by the aching in their ravished bodies, by the deterioration of their minds and spirits, by the realization that, had our luck been different, that could have been us or our children on the screen, etc. We are obligated, at least now and then, to become engrossed to an extent that is sufficient to motivate *some* passion-action on our part that is directed toward the alleviation of this anguish.

Why? Because we ought to promote human flourishing and to undermine human debilitation, and when we can do either at what practical wisdom indicates to be a reasonable cost to ourselves, we ought to do so. The fact that the other human being happens (accidentally) to be a distant stranger is not irrelevant to our cost-benefit analyses, but neither is it sufficient to let us off the hook automatically. We are obligated to promote flourishing and to undermine debilitation because (within a eudaimonistic framework) this is the best sort of life for a relational human being to live. The most worthwhile and satisfying life is one in which we "perform" distinctively human "functions," like exercising compassion and justice, with "excellence." Being compassionate and just within our modern global context requires recognizing that every human being is a "neighbor" who has *some* claim on us to be received and responded to with attention, affection, beneficence, respect, and fairness.

Noddings argues similarly that whether and how much we are obligated to care for the proximate stranger—in this case the stray teenager at our door—depends on whether and to what extent we can expect her to "complete" our caring. This, too, seems to be misguided. What if the teenager in question comes across as being bitter, resentful, ungrateful, cocky, likely to lie to us, and unlikely to reveal to us that our caring matters to her one way or another? Does this mean that we are not obligated to care for her? Are we not, rather, obligated (in cases where we have the wherewithal) to become engrossed with her to the point that we are *struck hard* by the loneliness, fear, and loss of hope that are ill concealed in her heavy eyes, and by the realization that, had our luck been different, it could have been us or our child who was simply left for dead? I believe that we *are* obligated (again, where we have the wherewithal) to be struck sufficiently hard to be motivated to do *something* on the other's behalf, even if only to speak a kind word.

Why? Because this teenager is in need of care, we are in a position to give that care at little cost to ourselves, and our care is likely to do some good, even if the teenager is too proud or too tough to realize or to reveal that good. Even if our care does not, in fact, do much good—even if the teenager laughs at us for being such a "sucker," takes the money that we give her, and uses it to buy illegal drugs—it is still good that we care. It is good that we feel, if only for a moment, that this child is a part of us, that whether she lives or dies matters to us personally, that if she does remain defensive and uses our money to injure herself, then we will be injured with her. Once again, feeling that a stranger's good is included in our own good is of benefit to *us* in that it contributes to the cultivation of our relational excellence: it gives us practice at being open, attentive, and sensitive to the needs of others; it gives us practice at weighing these needs in relation to the needs of others, including ourselves; it makes us practically wiser, perspectivally broader, and passionally richer.

When I think about my own "best moments of caring and being cared for,"[55] I think of the times when being cared for elicited in me a powerful sense of abundance, and a readiness to care for others out of this abundance. But I also think of the times when *I* was a teenager—when I was closed up, rebellious, resentful, and downright ugly toward my parents—yet they still continued to care. They gave their care freely and generously, knowing that all they would get from me was a door slammed in their faces. True enough, they hoped for the eventual "completion" of their parenting efforts, but their care did not seem to me to rest contingently upon the promise of this "completion." For this reason, I experienced their care as particularly good.[56]

Extending Compassion to the Stranger

We cannot feel compassion for every person who experiences pain. We cannot extend the compassion that we feel readily and cultivate deliberately in relation to our friends toward every stranger that crosses our path without suffering significant losses to our relational excellence and *eudaimonia*. And yet, we ought not to exercise compassion exclusively toward our friends. We ought, instead, to cultivate friendships that serve as stable resources for the long-term moral education of our loves, our patterns of perception, and our habits of reasoned reflection. We and our friends ought, for example, to teach each other to perceive that (as much as we might want to deny it) the stranger, and even the enemy, is more like us than s/he is unlike us in morally significant respects. S/he, too, is vulnerable, fragile, needful, frightened, ignorant, socially conditioned, self-deceptive about her/his limitations, and sometimes vicious. S/he, too, wants to live a good life, wants to love and to be loved, is capable of at least some reflection, conversation, and understanding, and sometimes manages to be virtuous. We and our friends ought, accordingly, to teach each other to feel that the stranger, and even the enemy, is part of us insofar as s/he, too, is a unique embodiment of the power in which each of us has the ultimate source of existence. We and our friends ought, in sum, to cultivate in each other's company friendships that enable and encourage us to extend the compassion that we feel toward each other toward those whom we are, again and again, tempted to relegate to otherness, invisibility, and death.

Why ought we to do this? As I have said, it is good to promote human flourishing and to undermine human debilitation, and the stranger/enemy is, after all, a human being. Sometimes it is best to concentrate our compassion on those whom we know and like the best, and are in the best position to assist, i.e., our friends,[57] but it is never appropriate to limit the category of "the human" to the category of "my friends," such that we fail to take seriously the interests of other, equally human beings. Why not? One answer (within a eudaimonistic framework) is that this is simply not the way that we would wish (upon reflection) to be, nor is it the kind of community of which we would wish to be a part. Instead, we wish to be persons who are open to making passional and cognitive connections with humans *qua* human—connections that give us a vivid, expanding sense that each of us belongs to the other, and each of us is responsible to promote (or at least not to inhibit) the other's flourishing. We wish to live in (and thus to contribute to) a community in which everyone feels bound by these connections because human beings are the sorts of beings that are able to live fully satisfying lives only within generous relational contexts.[58]

Granted that we ought to extend *some* compassion toward the stranger, how can we limit this extension appropriately? First, we can allow ourselves to feel reflectively the many desires that condition our affective awareness of a particular stranger, e.g., the desire to be good, the desire to be compassionate, the desire to alleviate this person's pain, the desire to alleviate the pain that we feel *at* this person's pain, the desire to be effective in the use of our limited resources, the desire to benefit our friends, the desire to be left alone to pursue our own private good, the desire to live in a community in which "strangers" are welcomed, etc. To the extent that we feel certain of these, we will already be feeling the initial stirrings of compassion. We can allow ourselves to feel these stirrings (and other, competing stirrings) reflectively, and we can re-feel our desires deliberately in light of our deepening understanding of relational selfhood, moved by our growing love of relational *eudaimonia*.

If compassion-constituting desires come to the fore of our affective awareness, then the second thing that we can do is to consider the benefits that could be achieved for the particular stranger, for ourselves, for persons to whom we have special obligations, and for the community as a whole, by our choosing to feel and to act in one way or another. We can also consider the many losses that we and each of these others would likely suffer if we were to choose to feel compassion in this way or that. Then we can weigh the most attractive possibilities and limit ourselves to the act of compassion that strikes us, all things considered, as the best.

We can check our feeling and reasoning against the critical questions that our friends ask us and have taught us, over the years, to ask ourselves in order to remain faithful to our best available visions and values.

The limits to our compassion for strangers are best set in response to different constellations of different factors in different situations, but guided by considerations such as the ones that we have raised. Feeling and reasoning about these general considerations, inside and outside of the contexts of particular painful predicaments, is likely to dispose us, over time, to make the appropriate extensions more or less spontaneously, so that a lot of this "figuring" becomes unnecessary.

THE MEAN OF COMPASSION

Can anything more specific be said about the mean of compassion? The principle of balance can serve as a helpful rule of thumb as we confront the messiness of the "real world." We must realize, however, that the balancing of certain desires usually requires the frustration of yet other desires, and the balancing of certain goods usually requires the loss of yet other goods. We must also realize that balance is something to be sought, not simply in this or that decision, but over the long haul. One decision might be out of balance in itself, but in balance relative to a prior decision, or one that we anticipate making in the future. Achieving balance in our overall pattern of decision making requires achieving balance in our character, which requires living reflectively with others in the pursuit of a life that we take, with good reason, to be good.

It can also be helpful to identify the extremes between which the mean of compassion is located. For example, feeling compassion toward the right end requires avoiding the extreme of collapsing the multiple goods that are at stake into a single good, and it requires, at the same time, avoiding the extreme of becoming so preoccupied with the multiplicity of goods that we cannot order or attach ourselves to any of them. Feeling compassion in the right manner requires avoiding the extreme of being "sucked into" the immediacy of another's painful experience such that we lose the capacity deliberately to pull ourselves out of it, yet it requires, at the same time, avoiding the other extreme of being so "removed" from the other that we have no sense of what she is experiencing and no desire to find out. Feeling compassion for the right persons requires avoiding the extreme of reserving all of our compassion for our closest friends, and yet it requires, at the same time, avoiding the other extreme of spreading our compassion so thin that it is of little value to anyone.

Note that these extremes (and other extremes that we have not discussed, such as the extremes relative to intensity and duration) can be combined in different ways. For example, a person can be disposed to become too engulfed in the experiences of friends, but not engulfed enough in the experiences of persons other than friends. It is therefore unhelpful, in my view, to identify the mean of compassion with reference to one character trait at the extreme of excess and one character trait at the extreme of deficiency, as Aristotle does in his discussion of other virtues. It is much more helpful to bring into perspective and then to "aim" with concerted effort at "targets" like these: remaining *attentive* to multiple particulars, yet *focused* on those that are most significant; remaining *vulnerable* to being moved by the desires of others, yet *centered* within the context of our own desiderative awareness; remaining *open* to feeling with and for any human being in particular, yet *decisive* with respect to how we will expend our finite human resources.

In conclusion, we have seen that it is possible to choose whether and how to feel compassion's complacency. It is also possible to choose whether and how to feel the rest of compassion in relation to compassion's complacency. We have considered how these choices can be made, and we have considered some of what is at stake in making these choices well. I have argued in an Aristotelian spirit that the best choices rest with well-educated, empassioned perception. At this point, we are poised to bring some theological concerns into perspective. If the choice to feel one way or another rests with perception, it behooves us to consider how habits of perception that have been formed via participation in Christian community can affect the choice to feel compassion.

Eleven

Compassion and the Christian Life

We have examined some of the impact that a friendship with God can have on the way in which a Christian believer stands to herself and to her "other selves." We have examined some of the impact that this change in standing can have on a believer's exercise of her relational moral agency. In this chapter, we will consider specifically some of the impact that a friendship with God can have on the way in which a believer stands to her "other selves" who are in pain, and the impact that this altered standing can have on the wanting, the believing and perceiving, and the acting-feeling that together contribute to the exercsie of compassion. Our focus will remain on compassion for friends, but we will attend to the way in which compassion for friends can be extended to those whom we might not ordinarily regard as friends. We will carry out our analysis with reference to one of the few texts of religious ethics that is devoted to an analysis of compassion, namely, *Compassion*, jointly authored by Donald McNeill, Douglas Morrison, and Henri Nouwen.[1]

FRIENDSHIP WITH THE COMPASSIONATE GOD

Recall that, according to our reconstruction and extension of Thomas's ethical thought, friendship with God is a sharing of our lives with God in which we are gifted with "elevated" moral agencies, such that we become participants in God's vision of the good of Godself and God's creatures, participants in God's desire to accomplish this good, participants in God's belief and perception of how this good could best be accomplished in a given situation, and participants in the action-passion with which God seeks to accomplish this good.[2] Elevated into the life of God, we are elevated into a new understanding of our relational selves. We understand that we stand in elevated relation to the One who elevates, and that, because we stand in this relation, we stand to other selves as to beings who, like us, have a condition of the possibility of their flourishing in an elevated relation to One who elevates. We stand to those whom God has elevated or is seeking presently to elevate as to "other ourselves" who are "other" by virtue of their particularity, but are "ours" by virtue of the fact that they, like us, have been befriended in their particularity by the same Friend.[3]

McNeill, Morrison, and Nouwen also speak of friendship with God as a "participation in the divine life." They speak of it as a participation in which it becomes possible for us "to see with others what we could not see before, to feel with others what we could not feel before, to hear with others what we could not hear before."[4] Rather than emphasizing the "elevation" of our moral agencies into the agency of God, however, the authors emphasize the "humiliation" of God relative to us. They speak of charity as a "participation in the divine life in and through Christ,"[5] whose life, death, and resurrection has made manifest that God is indeed "God-with-us."

> As soon as we call God, "God-with-us," we enter into a new relationship of intimacy with [God]. By calling [God] Immanuel, we recognize that [God] has committed [Godself] to live in solidarity with us, to share in our joys and pains, to defend and protect us, and to suffer all of life with us. The God-with-us is a close God, a God whom we call our refuge, our stronghold, our wisdom, and even, more intimately, our helper, our shepherd, our love. We will never really know God as a compassionate God if we do not understand with our heart and mind that "[God] lived among us" (Jn 1:14).[6]

For McNeill et al., faith in Christ consists partly in the trust that God has chosen to enter with us into the depths of human uncertainty and vulnerability.[7] Christians trust that God has chosen to enter with us into "the condition of powerlessness in which [we feel] victimized by uncontrollable events, anonymous influences, and capricious agents which surround and elude [our] understanding and control."[8]

When we trust that God is like us and with us in our uncertainty, our vulnerability, and our powerlessness, something happens to the way in which we stand in relation to ourselves. We are able to cast off the comforting illusion that everything is "under control and that everything extraordinary and improper can be kept outside the walls of our self-created fortress."[9] We are able to recognize our competitiveness for what it is, namely, the desperate attempt to defend ourselves against the threat of invisibility by "distinguishing" (i.e., separating and exalting) ourselves relative to "others."[10] We are able to discern the way in which clinging to "differences" disposes us to hate, torture, and exterminate what we can no longer recognize as the "same."[11] We are able to discern all of this, however, without succumbing to despair, for we trust that God is like us and with us even in our brokenness.[12]

When we suffer the full recognition of our finitude and our sinfulness in the presence of the broken God, we receive from God the assurance that "God has embraced everything human with the infinite tenderness of [God's] compassion."[13] We hear the "good news" that we are free to be "born again" with Christ out of the "womb" of God's compassion. Captivated by the promise of a new life, we are able to hear the "names" by which we are called to our divinely appointed destinies.[14] "This is the mystery of the Christian life: to receive a new self, a new identity, which depends not on what we can achieve, but on what we are willing to receive" from God.[15]

When we receive new selves from God, something happens, in turn, to the way in which we stand in relation to other selves. Encountering with Christ the reality of our own brokenness, we are able to encounter the brokenness of other human beings, and we are able to perceive their brokenness, not as something that makes them different from us, but rather as something that makes them like us. We are able to "discover each other as members of the same human family," as "sisters and brothers of the same Christ and daughters and sons of the same [Mother/]Father."[16] Accordingly, we are able to welcome our friends-in-pain "into the center of our hearts." We are disposed "to allow their pains and sufferings, their anxieties and loneliness, their confusion and fears to resound in our innermost selves."[17]

McNeill, Morrison, and Nouwen characterize the act of compassion as a gut-wrenching suffering-with:

Compassion asks us to go where it hurts, to enter into places of pain, to share in brokenness, fear, confusion, and anguish. Compassion challenges us to cry out with those in misery, to mourn with those who are lonely, to weep with those in tears. Compassion requires us to be weak with the weak, vulnerable with the vulnerable, and powerless with the powerless. Compassion means full immersion in the condition of being human.[18]

Although compassion also includes a seeking to alleviate the pain that we suffer with others, compassion requires that we not seek to relieve any pain that we have not first tasted as our own.[19]

CHARITY'S IMPACT ON COMPASSION'S COMPLACENCY

The implicit movement that I am seeking to draw out of the text is one that can be characterized in terms of compassion's complacency. Trusting that God is a God-with-us who has chosen to take in, or to be taken in by, the pain of being human, we are able to "rest" with a certain familiarity and accustomedness in our own pain constituents. For example, our uncertainty, our vulnerability, and our powerlessness continue to frighten us, and we continue to want to escape their constraints. But at the same time, our affective awareness is captivated by and turned toward our (frustrated) desire to control what no human being can, in fact, control. Turning in the company of God toward the face of our own desire, we are able to "rest" in that desire, which means that we are able to feel it, to recognize it for what it is, and to be honest about the maliciousness to which it gives rise. We are able to forgive ourselves for feeling the desire and the maliciousness, and we are able to give deliberate shape to both of these in light of the good that we believe to be—and long for as—possible. God's befriending presence in our midst assures us that it is always possible (and necessary) for us to begin anew the task of educating our desire.

When we recognize fully and confront honestly what is most disturbing about *ourselves,* it becomes possible for us to take complacency in other human beings. It becomes possible for our affective awareness to become attuned and accustomed to the pain that they, too, experience at being human, so that we find all too familiar, for example, the pain that another human being experiences in wanting (despairingly) to become someone other than who he is.[20] We are not surprised when the desperate desire to control pain-causing conditions drives the other to do something heinous. Rather, we are able to "rest" in the other's desire, i.e., we are able to be captivated by it and thus to feel it as a desire with which we, too, must struggle. Feeling it as our own, we can judge the desire without being judgmental, and we can seek its effective alteration without being controlling. In the company of the One whose nature it is to extend the hand of friendship to all of us unconditionally, we can feel "at home" with and doggedly hopeful toward those (like us) who repeatedly reject God's offer.[21]

Complacent in our own pain and in our vulnerability to being pained, we are disposed to become complacent in the pain of others and in their vulnerability to being pained. We are disposed to "rest" in their pain with the assurance that God "rests" with us in the pain that we share with others.[22] Putting the matter this way, however, raises a troubling issue: What if the pain that another human being feels is the pain of an evil desire? Doesn't "taking in" an evil desire of another make us, and God-with-us, evil? Briefly, it depends upon the way in which we stand to the desire that we experience as "our own."

As we have already seen, feeling compassion toward a friend involves (among other things) suffering with him something of the same desire that he suffers. It involves suffering with him a desire that is co-constituted out of some of the same building blocks of experience. It involves, for example, entertaining the intentional content of a desire that we are conceiving *with* the other partly on the basis of perceptual habits in whose formation each of us has had a hand. It involves entertaining this content more or less lucidly. If we suffer the same evil desire as another in the absence of an affective awareness that this desire is indeed distorted, i.e., if the desire commands our passional attention in such a way that our well-considered vision and love of the good ceases to frame our experience of it, then our feeling of the same desire reflects on us badly. If, however, we suffer the other's desire with the affective awareness that this desire has been poorly conceived, i.e., if we experience its intentional content *as* distorted in light of our well-deliberated habits of empassioned envisioning, then we are in a position to see through and to detach ourselves from that desire. We are in a position to feel the same desire as the other while, at the same time, feeling yet other desires of our own that provide a different perspective on the same. Choosing to co-feel an evil desire from an appropriate perspective does not reflect on us badly.[23]

Although I cannot develop here the theological implications of the assertion, the same point can be made with reference to God. Choosing to co-feel (say, in the person of Christ) the evil desires that are constitutive of considerable human pain does not make God evil. God suffers our evil desires *as* evil relative to God's desire for the good of Godself and God's creatures. God suffers a given human desire in order to be with us in that desire, but God entertains the intentional content of our desire in light of God's perfect wisdom (such that all distortions are transparent), and God entertains the passional movement of our desire bound by God's perfect love (such that all dissonance marks our desire as disordered). God can still be said to suffer with us the same desire; it's just that God suffers the same desire *as* other than God.[24]

Compassion is partly a disposition to "rest" with a sense of familiarity and accustomedness in the painful experience of being human. It is a disposition (courageously) to be so "at home" in our humanness that we discover ourselves to be similarly "at home" in the presence of other human beings. To be "at home" in the presence of others is not necessarily to like them (nor is it necessarily to condone their characters or their actions), but it *is* to recognize them as beings who are like us even in their unlikeableness. It is to recognize that they are one with us in an unlikeableness to which each of us contributes—directly or indirectly, knowingly or unknowingly—through our facial expressions, our words, our actions, and the incalculable consequences of these. Friendship with God can ease Christians into these difficult recognitions by humbling them and, at the same time, teaching them that the compassionate God recognizes them precisely in their humility.

Choosing Compassion's Complacency

Acquiring the virtue of compassion requires choosing to feel reflectively an array of perceptive, passional resonances in the company of those who suffer. It requires choosing to become the sorts of persons who are disposed to feel these resonances as a matter of habit. How can friendship with God contribute to the choice to become so disposed? McNeill,

Morrison, and Nouwen say that "Compassion is a divine gift and not a result of systematic study or effort," but they nevertheless suggest some things that persons can do "to unveil what has been covered, to bring to the foreground what has remained hidden, and to put on the lampstand what has been kept under a basket."[25]

One thing that we can do to become habitually more disposed toward inter-human complacency is to engage in the practice of voluntary displacement. We can "move away from the ordinary and proper places" where everything appears to be "under control" and into places of ambiguity, uncomfortableness, and powerlessness.[26] We can make geographical, economic, work-related, additudinal, or other "moves" intended to bring us into "the places where people hurt."[27] We can displace ourselves or we can simply "identify in our . . . lives where displacement is already occurring."[28] We can suffer the pain of our own displacements and we can "listen" *in* our suffering for the "first whispers" of the displaced Lord.[29] "Hearing" the "voice" of the Lord in the depths of our suffering disposes us to "listen" for the same "voice" in the suffering of others, i.e., it sets us up to be re-oriented by and made attuned to those who suffer.

Choosing to undergo this sort of displacement—choosing to become the sorts of persons who are habitually disposed to "take in" and to "stay with" our own and each other's experiences of "being lost or left alone"—requires a great deal of patience.[30]

> Patience means to enter actively into the thick of life and to fully bear the suffering within and around us. Patience is the capacity to see, hear, touch, taste, and smell as fully as possible the inner and outer events of our lives. It is to enter our lives with open eyes, ears, and hands so that we really know what is happening. . . . In short, patience is a willingness to be influenced even when this requires giving up control and entering into unknown territory.[31]

Patience is the effort to surrender rigidifying attachments to "clock time" and to make ourselves available to the grace-full experience of the "fullness of time."

Patience, in turn, can be cultivated through prayer. The authors insist that "prayer is not an effort to make contact with God, to bring [God] to our side." Rather, prayer is "the effort to remove everything that might prevent the Spirit of God, given to us by Jesus Christ, from speaking freely to us and in us."[32] Disciplining ourselves to "hear" what the already present Spirit has to say involves many things:

> It involves the constant choice not to run from the present moment in the naive hope that salvation will appear around the next corner. It involves the determination to listen carefully to people and events so as to discern the movements of the Spirit. It involves the ongoing struggle to prevent our minds and hearts from becoming cluttered with the many distractions that clamor for our attention. But above all, it involves the decision to set aside time every day to be alone with God and listen to the Spirit. The discipline of prayer enables us both to discern the presence of God's life-giving Spirit in the midst of our hectic lives and to let that divine Spirit constantly transform our lives.[33]

To pray is to allow ourselves to be made fit, by the Spirit, to welcome all of God's beloved "into the center of our hearts."

> To pray for others means to make them part of ourselves. To pray for others means to allow their pains and sufferings, their anxieties and loneliness, their confusion and fears to resound in our inmost selves. To pray, therefore is to become those for whom we pray, to become the sick child, the fearful mother, the distressed father, the nervous teenager, the angry student, and the frustrated striker. To pray is to enter into a deep inner solidarity with our fellow human beings so that in and through us they can be touched by the healing power of God's Spirit.[34]

Here, the authors capture well the way in which the act of prayer can actually constitute compassion's complacency.

As Fellow Friends of God

McNeill, Morrison, and Nouwen emphasize that we are limited as individuals in our separate capacities "to bring the whole world with all its suffering and pains around the divine fire in our heart."[35] Without assistance and encouragement from persons who share this fire with us, we can easily become "burned out," i.e., numbed, angered, or disgusted by the endless panoply of human miseries, to the point that we are no longer capable of seeing them for what they are.[36] The Christian community can "[mediate] between the suffering of the world and our individual responses to this suffering."[37]

> Since the Christian community is the living presence of the mediating Christ, it enables us to be fully aware of the painful condition of the human family without being paralyzed by this awareness. In the Christian community, we can keep our eyes and ears open to all that happens without being numbed by technological overstimulation or angered by the experience of powerlessness. In the Christian community, we can know about hunger, oppression, torture, and the nuclear threat without giving into a fatalistic resignation and withdrawing into a preoccupation with personal survival. In the Christian community, we can fully recognize the condition of our society without panicking.[38]

We can embrace our friends-in-pain without utterly suffocating in that embrace.

We can do this because, under the influence of the Spirit, our new selves have become knit together into a single, extended self that experiences in its midst the transformative presence of the divine Self. The authors put it this way:

> In the Christian community we gather in the name of Christ and thus experience him in the midst of a suffering world. There our old, weak minds, which are unable fully to perceive the pains of the world are transformed into the mind of Christ, to whom nothing human is alien. In community, we are no longer a mass of helpless individuals, but are transformed into one people of God. . . . While still subject to the power of the world and still deeply involved in the human struggle, we . . . become a new people with a new mind, a new way of seeing and hearing, and a new hope because of our common fellowship with Christ.[39]

As a single, extended self-with-Christ, our experience is that "there is unlimited space [in our presence] into which strangers from different places with very different stories can enter and experience God's compassionate presence."[40]

It is true that it is in relation to persons who share with us significant aspects of a working vision and love of the good that we are best able to carry out the hard work of compassion. It is in relation to persons who share with us a searching openness to what is ultimate that we are best able to cultivate openness to what is "other" in ourselves and in our "other selves." Speaking to members of diverse Christian communities, let me explore a bit further some of the ways in which participating in character-forming communities can assist us in becoming properly disposed toward compassion's complacency.[41]

Spending at least some of our days with persons who are committed to the cultivation of compassion, we can wade through the sorts of questions that have surfaced in the present inquiry. As fellow believers who are called to interpret, speak, hear, and interpret (again) the Word of God to each other and to yet others,[42] we can seek answers to the problems of co-suffering in light of our interpretations-in-process.[43] We can put our working interpretations into shared practice, and we can deliberate about the appropriateness of our practices in a way that refines our interpretations and, in turn, alters our future practices. We can embody our best-to-date understandings in rituals that form and re-form our characteristic patterns of thinking, perceiving, and desiring. We can help each other to develop the vulnerability, receptivity, attention, attunement, patience, and trust that are ingredient in complacency. We can help each other to undermine the guardedness, narrow-mindedness, arrogance, and bigotry that repeatedly thwart our efforts.

We can do all of this in such a way that our conceptions, deliberations, commitments, and practices become partly *shared* conceptions, deliberations, commitments, and practices. We can share these things in such a way that our agencies combine with the agencies of others to form a single, extended moral agency. Together, we can form a "mind" that presupposes that every human being is sufficiently like us in our fragility, our fearfulness, our sinfulness, and our God-befriendedness to count as "another self." Together, we can form a "heart" that is able to take in and resonate with the disagreeable sensations and frustrated desires of even the most disgusting "other selves." Together, we can form a "body" that is disposed to absorb and to disperse the shock of this resonance throughout its many "members." We can do all of this under the guidance of the Spirit in the hope that our interwoven interagencies will become (partial) manifestations of the "mind," the "heart," and the "body" of Christ.

Participating in an open-ended network of complacency-cultivating friendships, our relational moral agencies can be collectively enhanced. What is more, we can experience the intimacy of a "multiple indwelling" relative to each other and, through each other, relative to God. It is partly on account of our access to this intimacy with Ultimacy through particularity that we are motivated to risk, again and again, being taken in by hostile and abusive others. It is in this intimacy that we enjoy the fruition of our relational excellence. Believer-friends will likely feel closer to each other than they feel toward "other themselves" whom they encounter as "theirs" simply by virtue of being God's. After all, believer-friends will have constituted many of their character dispositions uniquely the "same," which means that they will have become like and one with each other in ways that they are like and one with no one else. Still, one of the dispositions that the believer-friends will have constituted the same is the disposition to invite other-than-friends to "dwell" with them in their "mutual indwelling." One of the respects in which the friends will remain closest to each other is in their shared enjoyment of the way in which inclusive "indwellings" draw them *and* their "other selves" into the abundance of the divine life.[44]

CHARITY'S IMPACT ON COMPASSION'S DESIRE

Compassion's complacency is only one aspect of compassion. Let us consider the impact that charity can have on aspects of compassion that are associated more directly with deliberation and choice. It will be helpful, once again, to organize our reflections in terms of a practical syllogism, where the major premise represents compassion's desire, the minor premise represents compassion's belief and perception, and the conclusion represents compassion's chosen action-passion (or the intention to act and to feel when the time is right). Keep in mind that compassion's complacency conditions both the major and minor premises and is, in turn, conditioned by them.

To begin with, friendship with God can condition the desires that are ingredient in the decision to show compassion. McNeill, Morrison, and Nouwen identify several context-unspecific desires that can frame the way in which Christians perceive the world, such that they are disposed to conceive context-specific desires that initiate compassion-related deliberative processes. First, compassionate Christians want to flourish. Specifically, they want to be "one" with the risen Christ. They believe that the way to be "one" with Christ is to follow the "self-emptying," humiliating way of Jesus, and they want, therefore, to follow this way.

> Radical servanthood does not make sense unless we introduce a new level of understanding and see it as the way to encounter God [God-self]. To be humble and persecuted does not make sense unless we can find God in humility and persecution. When we begin to see God [Godself], the source of all our comfort and consolation, in the center of servanthood, compassion becomes much more than doing good for unfortunate people. . . . [It becomes] a joyful way of life in which our eyes are opened to the vision of the true God who chose the way of servanthood to make [Godself] known.[45]

Compassionate Christians want to serve others, then, partly for their own sake: "what they seek is not misery and pain but the God whose compassion they have felt in their lives. Their eyes do not focus on poverty and misery, but on the face of the living God."[46]

Second, compassionate Christians want to contribute to the flourishing of others for others' own sakes. Specifically, they want to bring those who suffer to the center of their attention in such a way that those who suffer "begin to recognize their own value."[47]

> When someone listens to us with real concentration and expresses sincere care for our struggles and our pains, we feel that something very deep is happening to us. Slowly, fears melt away, tensions dissolve, anxieties retreat, and we discover that we carry within us something we can trust and offer as a gift to others. The simple experience of being valuable and important to someone else has a tremendous recreative power.[48]

Compassionate Christians want to bring those who suffer to the center of their attention in order to comfort and upbuild, but also in order to enter with them into a shared struggle against the causes of their suffering.

> We cannot suffer with the poor when we are unwilling to confront those persons and systems that cause poverty. We cannot set the captives free when we do not want to confront those who carry the keys. We cannot profess our solidarity with those who are oppressed when we are unwilling to confront the oppressor.

Compassion without confrontation fades quickly into fruitless sen-
timental commiseration.[49]

Compassionate Christians believe that the best way to alleviate human
suffering and its causes is to become "empty" relative to others, for "to be
able to receive others into our intimate inner space we must be empty."[50]
They look to Jesus as the one whose "self-emptying" was central to his
healing ministry, and they want to be "empty" like Jesus.[51]

Third, compassionate Christians want to promote the good of
God's creation for God's own sake. Specifically, they want to constitute themselves members of a community whose way of living and working together witnesses to God's compassionate presence in the world.
Together, Christians want to be "empty" enough relative to God that there
is "space" to receive God's presence into their midst, and they want to be
"empty" enough relative to others that there is "space" for others to bask
with them in the received presence of God. Christians want "to overcome
poverty, hunger, illness, and any other form of human misery," but they
want to do so partly in order to further God's own ends, i.e., in order "to
reveal the gentle presence of our compassionate God in the midst of our
broken world."[52]

What is the relationship between these desires, and what happens
when we find ourselves in conflicts of desire? McNeill, Morrison, and
Nouwen do not pursue these questions, but the texts to which we have
referred are suggestive of a likely response. The good Christian wants to
want what is good. She believes that God's desire is determinative of
what is good, and she therefore wants more than anything to want what
God wants as a participant in God's own wanting. She believes that the
best way to become this sort of participant is to "empty" herself of all
desire that is "other" than the desire of God. Empty of her own desire,
she discovers *as* her own God's desire that she become "empty" relative
to other human beings. In her "emptiness," she wants to promote the interests of others before her own.

The authors are right, in my judgment, to bring to attention the
multiplicity of desires that characteristically contribute to the Christian's
decision to show compassion. There are several concerns I have, however, with the way in which they characterize and order these desires, all
of which have to do with the notion of "emptiness." The authors are not
attempting in their book to present a nuanced understanding of "empti-

ness" that would stand up under philosophical scrutiny: they are (justi-fiably) seeking to address the hearts and minds of ordinary believers. Hence, I raise my concerns not so much in criticism of McNeill, Morri-son, and Nouwen, but as a cautionary response to some common Christian beliefs.

First, the authors suggest that the Christian wants in her compas-sion to be "empty" relative to God. In perfect obedience, she wants to be "empty" of her own desire so that she can want what she wants with the very desire of God. Like Jesus, she wants to be so open and attentive to the desire of God that she can "[know] without restriction the will of the one who commands and [have] only one all-embracing desire: to live out that will."[53]

One problem with construing a right relationship with God in this way is that it does not convey the impression that the self is always con-stituted in part by its own substantial desires, the intentional content and intensity of which are always changing. The self who enters into a char-acter-building friendship with God in the company of its other friends never ceases to have its own desires, and it never ceases to be driven by the desires that it has. Instead, its desires are (more or less) educated in ongoing conversation with a Friend whose nature it is to desire the good. Imaging God as Friend, we can describe the process of becoming con-formed to God as one in which the relatively un(re)formed self is moved by a desire for *eudaimonia* to deliberate with itself and with its "other selves" about the content of *eudaimonia*. Hearing the Word in the midst of its deliberations, and hearing *in* the Word the "name" by which it is called to become its divinely appointed self, the self considers what it would be like to answer to that "name," i.e., it feels as a possibility for itself the desire to become *this* relational self who is destined to flourish in *this* way. If the possibility strikes the self as sufficiently attractive rela-tive to other of its desires, then the self's desiderative orientation will be reformed in increased conformity to the perceived desire of God. Con-tinued engagement with the Word of divine desire through activities with "other selves" who have an interest in the self's moral education will help to specify further the intentional content of the self's desire and to make these specifications a matter of habit.

Another problem with construing a right relationship with God in terms of "emptiness" is that it does not convey well the active role that the self's (partially educated) desire plays in its deliberations concerning whether and how to feel compassion. Choosing to feel compassion in the right way requires seeking to integrate and to balance the wantings *with* and the wantings *for* that contribute to the self's passional awareness of (among other things) another's pain-filled predicament. That is to say, it requires heeding the way in which some of the self's desires draw it abruptly into the immediacy of the other's experience, even as other of its desires draw it into a broadening perspective on what is the case and how much it matters. It requires feeling and attending to this diverse and ever changing bundle of desires and seeking *in* this feeling and attending to discern which of them, in which configuration, are most consistent with the self's best-to-date vision and love of the good. Obviously, the self cannot carry out these assessments utterly unmoved by the desires that it already feels; it can only assess *as* it desires, feeling its way reflectively into yet other possibilities of desire, in searching openness to the Friend who determines the good, and with friends who keep the self from assuming too glibly that it knows what its Friend determines to be good.

Second, the authors suggest that the Christian wants in her compassion to be "empty" relative to "other selves" who are in pain: "To pay attention to others with the desire to make them the center and to make their interests our own is a real form of self-emptying, since to be able to receive others into our intimate inner space we must be empty."[54]

This suggestion, too, is problematic. To begin with, the call to "emptiness" does not sit well with the acknowledgment that it is partly the self's well-educated desire for *eudaimonia* that drives it to become good at being compassionate. To "empty" the self of this desire would be to undercut its reasons and motives for cultivating compassion. It will not do to specify that the self must be "emptied" of "its own" desire (so that it can become a cipher for God's desire), for the self's initial stirrings to become compassionate[55] remain in a morally significant sense "its own" even as they are healed of their distortions and elevated into a participation of God's desire. Nor will it do to specify that the self must be "emptied" of its "self-interested" desire, for the self has a legitimate and compelling interest in being good.

McNeill, Morrison, and Nouwen assume that the friend of God will be disposed always to put the interests of the other before the interests of the self. They appeal to the words with which Paul exhorted the Christians at Philippi, and render them as follows:

There must be no competition among you, no conceit; but everyone is to be self-effacing. Always consider the other person to be better than yourself, so that nobody thinks of his own interests first but everyone thinks of the other people's interests instead (Ph 2:3–4).

But this scriptural passage ought not to be taken literally and straightforwardly as normative for all human beings today.[56] First, the passage does not in itself make clear that the self cannot love its "other selves" *as* itself unless it first loves itself. We have seen that it is precisely in loving itself (in the right way) that the self discovers itself to be a relational self that is bound to promote the good of included others in the act of promoting its own good. Second, the passage does not without further discussion disclose the ways in which the good of the self and the good of its "other selves" interpenetrate, such that a sacrifice of the self's good counts as a sacrifice to the good of the other (inasmuch as the other includes the good of the self in its own good). The shared sacrifice may be worth it, all things considered, but all things *should* be considered (when possible) before making this judgment.

Third, the passage as such does not bring to light the fact that habitual self-sacrifice can injure the other. Repeatedly sacrificing the self's good on behalf of the other can give the other the sense that his or her interests are more important than the interests of other selves; it can give the other implicit permission to treat other selves as if they were of lesser or no account. Failing to require that the other treat the self with equal regard can thus contribute indirectly to his or her moral diminishment. Fourth, we must remain acutely aware of the ways in which texts like these have been and continue to be used by certain people in power to render the oppressed and marginalized submissive and obedient to the rule of the F/father. To tell a woman or a person of color whose interests have never been put "first" to continue to put the interests of other people "first" is, in effect, to discourage her from cultivating mature character-friendships in which she and her "other selves" bind themselves equally to the promotion of shared goods, including the goods of mutual respect, intimacy, and justice. Fifth, the text as such does not acknowledge that the self's good is worthy of pursuit in its own right. McNeill, Morrison, and Nouwen say that, "in the intimacy of prayer, God reveals [God-self] to us as the God who loves all members of the human family just as personally and uniquely as [God] loves us."[57] But this means that, as friends of God and participants in God's own desire, we will desire our own good just as personally and uniquely as we desire the good of others.[58]

None of this is to deny that the self's desire for its own good can be "selfish" in the strongest sense of the word (i.e., utterly oblivious to the interests of others) and that this kind of self-regard is morally problematic. It's just to say that an unqualified call to "self-emptying" or "selflessness" has its own problems. It seems to me that a helpful way to combat the problem of human "selfishness" would be to teach each other to conceive of and to experience ourselves as relational creatures who have a personal stake in the flourishing of every other human being. Unfortunately, Christians have not, on the whole, fared very well at becoming richly relational selves, partly because so many of them have believed that the "other" must be converted to the "same" belief in Christ in order to count as "another self." Fortunately, Christians have resources within their sacred texts, within the history of interpretation of these texts, within their traditions of religious practice, and beyond Christianity itself for dismantling the xenophobia that keeps them relationally so "small." Other authors have discussed these resources.[59]

Choosing Compassion's Desire

Choosing to feel compassion in the right way remains, for the Christian as for others, partly a matter of feeling, forming, integrating, and re-feeling in critical conversation with herself and her "other selves" the wantings *with* and the wantings *for* that constitute her affective awareness of and orientation toward particular persons in pain. It remains, for the Christian, partly a matter of training and habituating her desires to arise and to persist in coordination with her best-available vision and love of the good. The difference is that the virtuous friend of God seeks to form her desires and to have them formed in explicit friendship with God and with other-selves-with-God. She seeks the education of her desires for *eudaimonia* and the goods that contribute to *eudaimonia* partly by appropriating prayerfully Biblical and other narratives about the compassion (and the other excellences) of God, Jesus, and the followers of Jesus, i.e., by listening to, reflecting upon, conversing about, critiquing, reading, reciting, studying, singing, and enacting in ritual a variety of stories that disclose the compassionate God's engagement with human beings.[60] On account of this prayerful appropriation process, the desires that predominate over the compassionate Christian's passional awareness are likely to be deliberately God-referential.

CHARITY'S IMPACT ON COMPASSION'S BELIEF AND PERCEPTION

Friendship with God can condition many of the desires that contribute to the decision to exercise compassion. It can also condition our compassion-constituting beliefs and perceptions. The compassionate Christians that McNeill, Morrison, and Nouwen have in mind believe and perceive that radical servanthood is the way to encounter God. Christians perceive God, "the source of all ... comfort and consolation, in the center of servanthood," and it is on God that Christians keep their attention focused in their encounters with suffering others:

> The joy of those who follow their Lord on [the Lord's] self-emptying and humbling way shows that what they seek is not misery and pain but the God whose compassion they have felt in their own lives. Their eyes do not focus on poverty and misery, but on the face of the loving God.[61]

Christians keep their eyes focused on God partly because God is the source of their practical wisdom. They believe that, just as Jesus "reaches out to the suffering of the world from the silent center where he stands in full attentiveness to his Father[/Mother]," so Christians do best to reach out to those in pain while giving their "full undivided attention to the voice of [their] beloved Father[/Mother]."[62] Christians keep their eyes focused on God also because to do otherwise is to court burnout:

> As long as the help we offer to others is motivated primarily by the changes we may accomplish, our service cannot last long. When results do not appear, when success is absent, when we are no longer liked or praised for what we do, we lose the strength and motivation to continue. When we see nothing but sad, poor, sick, or miserable people who, even after our many attempts to offer help, remain sad, poor, sick, and miserable, then the only reasonable response is to move away in order to prevent ourselves from becoming cynical or depressed.[63]

The authors insist, then, that the eyes of compassionate Christians "are not focused on pain, but on the Lord."[64] But if the eyes of Christians are not focused to *some* extent on pain, it is difficult to see how the co-suffering of this or that pain is possible for them. The authors do acknowledge that, even as the Christian makes obedience to God her "first and only concern" in compassion, she "[pays] attention" to those who suffer, "with the desire to make *them* the center and to make *their* interests [her] own."[65] The authors do say that, even as the Christian gives her "full undivided attention" to what the Father/Mother is saying to her in a given situation, she attends with patience to those who suffer, where patience is defined as "the capacity to see, hear, touch, taste, and smell as fully as possible the inner and outer events of our lives . . . so that we really know what is happening."[66] The authors do not attend, however, to the tension in these remarks: Is it chiefly to the person in pain or to the Father/Mother that the Christian "listens" in her deliberations? (If the "voice" of God "speaks" to her partly through the voice of the other, how does she distinguish between the Word and mere words?) Is the Christian "looking" chiefly for the best way to alleviate this person's pain or for the best way to encounter her God? (What if she "sees" that God can be encountered more easily and more pleasantly through some other means?)

These are not easy questions to resolve. I want simply to argue that what marks an experience of ours as an experience of compassion is the fact that the intentional desires that are most prominent in our perceptive, passional awareness are ones that are focused on a particular person, her pain, and the possible means to its alleviation. To make *God* the focus (i.e., the object) of compassion is to reduce compassion to the love of God. It is, indeed, possible for a Christian's compassion to be composed of dispositions to desire, to believe, and to perceive that are all conditioned by her loving participation in the life of God. For example, it is possible for a Christian characteristically to "see" persons *as* God-related beings whose good includes the good of their God-relationships, and it is possible, accordingly, for her to "look for" and to "see" ways of helping persons with reference to their God-relationality. But if the Christian does not, in a given situation, have the alleviation of *this* (God-related) person's (God-related) pain at the center of her (God-related) attention, then what she is feeling is not properly characterized as compassion.

What about the danger of burnout? I agree that this is a serious danger, but I submit that focusing attention on God as object (to the point that we risk inadvertently relegating the particular other to the periphery) is not the only or the best way to avoid this danger. It seems to me that the Christian who is most effective at the long-term cultivation of compassion is someone who learns, within the context of character-friendships with other God-relational selves not to construe the goods to be achieved in compassion too narrowly. She is someone who believes and perceives that, even if she cannot alleviate certain sorts of pain in a given predicament, she can realize a number of other important goods through her compassion. For example, she can help those who suffer to feel less alone in their pain or to choose wisely how they will *be* in their pain; she can re-invigorate her own sense of connectedness; she can serve as an example for others who would be compassionate; she can embody and thus reinforce her commitment to community; she can cultivate character traits that are ingredient in a range of related excellences; she can deepen her character-friendships with those who share her commitment to compassion, and she can enjoy God's presence in the midst of these friendships. The Christian who is most effective at sustaining a commitment to the cultivation of compassion is the one who works in community with others to keep goods like these in perspective, so that when some of these goods go unrealized in a particular predicament, others come to the fore and maintain motivation.

My view is that friendship with God can and often does condition compassion's belief and perception by conditioning the way in which the self "sees" the other. When the friend of God perceives a particular person in pain, he "sees" that the other is like him in important respects—the other has been befriended by God, just as the self has, which means that God includes the good of the other in God's good, just as God includes the good of the self in God's good. Perceiving that God includes the good of all God's befriended in God's good, and wanting to be one with the inclusive Befriender, the friend of God perceives that, indeed, the good of the other is included in his own good. He perceives that the good of the other matters to him personally.

When the friend of God seeks to promote the good of the particular other whom he now perceives to be "another himself," he draws (ineluctably, but critically) on the practical wisdom that has been communicated by (various interpretations of) Christian scripture and tradition. He

228 | CHOOSING TO FEEL

discerns what is at issue in a particular case of suffering; he determines what would count, in this case, as "the alleviation of pain"; he weighs the good of pain-alleviation against other goods that he perceives to be at stake; he considers and assesses possible means for alleviating pain while promoting these other goods; and he attaches himself to the overall best possibility. He does all of this as someone whose habits of desiring, believing, and perceiving have been and continue to be formed by wrestling personally with who Jesus was, what he did and taught, what his followers believed of him, and how these beliefs have given shape to communities of persons who continue to gather in his name. He engages in all of these deliberative activities as someone who has wrestled with these and other questions in the company of "other selves" who seek, with him, to become available to and elevated into the insight and the passion of God.

Choosing Compassion's Belief and Perception

Choosing to feel compassion in the right way remains, for the Christian as for others, partly a matter of choosing here and now to attend to the alleviation of a particular person's pain by the best means available, while attending also to a broader range of goods that are at stake. It remains, for the Christian, partly a matter of choosing over time to cultivate (among other, related excellences) excellences in perceiving passionately that this or that person is experiencing pain, that he or she is experiencing *this* particular pain, and that *this* pain is most likely to be alleviated by *this* sort of action-passion. The difference is that the Christian chooses to construe persons, their pain, and the possible ways of alleviating their pain, in light of a faithful appropriation of certain Christian teachings. He chooses to "see" persons in pain as God-related persons who are like him and, indeed, part of him by virtue of their God-relatedness. He chooses to perceive their pain as being constituted, in part, by the experience of being in disrelation to God. He chooses to perceive the possible means for alleviating their pain partly *as* means for righting this disrelation. And so on. In sum, the Christian seeks to discern the best means for alleviating the pain that he perceives in the particular other; it's just that the way in which he perceives the other and her pain, and the habits of desire, belief, and perception that he brings to the discernment process, are all conditioned by his participation in a particular religious community.[67]

CHARITY'S IMPACT ON COMPASSION'S CHOICE

Qua virtue, compassion is a habitual disposition concerned with choosing both to act and to feel on the basis of deliberations that are constituted by desiderative, cognitive, and perceptual discernments of particular persons in pain and the best means available for alleviating their pain. To exercise the virtue of compassion is deliberately to *desire* in coordination with other goods the alleviation of a person's pain, to believe and to perceive that this alleviation could best be accomplished, while other of the goods at stake could be promoted or preserved, by means of a particular action-passion on our part, and to do-feel that action-passion when the time is right. The choice to act with compassion *is* the composite of compassion's desire (in coordination with other, re-lated desires) and the belief and perception that this desire can best be fulfilled in *this* way; the act follows immediately unless an obstacle of some sort gets in the way, in which case further deliberations will have to be carried out before a final choice can be constituted.

As we have seen, one obstacle that can keep us from choosing to act with compassion is the belief that we cannot exercise compassion toward every person who happens to be in pain, along with the judgment that we ought, therefore, to limit ourselves to exercising it toward this or that class of persons (e.g., those who are most likely to "complete" it). I wish to conclude this chapter by considering the impact that a friendship with God can have on a believer's decision regarding who is, and who is not, a proper object of her compassion.

We have already considered some of the ways in which ongoing conversations with God the Friend can condition a person's moral agency. McNeill, Morrison, and Nouwen argue that,

> In the intimacy of prayer, God reveals [Godself] to us as the God who loves all members of the human family just as personally and uniquely as [God] loves us. Therefore, a growing intimacy with God deepens our sense of responsibility for others. It evokes in us an always increasing desire to bring the whole world with all its suf-fering and pains around the divine fire in our heart and to share the revitalizing heat with all who want to come.[68]

The practice of prayer can evoke in us a habitual openness to the "other" and a growing desire to make every other "our own." It can even dispose us to take in, or to be taken in by, the painful experiences of "enemies," such that we stand to them, too, as to "other ourselves." As the authors put it: "Prayer converts the enemy into a friend and is thus the beginning of a new relationship."[69]

Once again, the authors recognize that finite human beings on their own cannot extend compassion toward all "friends," in all places, at all times. But they can participate in communities that are bound together by shared commitments to "converting" all human beings (in their own hearts) to "friends." As members of these sorts of communities, finite human beings can establish networks of extended befriending:[70] they can cultivate in each other's company "an intangible atmosphere resulting from a common life"—a "healing influence" under which every participant feels "understood, accepted, cared for, and loved."[71] They can also transcend their individual limitations in such a way that they are able to meet, if not all needs, then "a great variety of needs."[72] Speaking to Christians, the authors say that,

> By our life together, we become participants in the divine compassion. Through this compassion, we can take on the yoke and burden of Christ—which is all human pain in every time and place—while realizing that his yoke is easy and his burden light (Mt 11:30).

As participants in the divine compassion, "we can enter deeply into the most hidden corners of the world and perform the same works Christ did; indeed, we may perform even greater works (Jn 14:12)!"[74]

Strangers and Enemies as "Other Ourselves"

Throughout much of this project, we have explored the way in which the self stands to its intimate character-friends as to its "other selves." We have also explored the way in which charity can condition the self to stand to those other than character-friends, too, as to its "other selves." In this chapter, we have said of the compassionate Christian that she exercises compassion toward *all* selves as to her "other selves." Clearly, character-friends are "other ourselves" in a sense that strangers and enemies are not. A character-friend is "another oneself" in that he and the self have co-constructed many of the habits of desiring, believing, perceiving, etc., that each of them brings to situations of moral import, such that he and the self are disposed to feel much the same desires, to believe much the same things, to see from much the same angles, and thus to experience much the same pains in the same situations. But none of this can be said with respect to the stranger or the enemy (unless the enemy was once a friend). What sense does it make, then, to call the stranger or the enemy "another oneself?"

Compassion is, in part, a disposition deliberately to receive and respond to persons in pain *as if* they were persons with whom we share our lives. That is to say, it is partly a disposition to experience in the presence of persons in pain a sense of "mutual indwelling" or oneness that makes it possible for us to say meaningfully that we experience something of the same pain that they experience (and that we therefore desire and seek the alleviation of that pain as partly our own). We have accounted for this intimacy with respect to character-friends who have spent many of their days pleasurably in each other's company, but how can we account for it with respect to strangers and enemies?

We do not need to have spent our days with a particular stranger or enemy to presume with good reason and passion that he is like us in the way that he experiences certain pains: he, too, has life plans that he wishes to accomplish; he, too, fears the frustration of these plans; he, too, feels vulnerable when his plans are frustrated by awareness-consuming sensations of pain; he, too, is afraid of being abandoned in his pain; he, too, is afraid of having to abandon those who are depending upon him to stay well; he, too, gets tired of life's struggle, yet he, too, is afraid of dying. We do not need to have spent our days with a particular stranger or enemy to perceive that he is experiencing at least some of these (and other like) things in his pain, and to find these experiences so familiar that they seem to become our own.

Even if the stranger or the enemy has never contributed through conversation or other character-building activities to the co-configuring of our desiring, believing, and perceiving, our compassion is an openness to the possibility that he will do so in the future, to the extent that he is able and willing to engage us in conversation. Where conversation is not possible, our compassion for him is an always-open-to-being-corrected set of *presumptions* about what he is feeling and how he is feeling it, and a willingness to allow those presumptions to contribute to our perceptive, passional "take" on his situation, giving us a sense that the (presumed) other has become sufficiently one with us to give us *some* direct experience of what he is feeling. Some of our presumptions may turn out to be false, in which case our experience will turn out to have been much less the same in certain respects than we had imagined it to be. But if we are practically wise people, many of our presumptions will be right. Enough of them will be right to account for the sense that we and the other really have experienced something of the same pain. In any case, if our presumptions move us to turn our affective attention in the other's direction (and thus to discern whether or not our presumptions are right), then they serve a crucial moral function.

One could say that the act (i.e., the action-passion) of compassion is an act of "being a friend" to someone in pain, and one could say, accordingly, that the act of extending compassion toward persons other than character-friends constitutes an act of "befriending." Extending compassion does not, in itself, turn an object of compassion into a friend; friendship is a *relationship* of mutually known and reciprocated affection and benevolence that is cultivated over an extended period of time. However, it does constitute an initial, presently one-sided befriending in that it is a recognition of likeness; it is an extension of the affection that we feel toward beings who are "akin" to us and with whom we therefore feel "at home"; it is a desire that the other with whom we feel "at home" flourish under (and apart from) our influence; it is a readiness to allow the agential orientation that we adopt in our pursuit of the other's good to be constructed, in part, out of contributions from the other or, at least, out of our best guesses about the other. It is a preparedness to allow our broader patterns of wanting, thinking, and perceiving to be altered by the other, such that the other really does become (and remains) an integral part of us.

To construe compassion for strangers or enemies as an act of befriending has some pluses and some minuses. On the minus side, it seems to say too much. It suggests that the person who acts compassionately wants in her compassion to develop a long-term relationship with the other, and that she wants to promote the other's good partly in the interest of promoting the shared good of their relationship. But often we feel compassion for people on the other side of the world whom we know of only via a thirty-second clip on the evening news. We realize that we will never have the chance to get to know these people very well, that they will never become acquainted with us, and that the prospects of our coming to share a life with them are virtually nil. We also feel compassion for mass murderers, racists, and other offensive people in whose company we would not wish to spend our days, even if we could.

Also on the minus side, construing compassion for strangers and enemies as a befriending runs the risk of diluting the concept of friendship, i.e., using it to describe such a wide range of relationships that it no longer functions to mark out certain intimate relationships as unique in kind and in moral value. To call a complete stranger a "friend" is to deny that friendship is necessarily the sort of relationship that requires intimate knowledge of each other's particularity and an affection that is based on this knowledge. To call an enemy a "friend" is to deny that friends are the sorts of persons who are attracted to each other partly on the basis of excellences that each of them has acquired and wishes to cultivate further in each other's company. It is to deny character-friendship's distinctive value as a locus for cultivating mutual affection and benevolence.

On the plus side, however, to construe an act of compassion for a stranger or an enemy as an act of befriending is to suggest that compassion is not something that we can do-feel for people "in general." It is something that we must do-feel for them "in particular." That is, it requires encountering persons in pain *in* their particularity, feeling attracted to them, wanting to be with them, and wanting to benefit them *as* the unique persons that they are. For the friend of God, acting-feeling with compassion requires being attracted to, wanting to be with, and wanting to benefit persons in pain because they are friends of God (and because God is a friend of ours), but not simply on the basis of their God-befriendedness. It requires feeling a friendship-love toward them on the basis of who they are as *these* particular God-related selves. It requires wanting to learn more about who they are, such that we can become even more accustomed to them as we pursue the alleviation of their-our pain.

This may seem too strong. There is a passive element to our affection for others, which means that we cannot simply *choose* to feel affection for people whom we naturally find uninteresting, strange, or repugnant. Or can we? I have argued that we can sometimes learn to love an activity (e.g. watching basketball) by focusing passionate attention on aspects of the activity that are significantly like aspects of another activity that we already love (e.g. watching dance). Doing this does not reduce the one activity to the other; it simply establishes a basis of likeness that disposes us to encounter differences in the two activities as potentially much more interesting and attractive than we had previously perceived them to be. Similarly, we can sometimes learn to love a person (with a love of friendship) by focusing our attention on aspects of her that are significantly like aspects of other persons (e.g. ourselves and our friends) whom we already love. Focusing on aspects of likeness does not reduce the "other" to the "same"; it simply disposes us to feel comfortable enough in her presence that we are able to attend to her differentness in a way that does not drive a wedge between her and us affectively (and thus morally).[75]

To say that the act of compassion is an act of befriending persons in pain *in* their particularity is not to say that doing-feeling compassion well requires befriending every human being who happens to be in pain. First, it is *because* the compassion that we extend toward strangers and enemies *as* befriendables has to be a particularized compassion that it can be extended toward only a few persons at a time, for only a limited period of time. If we are compassionate Christians, we regard any human being as being, in principle, befriendable by us because every human being is befriended by God (and God is a friend of ours), but not every human being can or should be befriended by us individually. Past a point of critical mass, the more people we try to befriend, the weaker all of our friendships get, to the point that none of them fulfills the needs that they were originally intended to fulfill. It is better to extend compassion toward a handful of people with attention to their particularity than it is to extend what can no longer even be called compassion to too many.

Second, to say that the act of compassion is an act of befriending particular persons in pain is not to say that doing-feeling compassion well requires befriending all whom we choose to befriend in the same way and with the same intensity. I have argued, along with Thomas, that friendship with God does not function to level our special relationships in favor of equal friendships with all. It *could* not, for in the life of Christian faith, as in any other life, it is precisely in the intimacy and the relative exclusivity of our closest character-friendships that we learn to become vulnerable, permeable, and expandable vis-à-vis others. It is in the comfort of our homiest relationships that we discover what it is to share with other human selves a single, flexible, extensible flesh that is strong and supple enough to resonate with the aching flesh of yet other human selves. It is *because* we are in the habit of cultivating a trusting openness and attentiveness in relation to our suffering friends that we are capable of being grasped by so much other suffering.

It is also in the intimacy of our closest friendships that we are (or should be) "reciprocated" in our compassion; it is in these relationships that we are able to be restored and strengthened in our struggle to remain compassionate. Friendship with God disposes Christians to regard *God* as the ultimate source of compassion, but it is (for Christians) in Spirit-filled communities of faithful character-friends that God's compassion is continually and most reliably given flesh. To weaken the bonds of these friendships is to weaken a basis for compassionate resolve.

Finally, the (God-relational) intimacy that we experience with our closest friends is of intrinsic, as well as instrumental value. It is good in itself, even apart from the ways in which it contributes to the cultivation of compassion. It is part and parcel of our relational flourishing. To sacrifice this intimacy is thus to consent to our moral diminishment.

Choosing Compassion

Choosing to feel compassion in the right way remains, for the Christian as for others, partly a matter of acting with passion on the basis of what one perceives will best contribute to (among other goods) the alleviation of a particular person's pain. It remains, for the Christian, partly a matter of choosing not to let another's differentness, strangeness, threatfulness, or repulsiveness interfere with the self's intention to act-feel toward the other on the basis of the self's deliberations. The difference is that the virtuous Christian's character is formed in accordance with the Word: *You shall* be disposed to regard and to treat every person in pain, *in* her particularity, *as* "another yourself."[76] Or, to put it eudaimonistically: it is precisely in being disposed to regard and to treat every person in pain *as* "another yourself" that you are made one with God (and it is precisely in being made one with God that you flourish). The virtuous Christian's character is formed in accordance with this Word to such an extent that no experience of otherness can possibly count for her as evidence for a particular person's unbefriendability. To be sure, an experience of otherness can keep the compassionate Christian from choosing to spend her days cultivating a friendship with the other beyond the requirements of compassion, but it cannot keep her from choosing to take the other in to the minimal extent that she must in order to make a practically wise decision on the other's behalf.

Friendship with God does not provide the Christian with ready-made solutions to the problem of distributing compassion rightly among her intimate and much less intimate "other selves." It does not abrogate the need for the sort of practical wisdom that is cultivated through years and years of experience and critical reflection upon experience aimed at living, and helping others to live, the best sort of life possible for relational human beings. The decision still rests with perception. Communally-supported faith and practice may, indeed, help to "elevate" a Christian's habits of perception into the perception of God, but as long as she remains other than God (and other than others-with-God), she (like everyone else) will have to make decisions about how to construe what she perceives and how to act-feel on the basis of those construals— decisions that emanate from the aspect of her extended moral agency which she has learned to recognize as most intimately, irreducibly, and continuously "her own."

CONCLUSION

In conclusion, we can define the virtue of compassion as a habitual dis-position concerned with choosing both to act and to feel on the basis of our wanting *with* others the alleviation of their pain, our wanting *for* others this alleviation as one among many of the goods that are at stake in a given situation, and our perceiving partly *in* our wanting the best means for promoting the alleviation of pain in coordination with other of the goods at stake. Each section of this project has been designed to cover some aspect of this definition, either from a secular or from a Christian ethical point of view. We considered, to begin with, some elements of virtue, and the impact that charity can have on the exercise of virtue. We considered next some features of friendship, and the impact that a friend-ship with God can have on the way in which we stand to ourselves and to our "other selves" in the exercise of our relational moral agencies. We considered finally the way in which the particular virtue of compassion for friends is exercised by certain selves in relation to their "other selves," and the way in which charity can form selves-in-relation to perceive *all* selves as "other themselves" in whose pain-alleviation they have a per-sonal interest.

I hope to have shown that and how we can *choose* (within the con-text of a secular or a religious worldview) to become persons who are disposed, as a matter of habit, to take in, or to be taken in by, the pain of those to whom we stand as to "other ourselves." I hope to have shown that and how we can *choose* to become persons who are deliberately disposed to be wanters *with* and wanters *for* particular persons in pain, such that we are prone to deliberate, to act, and to feel as persons who are, in certain respects, one and the same relative to those who suffer and yet, in other respects, separate and different. I hope also to have provided some compelling reasons and motives for cultivating the virtue of compassion in our own lives and in the lives of those with whom we share our complex, relational selves. In the end, I cannot prove that the best sort of life is one that includes the exercise of compassion. All I can do is to present a life-option that is interesting and compelling enough to spark empassioned, thoughtful moral reflection and debate on the part of character-friends who share an interest in living well and in figuring out together just what this involves.

There is no question that being a compassionate person is a difficult thing to do. Every aspect of every relational activity that I have described in this project can be and often is subverted by ignorance, weakness, self-deception, maliciousness, and callousness. All of these failings can be and often are encouraged by "other ourselves" who are themselves caught up in personal and social structures of moral evil. In the end, we cannot transcend these trappings to the degree that we would need to in order to have a great deal of confidence in our efforts at even conceiving what it would be like to live a good human life. And yet, we have no choice but to step up to the drawing board, again and again. We cannot do without a working vision and love of the good.

Notes

1. INTRODUCTION

1. Many feminists understandably regard ethics of care or compassion with suspicion. Within the context of patriarchy, ethics of care or compassion often have the (unintended) effect of encouraging women to do the caretaking of the world and enabling men to fail to cultivate this aspect of their humanity. These are serious negative effects. It would be a mistake, however, to avoid such effects by discouraging women from cultivating compassion. Instead, women must educate ourselves about this moral excellence so that we can become clear, incisive, and deliberate about when and how we exercise it. We must exercise it in a way that makes us progressively wiser, stronger, more centered, yet at the same time more deeply and powerfully connected to others. We must also do what we reasonably can to help the men and boys in our lives to grasp what compassion is, how it can be cultivated, and why it ought to be cultivated by them. We must encourage men and boys not to tolerate in themselves and each other the failure to develop this aspect of their humanity. These are a few of the effects that I intend with this book.

2. See, e.g., Gene Outka's classic, *Agape: An Ethical Analysis* (New Haven: Yale University Press, 1972).

3. I offer, with the help of recent scholars, a selective, critical reading of Aristotle and Thomas on the topics of virtue and friendship. I seek to get as much out of Aristotle and Thomas as I can, to clarify certain shortcomings of their accounts, to begin correcting a handful of these shortcomings, and then to use these corrected accounts as a foundation upon which to set my own analysis of compassion. The thrust of my efforts throughout this project are constructive, rather than historical or exegetical.

4. Neither Aristotle nor Thomas analyze the virtue of compassion per se (although they discuss some related virtues and passions); hence the shift to more recent scholarship.

5. Lawrence Blum, "Compassion," in *Explaining Emotions*, ed. Amelie Oksenberg Rorty (Berkeley: University of California Press, 1980), pp. 509, 513.

1. ARISTOTLE ON CHARACTER VIRTUE

1. Unless otherwise noted, references to Aristotle included in the body of the text refer to Aristotle, *Nicomachean Ethics* [*NE*], trans. Terence Irwin (Indianapolis: Hackett Publishing Company, 1985). The *NE* is probably an edited collection of some of Aristotle's lecture notes on ethics, but it is widely regarded as the most complete, accurate, and compelling representation of Aristotle's ethical views available.

2. *Ethica Nicomachea*, trans. W. D. Ross in *The Basic Works of Aristotle*, ed. Richard McKeon (New York: Random House, 1941).

3. We cannot address here the difficulties involved in squaring Aristotle's apparently inclusive understanding of *eudaimonia* throughout most of the *Nicomachean Ethics* (and in the *Eudemian Ethics*) with his apparently exclusive emphasis on contemplation (*theoria*) in bk. 10. I agree with John M. Cooper that Aristotle's understanding of *eudaimonia* is an inclusive one: "despite a certain initial plausibility . . . an intellectualist interpretation cannot make coherent sense of Aristotle's theory in the *Nicomachean Ethics* taken as a whole." *Reason and Human Good in Aristotle* (Cambridge: Harvard University Press, 1977) p. 90. See also J. L. Ackrill, "Aristotle on *Eudaimonia*" in *Essays on Aristotle's Ethics*, ed. Amelie Oksenberg Rorty (Berkeley: University of California Press, 1980), pp. 15–33.

4. As Nancy Sherman notes, "the excellences of character cover a gamut that is more than merely moral," hence, the term "character virtue" as opposed to "moral virtue." *The Fabric of Character: Aristotle's Theory of Virtue* (Oxford: Clarendon Press, 1989), pp. 1–2.

5. This is Nancy Sherman's rendering of *NE* 1107a1. *The Fabric of Character*, p. 5.

6. On the meaning of *hexis* in Aristotle, see D. S. Hutchinson, *The Virtues of Aristotle* (London: Routledge and Kegan Paul, 1986), chap. 1.

7. Gilbert Ryle, *The Concept of Mind* (London: Hutchinson, 1949), p. 43, quoted in Hutchinson, *The Virtues of Aristotle*, p. 35.

8. Aristotle acknowledges the role that legislators, in addition to parents, ought to play in the training of citizens' pleasures and pains at *NE* 1179b20–1180a33. For more on Aristotle's theory of moral education, see Sherman, *The Fabric of Character*, chap. 5.

9. See Martha C. Nussbaum, *The Fragility of Goodness: Luck and Ethics in Greek Tragedy and Philosophy* (Cambridge: Cambridge University Press, 1986), on Aristotle's recognition of the vulnerability of even our deepest and most characteristic dispositions.

10. Aristotle, *Eudemian Ethics*, trans. Michael Woods (Oxford: Clarendon Press, 1982), 1227a5.

11. Nussbaum, *The Fragility of Goodness*, p. 307.

12. See Aristotle's *De Motu Animalium* 701a6–39 in Martha C. Nussbaum, *Aristotle's De Motu Animalium* (Princeton: Princeton University Press, 1978). See also *NE* 1113b3–8, 1139a32–1139b6. We cannot concern ourselves here with the diversity of scholarly opinion regarding the meaning and significance of the practical syllogism in Aristotle. My own view is influenced by and broadly consistent with the views of Sherman, *The Fabric of Character*, chap. 3, and Nussbaum, *Aristotle's De Motu Animalium*, Essay 4, "The Syllogism in *EN* VII and *DA* III."

13. Readers who are not familiar with philosophical logic should not be put off at this point. For our purposes, the practical syllogism is simply a way of representing the idea that human beings are both desiring beings and thinking/perceiving beings who deliberate and decide as such.

14. On the meaning of desire (*orexis*) in Aristotle, see Sherman, *The Fabric of Character*, chap. 3. See also Troels Engberg-Pedersen, *Aristotle's Theory of Moral Insight* (Oxford: Clarendon Press, 1983), who argues that for Aristotle, "any type of desire [whether it be a desire which includes rational, i.e. deliberative or calculative, *phantasia* or non-rational, i.e. perceptual, *phantasia*] presupposes an evaluative cognitive state on the part of the person who has the desire," pp. 136, 139.

15. This is Nussbaum's translation. See "The Discernment of Perception: An Aristotelian Conception of Private and Public Rationality" in *Proceedings of the Boston Area Colloquium in Ancient Philosophy*, vol. 1, ed. John J. Cleary (Landham, Md.: University Press of America, 1986), p. 162. Cf. W. D. Ross, *The Basic Works of Aristotle*: "We deliberate not about ends but about means."

16. Nussbaum, *The Fragility of Goodness*, p. 297 and "The Discernment of Perception" in *Proceedings of the Boston Area Colloquium in Ancient Philosophy*, ed. Cleary, fn. p. 162; Sherman, *The Fabric of Character*, chap. 3, secs. 3 and 4; David Wiggins, "Deliberation and Practical Reason" in *Essays on Aristotle's Ethics*, ed. Rorty, p. 227. See Aristotle, *Eudemian Ethics* 1226b10–13.

17. Sherman, *The Fabric of Character*, p. 71. Cf. Richard Sorabji, "Aristotle on the Role of Intellect in Virtue" in *Essays on Aristotle's Ethics*, ed. Rorty, p. 204; Nussbaum, *The Fragility of Goodness*, pp. 296–97.

18. Sherman, *The Fabric of Character*, p. 33. See *NE* 1114b1–3, 1114b13–25.

19. See "The Discernment of Perception," sec. III in *The Fragility of Goodness*, pp. 308–9, and *Aristotle's De Motu Animalium*, Essay 5. See also Wiggins, "De-

liberation and Practical Reason," p. 234. Relevant texts include *NE* 1113a10–13, 1139a20–1139b6; *De Motu Animalium* 702a18–21; *De Anima* 431b2 ff.

20. Nussbaum, *The Fragility of Goodness*, p. 308.

21. Cooper, *Reason and Human Good in Aristotle*, p. 10. See also Sherman, *The Fabric of Character*, p. 82.

22. L. A. Kosman, "Being Properly Affected: Virtues and Feelings in Aristotle's Ethics" in *Essays on Aristotle's Ethics*, ed. Rorty, p. 109. See also J. O. Urmson, "Aristotle's Doctrine of the Mean" in *Essays on Aristotle's Ethics*, ed. Rorty, pp. 157–70.

23. Aristotle, *Rhetorica*, trans. W. Rhys Roberts, *The Basic Works of Aristotle*, ed. McKeon, 1378a31.

24. Are beliefs and evaluative judgments constitutive parts of the passion or are they merely necessary, prior bases for the passion? Aristotle seems here to be saying the former. Anger is an impulse *to* revenge: the impulse cannot be separated from its intentional content and still be identified *as* an impulse of anger. Aristotle does not, to my knowledge, address this question directly in the *Nicomachean Ethics*. He says of the relation between reason and passion *generally* that the part of the soul with which we suffer passion "is by nature something besides reason, conflicting and struggling with reason. . . . However, this [part] as well [as the rational part] appears, as we have said, to share in reason—at any rate, in the continent person it obeys reason and in the temperate and the brave person it presumably listens still better to reason, since there it agrees with reason in everything" (1102b25). Regarding the more *precise* relation between reason and passion, however, Aristotle says that it "does not matter for present purposes" (1102a32, cf. 1102b25).

25. In *Aristotle's Philosophy of Action* (Ithaca: Cornell University Press, 1984), p. 187, David Charles translates *NE* 1117a19–22 in a way that illuminates Aristotle's fuller notion of choice: "Their actions [those of brave men] spring more from character because less from preparation. They *choose* to act courageously in line with their character in sudden danger and not from calculation, i.e. general reasoning" (my emphasis).

26. Aristotle says that certain sorts of conduct contribute to certain habits of passion (*NE* 1104a19–21), but he does not explain how this works. He does not say, e.g., that choosing certain actions will effect certain passions because, when we choose certain actions in light of certain desired passions, we engage a number of the perceptions, beliefs, evaluative judgments, and intentional desires that partly constitute the passions we desire. This is, however, an explanation that his larger understanding of choice would allow.

27. I refer to Aristotle's person of practical wisdom as though this person could be either male or female. Although there exists disagreement among scholars regarding Aristotle's considered judgment of women's deliberative capacities,

many agree that, for Aristotle, the practically wise person could only have been male. At least one text indicates that he judged the deliberative faculties of women to be by nature "without authority" and capable of supporting only a diminished measure of virtue [*Politica*, trans. Benjamin Jewett, in *The Basic Works of Aristotle*, ed. McKeon, 1260a10–30]. This poses a serious problem for feminists like myself who want to reject Aristotle's sexism without rejecting his theory of virtue as a whole. If I refer to the practically wise person as the practically wise *man*, then I perpetuate Aristotle's sexism. If I refer to the practically wise person as male, but continually mark the sexism inherent in this characterization (e.g., with *sic*), then I promote frustration and impatience with a man who was perhaps obtuse about women, but whose theory of virtue has immense contemporary relevance for both women and men. In this project, I opt for some generous-minded interpolation at the possible cost of some historical accuracy. I do the same in my treatment of Thomas Aquinas, for the same reasons.

28. On the distinction between the doctrine of moderation and Aristotle's doctrine of the mean see J. O. Urmson, "Aristotle's Doctrine of the Mean" in *Essays on Aristotle's Ethics*, ed. Rorty, pp. 161–62.

29. Nussbaum, *The Fragility of Goodness*, p. 299. See *NE* 1109b13–23, 1107a29–32, 1137b13–32.

30. Ibid., p. 301. See *NE* 1109b22–3, 1107a29–32, 1137b13–32, 1104a1–11, 1142a12–24, 1143a25–b6, 1143b11–14.

31. Nussbaum recalls these words of Henry James in "Finely Aware and Richly Responsible: Moral Attention and the Moral Task of Literature," *Journal of Philosophy* 82/10 (Oct. 1985): 516.

2. THOMAS AQUINAS ON ACQUIRED MORAL VIRTUE

1. Unless discussion is required, references to St. Thomas Aquinas, *Summa Theologica*, parts I, I–II, and II–II, trans. Fathers of the English Dominican Province (Westminster, Md.: Christian Classics, 1981), will be included in the body of the text. References to the Latin are to S. Thomae Aquinatis, *Summa Theologiae* (Taurini, Romae: Marietti, 1950).

2. Scholars disagree as to whether Thomas had an inclusive understanding of human flourishing or an exclusive one, i.e. whether he thought that the best human life consisted in the active exercise of all the full range of intellectual and moral virtues or in contemplation alone. While Thomas, like Aristotle, sometimes appears to embrace the latter position (e.g., I–II 3.2 *ad* 4), his larger ethic of virtue commits him to the former (e.g., I–II 3.5, 65.1).

3. Grace will be defined subsequently when we consider how Thomas's Christian perspective conditions his Aristotelian understanding of virtue.

4. There should be no direct conflict between the dictates of natural and eternal law, for the natural law is a principle implanted in the rational creature by God, giving it "a natural inclination to its proper act and end." The natural law is "the rational creature's participation of the eternal law (I–II 91.2). This participation is limited, however; the eternal law in its uncreated perfection sometimes dictates via revelation and the infusion of supernatural principles activities of soul that natural reason alone would not dictate (I–II 63.2).

5. We will account below for the way in which Thomas distinguishes the intellective appetite from the sense appetite. Thomas thinks that he is following Aristotle's *De Anima* iii.9 in distinguishing between the two (I 80.2).

6. I–II 22.3. Richard R. Baker, *The Thomistic Theory of the Passions and Their Influence Upon the Will* (Dissertation: University of Notre Dame, 1941), is a good place to begin an inquiry into the interrelationships between intellect, will, and passion in Thomas. A more recent resource is G. Simon Harak, S.J., *Virtuous Passions: The Formation of Christian Character* (New York/Mahwah: Paulist Press, 1993). I have been strongly influenced by the latter book and by stimulating conversations with its author.

7. I 78.4. By "senses," Thomas means not only the external senses, but also the internal senses, which include "the common sense, the imagination, and the estimative and memorative powers."

8. For a detailed analysis of Thomas's theory of anger, see Diana Fritz Cates, "Taking Women's Experience Seriously: Thomas Aquinas and Audre Lorde on Anger" in *Aquinas and Empowerment: Classical Ethics for Ordinary Lives*, ed. G. Simon Harak, S.J. (Washington, D.C.: Georgetown University Press, 1996), pp. 47–88. See also J. Giles Milhaven, *Good Anger* (Kansas City, Mo.: Sheed & Ward, 1989). I am indebted to Professor Milhaven for, among other things, many hours of conversation on Thomas's theory of anger.

9. I draw this implication from St. Thomas Aquinas, *The Disputed Questions on Truth*, vol. III, trans. Robert W. Schmidt (Chicago: Henry Regnery, 1954), 26.7.

10. Here I draw on Thomas's statement that a person sometimes "chooses to be affected by a passion in order to work more promptly with the co-operation of the sensitive appetite" (I–II 24.3 *ad* 1).

11. G. Simon Harak, S.J., clarifies that, for Thomas, the passions of rational animals are "*already* (by virtue of creation) ordered to reason. Of course, in another sense they are *not yet* fully governed by reason, since then we would be in union with God. The morality of the passions refers to a process of finalizing or completing or fully integrating passions that are already disposed toward rationality by virtue of their participation in a composite, rational being. That process is hardly captured by the phrase, 'submitting passions to rational control'" (*Virtuous Passions*, p. 91).

12. St. Thomas Aquinas, *The Disputed Questions on Truth,* vol. III, trans. Schmidt, 25.2.

13. We will consider the *sense* in which the beloved is "part" of the lover when we discuss in subsequent chapters the meaning and value of Thomistic *complacentia*.

14. On the nature of "connatural knowledge," according to Thomas, see W. E. May, "Knowledge, Connatural" in *New Catholic Encyclopedia*, vol. 8 (New York: McGraw-Hill, 1967), pp. 228–29; and Etienne Gilson, *The Christian Philosophy of St. Thomas Aquinas*, trans. L. K. Shook (New York: Alba House, 1985), pp. 347–50.

15. For a related discussion of the *body's* contribution to knowledge, see J. Giles Milhaven, "Ethics and Another Knowing of Good and Evil" in *The Annual of the Society of Christian Ethics,* ed. D. M. Yeager (Washington D.C.: Georgetown University Press, 1991), pp. 237–48.

16. Thomas says at II–II 58.9 that the acquired moral virtue of justice, in particular, is "not about the passions, as are temperance and fortitude, which are in the irascible and concupiscible parts." While justice may not be specified by a particular passion, it is nevertheless the case that justice, along with every other moral virtue "is directed to pleasure and pain, as to ends to be acquired, for as the Philosopher says (*Ethic.* vii.11), *pleasure and pain are the principal end in respect of which we say that this is an evil and that a good*: and in this way too they belong to justice, since *[one] is not just unless he rejoice in just actions* (*Ethic.* i.8)" (II–II 58.9 *ad* 1; cf. I–II 59.4 *ad* 1). See J. O. Urmson, "Aristotle's Doctrine of the Mean" in *Essays on Aristotle's Ethics,* ed. Rorty, p. 166, for a discussion of a parallel ambiguity in Aristotle. Urmson argues that, because justice is not and cannot be specified by a particular passion, it does not count as a virtue in the strict sense.

17. We shall observe Thomas's distinction between the sense and intellective appetites. Keep in mind, however, that the distinction becomes rather fuzzy within the context of his theory of the passions. I will have no use for this distinction in my account of compassion.

18. Recall Thomas's analysis of anger (I–II 47).

19. Thomas repeatedly quotes Aristotle (*NE* iii.5) as saying, "*according as a [person] is, such does the end seem to him* (1–11 9.2)." If virtue is partly a disposition to see the world in a certain way, then choosing virtue involves choosing habits of perception.

20. Thomas seems to have in mind here both long-term dispositions of the bodily organs (ones that we are born with) and short-term dispositions (like ones that arise when we get tired or sick). See I–II 17.7 *ad* 2.

21. Ibid. Thomas suggests that we can sometimes alter at least some of our passions by seeking to alter our bodily states directly. Sorrow, for example, can sometimes be assuaged via sleep and baths (I–II 38.5).

22. I 81.3 *ad* 2; cf. I–II 17.7. There are serious problems with imaging the relation between reason and passion in terms of the relation between ruler and

subject, or master and slave. It can be helpful to distinguish different sorts of things that occur within human experience with reference to the terms of reason and passion, but this distinction must be drawn in a way that captures the mutual dependence and influence that obtains between these two sorts of things. The distinction ought not to be made in a way that encourages persons to value reason over emotion or to inscribe this dualistic evaluation onto the structure of society or the universe.

23. See W. E. May, "Knowledge, Connatural" in *New Catholic Encyclopedia,* vol. 8, pp. 228–29.

3. THOMAS AQUINAS ON THEOLOGICAL AND INFUSED VIRTUE

1. Just as we are limited in the pursuit of natural human virtue, so we are obviously and seriously limited in our pursuit of supernaturally elevated human virtue. The following account, like that which precedes it, is not true to life in that it considers only abstractly and ideally what virtue is and how its exercise contributes to human flourishing. It does not consider the subtle, complex, and sometimes overwhelming ways in which vice can and does inhibit and under-mine the exercise of virtue. Nevertheless, I believe that an examination of virtue and of compassion, in particular, is prerequisite to an examination of moral evil (partly because a principal cause of moral evil is the failure to become the sort of person who is habitually affected by the weal and woe of others). Hence, this book serves as a first step in a much broader inquiry.

2. For a discussion of the different kinds of grace recognized by Thomas, see Reginald Garrigou-Lagrange, *Grace: Commentary on the Summa Theologica of St. Thomas, IaIIae, q. 109–14,* trans. the Dominican Nuns of Corpus Christi Monastery (St. Louis, Mo.: B. Herder Book Co., 1958). Thomas is concerned in the *Summa* mainly with what Lagrange calls habitual grace and actual grace. Actual grace is the movement of the soul by God by virtue of which a person knows, will, or feels anything. Habitual grace is defined below.

3. Paul Wadell, *Friends of God: Virtues and Gifts in Aquinas* (New York: Peter Lang, 1991), p. 129. Wadell realizes that this way of describing the gifts raises questions about the nature of human freedom under the influence of grace. He argues that, "To act in virtue of God and not ourselves, to be moved by divine agency instead of our own, did not signify a loss of freedom for Thomas, but free-dom's highest possibility, freedom's perfection, because to be absorbed wholly in God was what charity always desired," p. 131.

4. That is to say, they have to do with "eternal or necessary matters," (i.e., things which cannot be otherwise than they are) (II–II 8.3 *ad* 2).

5. Filial fear is distinguished from worldly, servile, and initial fear according to different specifications of the evil feared (II–II 19.2). Only filial fear is a gift of the Holy Spirit (II–II 19.9).

6. As we shall see in later portions of this project, the person of faith, hope, and charity does not seek "her own" supernatural happiness as though "her own" could be conceived of in isolation from the happiness of others. Rather, she seeks *as* "her own" the supernatural happiness of all whom she regards as her "other selves."

7. See Jean Porter, "Desire for God: Ground of the Moral Life in Aquinas," *Theological Studies* 47 (1986): 48–68.

8. Etienne Gilson, *The Christian Philosophy of St. Thomas Aquinas*, trans. L. K. Shook (New York: Random House, 1966), pp. 318–19.

9. Again, this means that it concerns things that are eternal and necessary (II–II 45.3 *ad* 2).

10. Thomas says that, "All the moral virtues are infused together with charity. . . . It is therefore clear that . . . whoever loses charity through mortal sin forfeits all the infused moral virtues" (I–II 65.3).

11. It is important to keep in mind that, for Thomas, grace does not overcome nature; rather, it perfects it (I 2.2 *ad* 1). It is also important to keep in mind that in perfecting nature, grace does more than promote a natural perfection; it also promotes a higher-than-natural perfection (I–II 62.2 *ad* 1). I use the term "perfection," as Thomas does, to include "supernatural elevation."

12. This reading is consistent, in my judgment, with what Thomas says at I–II 65.2.

13. Thomas says that, "Accordingly charity increases only by its subject partaking of charity more and more, i.e., by being more reduced to its act and more subject thereto. For this is the proper mode of increase in a form that is intensified, since the being of such a form consists wholly in its adhering to its subject" (II–II 24.5). Being more and more "reduced" to charity, however, takes practice. Paul Wadell makes the striking claim that "Friendship with God is *acquired*" (my emphasis) seemingly in order to make the point that, while charity is gratuitously infused by God, it can form us only inasmuch as we choose to be formed by it: "Only charity makes us God's friend, and becoming God's friend is a transformation only gradually achieved the more the will is determined to God" (*Friends of God*, p. 95).

14. Jean Porter, "The Subversion of Virtue: Acquired and Infused Virtues in the *Summa theologiae*" in *The Annual of the Society of Christian Ethics*, ed. Harlan Beckley (Washington D.C.: Georgetown University Press, 1992), p. 34. Porter makes the interesting observation that, for Thomas, "the individual who possesses infused prudence is not necessarily capable of good judgment on earthly matters, but only with respect to matters pertaining to salvation. Indeed as he

[Thomas] explains further, the prudence of the really dull saint may extend only as far as an ability to recognize that one needs to submit to the judgment of others, combined with an ability to discriminate between good and bad advice," (p. 34; cf. *ST* II–II 47.14 *ad* 1, *ad* 2). Thomas's statement to this effect suggests that he might not have thought of the infused virtues as gratuitously elevated forms of their acquired counterparts (or as having their basis in the same powers *qua* elevated). He might have thought of the infused virtues as functioning in considerable isolation from the acquired virtues (such that the infusion of, say, infused prudence could not be expected to have any effect on the acquisition or exercise of acquired prudence). The question, of course, is whether or not such a construal of the relation between the infused and the acquired virtues makes sense and whether it is consistent, finally, with Thomas's own insistence upon the unity of the moral life in grace.

15. Joseph Pieper discusses this briefly in *The Four Cardinal Virtues* (New York: Harcourt, Brace & World, Inc., 1967), pp. 37 ff.

16. This point, as I elaborate it below, follows from Thomas's assertion that "All the moral virtues [and thus, by implication, prudence (II–II 47.8)] are infused together with charity" (I–II 65.3), together with his assertion that faith, hope, and charity actually elevate our human capacities to reason and to love (II–II 23.2 passim and *ad* 1, II–II 45.3 *ad* 1).

17. The passions are divided by Thomas into the irascible and the concupiscible. The concupiscible passions (love, desire, joy, and their contraries) take as their object "sensible good or evil, simply apprehended as such, which causes pleasure or pain." The irascible passions (hope, despair, fear, daring, and anger) take as their object "good or evil inasmuch as it is of an arduous or difficult nature" (I–II 23.1).

18. We might expect this if we were to lose sight of the fact that Thomas's theory of the virtues is deeply Aristotelian. Repeatedly, Thomas defends the Aristotelian view of the goodness of well-ordered habits of passions against competing views (I–II 59.2). It is easy to lose sight of this, however, when Thomas himself reveals the power that Neoplatonism exercised over his thought. Arguing that we ought to strive onward in this life toward divine things, he turns to Plotinus: "Human virtues, that is to say, virtues of [humans] living together in this world, are about the passions. But the virtues of those who have attained to perfect bliss are without passions. Hence Plotinus says . . . that *the social virtues check the passions*, i.e., they bring them to the relative mean; *the second kind*, viz., the perfecting virtues, *uproot them; the third kind*,viz., the perfect virtues, *forget them; while it is impious to mention them in connection with virtues of the fourth kind*, viz., the exemplar virtues" (I–II 61.5 *ad* 2). The temptation to urge people to live in this world in a way that anticipates, as fully as possible, the strictly passionless life of the world to come is, for the most part, resisted by Thomas. But here, a ten-

sion is visible. It leads Thomas to offer what I regard as a Neo-Platonic reading of Aristotle (I–II 61.5).

19. G. Simon Harak, S. J., captures this understanding powerfully in *Virtuous Passions*, chap. 4.

20. Part of the problem here is that, in Thomas's view, God is incorporeal, but passion is defined as a movement of the sense appetite in response to some corporeal object. Hence, we cannot, in a strict sense, have a passion for God (I 12.3, 12.12). I expect that a consideration of Thomas's theory of the sacraments, however, would reveal that his understanding of the passion for God is richer than Part I of the *Summa* leads us to think. Along these lines, see L. Gregory Jones, "The Theological Transformation of Aristotelian Friendship in the Thought of St. Thomas Aquinas," *The New Scholasticism*, Autumn 1987, 61/4, pp. 387–90.

21. Recall the discussion of passion in chapter 2.

22. John Giles Milhaven explores the medieval mystic Hadewijch's reflections on the body's contribution to the knowledge and love of God in his *Hadewijch and Her Sisters: Other Ways of Loving and Knowing* (Ithaca: State University of New York Press, 1993). Consider also Milhaven's "Ethics and Another Knowing of Good and Evil" in *The Annual of the Society of Christian Ethics* (1991), ed. Yeager, pp. 237–48.

23. I may be pressing for something that Thomas would allow, but would want to describe differently, in accordance with the (unfortunate) constraints of his faculty psychology, in general, and his distinction between intellective and sense appetite, in particular. My point is that the value of rightly-ordered passion should be affirmed, not simply "from the top down" (as overflow from a movement of the will), but also "from the bottom up" (as valuable in itself and in its ability to open us up to a richer experience of God as God discloses Godself in ordinary objects of sense).

4. ARISTOTLE ON FRIENDSHIP

1. Twentieth century Scottish philosopher John MacMurray argues for "persons in relation" as a model for understanding persons in *Persons in Relation* (New York: Harper and Brothers, 1961). According to this model, as Frank Kirkpatrick relates it in *Community: A Trinity of Models* (Washington, D.C.: Georgetown University Press, 1986), what makes a person a person is "a consciousness of being in relation to that which is not oneself and an ability to initiate actions in accord with consciously chosen intentions which seek to develop that relationship" (p. 167). The following understanding of persons *as* persons in relation is similar to MacMurray's in many respects, but was arrived at independently. There are other authors, too, who make use of a relational understanding of the person in

their work. See, e.g., H. Richard Niebuhr, *The Responsible Self* (New York: Harper & Row, 1963); Catherine Keller, *From a Broken Web: Separation, Sexism, and Self* (Boston: Beacon Press, 1986) and "Feminism and the Ethic of Inseparability" in *Women's Consciousness, Women's Conscience: A Reader in Feminist Ethics,* Barbara Hilkert Andolson, Christine E. Gudorf, Mary D. Pellauer, eds., (San Francisco: Harper & Row, 1985), pp. 251–63; Ruth L. Smith, "Feminism and the Moral Subject" in *Women's Consciousness, Women's Conscience: A Reader in Feminist Ethics,* Barbara Hilkert Andolson, Christine E. Gudorf, Mary D. Pellauer, eds. pp. 235–50.

2. *Philia,* for Aristotle, refers not only to love relationships between friends as we tend narrowly to understand this term today, but also to love relationships between parents and children, spouses, siblings, lovers, and fellow citizens (where these relationships possess the requisite features to be discussed below). See Nussbaum, *The Fragility of Goodness,* pp. 354 ff. Aristotle goes so far as to speak of friendship between persons *qua* fellow human beings. He says that "Members of the same race, and human beings most of all, have a natural friendship for each other; that is why we praise friends of humanity. And in our travels we can see how every human being is akin and beloved to a human being" (1155a20). Julia Annas argues, however, that "if this [statement] is seriously meant as praise of those who feel commitment to other humans just as such, and regardless of any shared context, then not only does it find no echo elsewhere in Aristotle's ethics, it seems incompatible with the importance given elsewhere to the contexts of family and polis. . . . Aristotle's reflective theory emphasizes the importance and ethical potential of particular commitments, taking no serious account of unrestricted other-concern." *The Morality of Happiness* (New York: Oxford University Press, 1993), p. 253.

3. Aristotle says, "it would presumably be ridiculous to wish good things to wine; the most you wish is its preservation so that you can have it. To a friend, however, it is said, you must wish goods for his sake" (1155b29–32). On the importance of separateness and respect for separateness in Aristotle's account of *philia* see Nussbaum, *The Fragility of Goodness,* pp. 354–55.

4. Well-wishing differs from affection (or loving) in that the former lacks intensity of desire relative to the latter. Moreover, "goodwill can . . . arise in a moment," whereas "loving requires familiarity" (1166b33).

5. Aristotle, *Rhetorica (Rhetoric),* trans. W. Rhys Roberts, in *The Basic Works of Aristotle,* ed. McKeon, 1381a1.

6. For a critique of this aspect of Aristotle's understanding of friendship see Irving Singer, *The Nature of Love, 1: Plato to Luther,* second edition (Chicago: University of Chicago Press, 1984). Singer argues that "loving a friend means more than wishing him well or enjoying his noble character; it also means caring about him despite his imperfections, treating him in a way that is *incommensu-*

rate with his actual goodness, assuming a virtue though he have it not" (p. 90). In the *Rhetoric,* Aristotle says, along similar lines, that we regard with friendliness those "who are aware of neither their neighbours' bad points nor our own, but of our good ones only, as a good [person] always will be" (1381b8). My impression is that Aristotle recognizes the value of forming our perceptions of others in such a way that we highlight their best qualities and downplay or put the best light on their worst. But Aristotle would likely not want to say that friends assume that good qualities of character exist in each other when in fact they do not. Among other things, by ignoring our friends' character weaknesses, we become unable lovingly to challenge our friends to overcome these weaknesses and to pursue, with us, their distinctive human good.

7. On the distinction between the *basis,* the *object,* and the *goal* of friendship see Nussbaum, *The Fragility of Goodness,* p. 355.

8. This seems to be the most generous and sensible interpretation of Aristotle on friendships of advantage and pleasure. It is put forth by Nussbaum, *The Fragility of Goodness,* pp. 355–56; and John M. Cooper, "Aristotle on Friendship" in *Essays on Aristotle's Ethics,* ed. Rorty, esp. section IV. See Cooper for a thorough discussion of interpretive difficulties in which we cannot become enmeshed here. See also A. W. Price's treatment of Cooper in *Love and Friendship in Plato and Aristotle* (Oxford: Clarendon Press, 1989), pp. 148–54.

9. In order to be attached to someone with a love of character-friendship, it is necessary that we love her or him on the basis of *some* good quality or qualities of her or his character, "even though," as John Cooper puts it, "these qualities may be, and may be known to be, limited in their goodness and/or conjoined with other not so good, or even positively bad, personal characteristics." The best character friendships, however, are those between the perfectly virtuous. "Aristotle on Friendship" in *Essays on Aristotle's Ethics,* ed. Rorty, pp. 306–8.

10. This seems to be implied by 1156b9–33, 1157b3, and is supported by the analysis of Aristotle on virtue presented in Part I. See Cooper for a defense of this interpretation: "And since individual persons are what they essentially are by being human beings, it can be said that a person (any person) realizes his own essential nature more fully the more completely and adequately he possesses the moral excellences. So if one is the friend of another person and wishes him well, because of good moral qualities he possesses, one will be his friend because of something that he is essentially and not incidentally" ("Aristotle on Friendship" in *Essays on Aristotle's Ethics,* ed. Rorty, p. 312). Cf. Nussbaum, *The Fragility of Goodness,* pp. 356–57.

11. If Irving Singer's characterization of Aristotelian friendship is correct, then relations between sisters and brothers, parents and children, wives and husbands, do not look much like friendship at all. According to Singer, "The Aristotelian friends are [paradigmatically] businessmen who share a partnership

in virtue. They admire one another's goodness and they mutually benefit from overlapping interests; but their feelings rarely issue into emotional response. However intimate it may be, their friendship is purely professional. Philia is rational through and through" (*The Nature of Love, 1: Plato to Luther,* p. 92). I think that Singer's characterization of Aristotelian friendship is incorrect. In what follows, I will offer an account of Aristotelian character-friendship that identifies friendships between family members as character-friendships and, at the same time, recognizes the deeply emotional content of these relationships.

12. As we shall see, there is a difference between loving others as "other selves" and loving them as "other ourselves" or as *our* "other selves." The former involves loving others whom we regard as like us in that they, too, are selves. The latter involves loving others whom we regard as like us and, indeed, part of us in a more substantial sense to be developed throughout the rest of the book.

13. See Nancy Sherman, *Aristotle's Theory of Moral Education* (Dissertation: Harvard University, 1982) and *The Fabric of Character,* chap. 5. See also M. F. Burnyeat, "Aristotle on Learning to be Good" in *Essays on Aristotle's Ethics,* ed. Rorty.

14. Carol Gilligan, *In a Different Voice: Psychological Theory and Women's Development* (Cambridge, Mass.: Harvard University Press, 1982).

15. See Janice G. Raymond, *A Passion for Friends: Toward a Philosophy of Female Affection* (Boston: Beacon Press, 1986), esp. chap. 5. Raymond presents a vision of female-female friendship that is deeply Aristotelian in theory, even as she criticizes Aristotle for his obtuseness regarding the moral and psychological reality of women and their relationships.

16. My own experience indicates that more and more men and women in the United States are deliberately confounding the constraints of gender stereotyping, to the point that distinguishing in an accurate, thick, and fair way between "men's relationality" and "women's relationality" has become extremely tricky, if not impossible.

17. I am indebted in what follows to Sherman, *The Fabric of Character,* chap. 4. Her insightful treatment of nonfamilial character-friendship led me to consider, in an expanded way, features in sibling friendship similar to those in nonfamilial character-friendship.

18. Notice that what siblings share in the sharing of a life are most notably activities that are central to the exercise of moral agency. As we have already seen, it is more than anything else the manner in which persons exercise moral agency, for Aristotle, that makes them who they are as persons. Again, I expand on Aristotle's explicit statements regarding sibling friendship by drawing on his theory of virtue. The following reflections on the sharing of a life will be extended progressively throughout the project.

19. I develop this point in anticipation of what Aristotle says about adult friendship at 1167a23–b9 and 1172a1–7. The notion of *sharing* presupposes proportional equality with respect to the power to act, i.e., the freedom of each person to act in accordance with the level of moral development appropriate to her age. Inappropriate power imbalances within the context of shared living are all too common, and they deserve the attention of ethicists. However, I must limit myself in this project to conceptualizing certain features of relationships in which proportional equality is presumed to exist. To do anything else would be to complicate this analysis beyond measure. For an introduction to issues of power in ethics see Christine Firer Hinze, "Power in Christian Ethics: Resources and Frontiers for Scholarly Exploration," *The Annual of the Society of Christian Ethics* (1992), ed. Harlan Beckley, pp. 277–90.

20. I may be pressing Aristotle's ethic a bit far here. While it is important, for him, that friends be separate from one another in certain respects, it is not clear how much *difference* in vision and value can be tolerated between character-friends. See Sherman, *The Fabric of Character*, pp. 138–44. Also, a sense of common biological heritage as well as a sense of shared history can undoubtedly bind siblings together and keep them together despite major differences in vision and value. Unless the siblings are attached to each other on account of at least some aspect of each other's character, however, their attachment will not be characterized well, in Aristotle's scheme, as a friendship of character.

21. See Sherman's discussion of the importance, to Aristotle, of relatively exclusive familial friendships in *The Fabric of Character*, pp. 144–51.

22. I develop this point in light of what Aristotle says at 1167a23–b9 and 1172a1–7 about adult friendship.

23. I make this point in light of 1167a23–b9 and 1170b8–13.

24. Toni Morrison, *Sula* (New York: New American Library, 1973), p. 95.

25. I develop this point in light of 1166a7 and 1171a6, 1171a28 ff.

26. Here I expand on what Aristotle has to say about the importance of living together and sharing activities in friendship (1172a1–14).

27. Sherman, *The Fabric of Character*, p. 128.

5. ARISTOTLE ON FRIENDSHIP AND CHOICE

1. Note that for Aristotle, the best human life is a self-sufficient one, but "what we count as self-sufficient is not what suffices for a solitary person by himself, living an isolated life, but what suffices also for parents, children, wife and in general for friends and fellow-citizens, since a human being is a naturally political [animal]" (1097b8–11). Hence, the good at which we aim in the life of

complete virtue is not simply a private good. It is a shared good that we seek and enjoy especially with those who have an interest in seeking and enjoying the same.

2. Sherman, *The Fabric of Character*, p. 149. Sherman seems to be drawing here on Aristotle, *De Generatione Animalium*, 730a24–30.

3. Aristotle, *De Generatione Animalium (The Generation of Animals)*, trans. Arthur Platt in *The Basic Works of Aristotle*, ed. McKeon, 730a26, 730b15.

4. Ibid., 730b5–9.

5. Aristotle may simply be saying here that mothers love their children more because they spend more time with them *after* they are born. However, if Aristotle did not recognize that a woman labors over her fetus throughout pregnancy, he should have.

6. Many women confess that they treat themselves better while pregnant than they do at any other time. Many of us have come to believe, as we have been taught, that self-with-fetus is worthy of loving attention, but self-without-fetus is not. If society's sexism is to be resisted, it must be resisted by women partly in the construction of our own self-regard.

7. Paul Ricoeur explores "the enigmatic nature of the phenomenon of one's own body," focusing on various dimensions of the body's otherness and ownness, in *Oneself as Another*, trans. Kathleen Blamey (Chicago: The University of Chicago Press, 1992), pp. 319–29. The phenomenon of another body moving through one's own body in birthing is worth exploring as well.

8. See David O. Brink, "Rational Egoism, Self, and Others" in *Identity, Character, and Morality: Essays in Moral Psychology*, Owen Flanagan and Amelie Oksenberg Rorty, eds., (Cambridge: MIT Press, 1990), pp. 339–78, for an interesting neo-Aristotelian discussion of how it is that a child extends his or her parent's interests.

9. Aristotle says that friendship is a relationship, yet he implies that a mother can remain a friend to her child even though the child does not reciprocate her affection and good will. Aristotle may be thinking of friendship here less as a relationship and more as a virtue (1155a1): "hence, it would seem, loving is the virtue of friends" (1159a35). Perhaps he has in mind a love of friendship on the part of the mother which is necessary but not, in itself, sufficient for a relationship of friendship.

10. Here it is also clear that for Aristotle the flourishing life is a life lived within the context of a flourishing community. As Paul Wadell puts it, "Eudaimonia is the group activity of the virtuous life . . . not just the life of each member singly, but the life of all together. The happiness and well-being of each is this ongoing collective nurturing of the good. The interconnection between the virtues and eudaimonia and friendship demands that happiness is always a

group affair." *Friendship and the Moral Life* (Notre Dame, Ind.: University of Notre Dame Press, 1989), pp. 65–66.

11. Aristotle says that, "In all the friendships corresponding to superiority, the loving must be proportional, e.g. the better person, and the more beneficial, and each of the others likewise, must be loved more than he loves; for when the loving reflects the comparative worth of the friends, equality is achieved in a way, and this seems proper to friendship" (1158b24–29). His main point, however, is that "[e]quality and similarity, and above all the similarity of those who are similar in being virtuous, is friendship" (1159b3).

12. Cooper, "Aristotle on Friendship" in *Essays on Aristotle's Ethics,* ed. Rorty, p. 330.

13. Ibid., pp. 330–31.

14. Ibid., pp. 328–29. Cooper clarifies, "Now I do not claim that these considerations were actually in Aristotle's mind when he said that it is easier to be continuously active with others and toward others than in isolation. His failure to explain why he held this view makes it impossible to say with certainty what his reasons were. But it is hard to imagine what he could have meant if he did not have in mind at least some of these points" (p. 328).

15. *Friendship and the Moral Life*, p. 62.

16. Ibid., p. 61.

17. Recall Aristotle's example of the mother who allows her child to be raised by another in cases where the other is better able to meet the child's needs and interests. With respect to adult friends of good character, both friends have an interest in continuing to be good; hence, it is unlikely that they will grow apart with respect to what matters to them most. It is possible that equally virtuous adults will embrace different ideals or exhibit different patterns and points of emphasis in their exercise of complete virtue, but it is unlikely that such differences will diminish significantly the level of their intimacy. On Aristotle's recognition of character differences between friends, see Sherman, *The Fabric of Character*, pp. 141 ff.

18. See Anders Nygren, *Agape and Eros: The Christian Idea of Love*, trans. Philip S. Watson (Chicago: The University of Chicago Press, 1953).

19. I develop further the notion of sharing a vision of the good in "Toward an Ethic of Shared Selfhood," *The Annual of the Society of Christian Ethics* (1991), ed. Yeager, pp. 249–57.

20. See Sherman, *The Fabric of Character*, pp. 133–34.

21. We cannot do so here, but it would be interesting to ponder the way in which children become integral components of their parents' extended selves such that their parents, who are themselves integral components of each other's extended selves, love their children partly in loving each other and each other

partly in loving their children. Part of what parents love in each other is their shared love for their children. Part of what parents love in their children is the love for both parents that they and their children share.

22. The boxing example points to the difficulties involved in sharing a life with someone, some of whose interests one regards as morally suspect or bad. See Cates "Toward an Ethic of Shared Selfhood" in *The Annual of the Society of Christian Ethics* (1991), ed. Yeager, pp. 249–57.

23. See *Rhetorica* (*Rhetoric*), trans. W. Rhys Roberts in *The Basic Works of Aristotle*, ed. McKeon, 1385b13 ff.; *De Poetica* (*Poetics*), trans. Ingram Bywater in *The Basic Works of Aristotle*, ed. McKeon, 1453a1 ff.; and Nussbaum's discussion of these in *Fragility of Goodness*, pp. 383–85.

24. For a profound expression of this fear in its modern guise, see Steven Lewis, "The Remains of One Man's Day," *Commonweal* 16 (1995): 31.

25. Feeling compassion for someone requires (among other things) sharing her pain, i.e., suffering it as partly one's own. This requires discerning the kind of pain she suffers and the significance she attaches to suffering that kind of pain. Such discernment is hindered by deliberate hiddenness on the part of the other.

26. See Audre Lorde, "Uses of the Erotic: The Erotic as Power" in *Sister Outsider* (Freedom, Calif.: The Crossing Press, 1984).

27. This is how Irving Singer characterizes Aristotelian character-friendship in *The Nature of Love*, vol. I, p. 92.

28. Shelly Hall has raised an excellent question on this point: "What are the criteria for determining the legitimacy of particular responses to physical traits? How do we know that our responses are, in fact, to sensible manifestations of character, and not simply reactions to the preconceived—and more often than not erroneous—associations that a culture makes about physical characteristics (the term itself is telling here!) such as size, mode of dress, style of hair, complexion, make-up (or lack of it), etc., and a person's character?" (personal correspondence, 1993). I cannot answer this question here (related, as it is, to the broader question of how I can know anything about the inner life of anyone other than myself), but let me say this much: It is crucial for a person of practical wisdom to be aware of the fact that "character readings" of the body are subject to the manipulations and distortions of media misrepresentation. But it is also crucial that a wise person not attempt to separate "the real person" from her body. A person is not someone behind or beneath or hidden within her body; she is someone who appears to others and therefore must, of necessity, be "read" *as* body. She is someone who appears to herself, and must be "read" by herself, as body reflected in the bodies of others. There is no way for a person to avoid this often painful reality and, at the same time, become a well-integrated and intimately related body-self.

6. THOMAS AQUINAS ON FRIENDSHIP

1. My chartacterization of complacency is influenced by Frederick E. Crowe, S.J., "Complacency and Concern in the Thought of St. Thomas," *Theological Studies* 20 (1959): 1–39, 198–230, 343–95. Crowe argues that, for Thomas, "love has two quite distinct but complementary roles. . . . [I]n one role love is passive, quiescent, complacent; in the other it is active, striving, tending to an object. It is the latter role that is regularly to the fore in St. Thomas, but it is the former, often only implicit in his thought, that is basic both psychologically and ontologically. And the real problem is that St. Thomas never brought these two notions into careful confrontation or worked out extensively their relations to one another, with the result that two contrasting and unintegrated lines of thought show up in a whole series of questions" (p. 3). I assume in this project that, strictly speaking, Thomas understands the *passion of love* to consist in complacency; when he speaks of love as a tending or a leaning, he is sliding past the passion of love proper and into desire, which is the second moment of the broader *love of friendship* (i.e., the love of friend for friend). The third moment is joy.

2. Keep in mind that we will discuss the ways in which the self stands to its other selves as "other" as well as "the same." We must, however, proceed one step at a time.

3. In what follows, our concern will be focused on the self that loves itself (and its included others) in the right way. To introduce complications posed by the problem of moral evil or sin would be to make this project insurmountably complex. Besides, it makes good sense to try to conceptualize a relational human self that is "in good working order" before trying to conceptualize the ways in which the self "breaks down" or goes awry.

4. By "power of being" (lower case) I mean simply the power that makes whatever is, to be (and to be what it is). I assume that this power is something in which humans participate, but that it is ultimately other (or more) than human power. The notion will undergo development as our inquiry proceeds.

5. Keep in mind, as we have already seen, that the drives themselves give shape to this inquiry, partly by determining which cognitions will "fit" with our experience and which will not.

6. To say that love as complacency is an enduring moment that is experienced by the lover and the beloved in the context of their friendship is not to say that it is something of which the lover and the beloved are always explicitly aware. I take it to be an intimacy of which the lover and the beloved are ordinarily, in the midst of their private and relational activities, only implicitly aware.

7. There is no denying that this kind of openness leaves a person vulnerable to serious injury. But the threat of injury is not in itself sufficient to justify a general policy of closed-upness. It is only sufficient to justify the use of practical wisdom in determining *how* open one will be toward *whom* in order to attain *which* goods for oneself and for one's "other selves."

8. Steven Anthony Edwards, *Interior Acts: Teleology, Justice, and Friendship in the Religious Ethics of Thomas Aquinas* (Landham, N.Y.: University Press of America, 1986), p. 103. I would replace "will" in this statement with the more inclusive term, "appetite."

9. We find in Thomas an ambiguity that is also present in Aristotle. Both speak of friendship as a mutual relationship between persons, on the one hand, and as a virtue or something involving virtue, on the other, without clarifying the relationship between these different characterizations (*NE* 1155a1; *Summa* II–II 23.3 *ad* 1). In the case of friendship with God, it turns out that a habitual disposition of the intellective appetite to be united with God in the shared love of friendship is, in fact, a response to God's offer of friendship to the self. It is therefore sufficient for the completion of a relationship of friendship with God.

10. Thomas would likely insist that the bodily-appetitive fitness to which I point can only be regarded as an effect, and not as a constitutive component, of the self's complacency in God, given that "the object of charity is not a sensible good, but the Divine good which is known by the intellect alone," and given that "the subject of charity is not the sensitive, but the intellective appetite, i.e., the will" (II–II 24.1).

7. THOMAS AQUINAS ON FRIENDSHIP AND CHOICE

1. Leo M. Bond, "A Comparison Between Human and Divine Friendship" *The Thomist* 3/1 (January 1941): 58.

2. Thomas cites Jerome in objection 3 of II–II 23.1, but his reply to the objection gives no indication that he disagrees with Jerome's characterization of Christian friendship. In any case, this characterization is certainly consistent with Thomas's theories of Christian virtue and of friendship. See II–II 24.8.

3. Robert O. Johann, S.J., *The Meaning of Love: An Essay Towards a Metaphysics of Intersubjectivity* (Glen Rock, N.J.: Paulist Press, 1954).

4. Ibid., p. 42.

5. By "incommunicable," Johann means that which resists appropriation by another. See Ibid., p. 24.

6. Ibid., p. 36.

7. Ibid., pp. 38, 48.

8. Ibid., pp. 38–39.

9. Ibid., pp. 42–43. Johann quotes M. Madinier, *Conscience et amour: essai sur le "nous"* (Paris: Alcan, 1938), p. 99.

10. Martin Buber, *I and Thou*, trans. Walter Kaufmann (New York: Charles Scribner's Sons, 1970), p. 163.

11. Johann, p. 52.

12. Ibid., p. 54.

13. Ibid., p. 50.

14. Bond, p. 57. There is a difference, in Thomistic theology, between names that are predicated of God analogically and names that are predicated of God metaphorically. Names of God that are predicated *analogically* "are predicated substantially of God, although they fall short of a full representation of [God].... these names express God, so far as our intellect knows [God]" (I 13.2). They point to what really exists in God, but what exists in God in a more excellent way than it exists in the created order. On the other hand, names of God that are applied *metaphorically* "are applied to creatures primarily rather than to God, because when said of God they mean only similitudes to such creatures. For as *smiling* applied to a field means only that the field in the beauty of its flowering is like . . . the beauty of the human smile by proportionate likeness, so the name of *lion* applied to God means only that God manifests strength in [God's] works, as a lion in his" (I 13.6).

15. Bond, p. 54.

16. Ibid., p. 56.

17. Ibid., p. 60.

18. Ibid.

19. Ibid., p. 61.

20. Bond does not discuss the love of God that is possible for human beings according to their natural human powers or the sort of similitude that is constituted by such love. I include this brief discussion for the sake of balance and completeness.

21. Bond, p. 61.

22. Ibid., p. 63.

23. Ibid.

24. Ibid., p. 64.

25. Johann, p. 42.

26. Ibid., p. 50.

27. Ibid., p. 51. Johann refers here to J. de Finance, S.J., "Etre et Subjectivité," *Doctro Communis* II (May-August 1948), pp. 240–58.

28. Johann, p. 49.

29. Bond, p. 71.

30. Ibid.

31. Wadell, *Friendship and the Moral Life*, p. 122. Thomas says, more precisely, that by the Holy Spirit, "the Father and the Son love each other *and us*" (I 37.2, my emphasis).

32. Bond, p. 72.

33. Ibid., p. 73.

34. It is beyond the scope of this project to examine Thomas's doctrine of God. See I 2 ff. The notion of God as immutable is a matter of contemporary theological debate. See, e.g., Warren McWilliams, *The Passion of God: Divine Suffering in Contemporary Protestant Theology* (Macon, Ga.: Mercer University Press, 1985), who analyzes doctrines of God developed by Jürgen Moltmann, James Cone, Geddes MacGregor, Kizoh Kitamori, Daniel Day Williams, and Jung Young Lee.

35. Cf. Wadell, *Friendship and the Moral Life*, pp. 127–29.

36. Bond, p. 57.

37. Ibid., pp. 79–82.

38. II–II 25.7. What Thomas says about proper self-love applies to love of the neighbor.

39. See I–II 69.3 and 61.5, and the discussion of these on pp. 42–45.

40. See pp. 42–48.

41. Actually, the spectrum is broader than this, for it includes the "natural appetite" as well. On the relation between natural, sense, and intellective appetite, see Harak, *Virtuous Passions*, pp. 56–67.

42. Recall our analysis, in chapter 3, of the contribution that passion can make to our knowing and loving of God.

43. G. Simon Harak, S.J., puts it this way: "The most rational act for composite beings, who can delight in [both] the particular and the eternal, is to fuse" their sense and intellective appetites so that they are disposed to "*see the eternal in every particular.*" "Our movement toward God," says Harak, "integrates our higher and lower desires, such that we can, literally, physically '*hunger and thirst* for justice'— and be satisfied" (pp. 93–94).

44. A God who "suffers with" the world need not, as Wendy Farley suggests, be construed as "a benevolent but impotent God." There is no reason why a God who "suffers with" the world cannot also be a God that "struggles to transform evil into a locus of healing." Wendy Farley, *Tragic Vision and Divine Compassion: A Contemporary Theodicy* (Louisville: Westminster/John Knox Press, 1990), p. 112.

45. This sense could possibly be promoted by thinking of God as having a body that comprises the earth. See Sallie McFague, *The Body of God: An Ecological Theology* (Minneapolis: Augsburg Fortress, 1993). McFague only hints at the implications that the metaphor of the world as God's body could have for helping us to image the suffering of God-with-us.

46. Of course, such a view must wrestle with the problem of evil, and Thomas's does. See, e.g., I–II 79–81.

47. Bond, p. 91. This is tricky. God does seem to lack something here which only God's creatures can supply for God, namely, the free reciprocation of God's love by God's creatures. Thomas (and Bond) might say that, still, God does not *need* this reciprocation for the fullness of God's own self-enjoyment, but then the strength of the friendship analogy is, in my judgment, sorely weakened. Cf. II–II 31.1: "Hence it is not for us to benefit God, but to honor [God] by obeying [God], while it is for [God], out of [God's] love, to bestow good things on us."

48. Bond, p. 84.

49. Sallie McFague argues in her *Models of God: Theology for an Ecological, Nuclear Age* (Philadelphia: Fortress Press, 1987), that what binds God and humans together as friends is a common vision and a common commitment to its realization (p. 163). I seek, in effect, to deepen and extend this insight.

50. There is a long history of debate in Christian ethics regarding the relationship between *philia* as "preferential love" and *agape*. Recent contributions to this debate include Gene Outka, *Agape: An Ethical Analysis* (New Haven: Yale University Press, 1972); Gilbert C. Meilaender, *Friendship: A Study in Theological Ethics* (Notre Dame, Ind.: University of Notre Dame Press, 1981); Paul Wadell, *Friendship and the Moral Life*; and *The Love Commandments: Essays in Christian Ethics and Moral Philosophy,* ed. Edmund N. Santurri and William Werpehowski, (Washington D.C.: Georgetown University Press, 1992). Thomas is deeply Aristotelian in his reasoning about how the competing claims of friends and more distant neighbors are to be adjudicated. See II–II 31.3 *ad* 1.

51. In other words, under the healing and empowering influence of charity, there will remain some exclusivity with respect to our closest friendships, but this very exclusivity will serve to strengthen us in our love for God and for persons other than our most intimate friends.

8. COMPASSION'S COMPLACENCY

1. Nel Noddings, *Caring: A Feminine Approach to Ethics and Moral Education* (Berkeley: University of California Press, 1984).

2. Donald P. McNeill, Douglas A. Morrison, and Henri J. M. Nouwen, *Compassion: A Reflection on the Christian Life* (Garden City, N.Y.: Doubleday & Company, Inc., 1983). A reader need not be familiar with *Caring* or *Compassion* to follow the argument of this book.

3. Thomas says that, "since he who loves another looks upon his friend as another self, he counts his friend's hurt as his own, so that he grieves for his friend's hurt as though he were hurt himself" (II–II 30.2).

4. Ordinary language indicates a difference between the notions of "caring" and "compassion." (Noddings speaks, for example, about caring for ideas). As we shall see, however, Noddings tends to describe central elements of caring for human beings in ways that make her analysis directly relevant to our own. We shall be focusing on these elements. Our chief concern is to illuminate a characteristic way of being human in the presence of persons in pain—a way that I take to be virtuous.

5. My method is weakly Aristotelian in that I begin repeatedly by "setting down" some of the "appearances," and I proceed by "setting out the puzzles or dilemmas with which they confront us" in order to determine and "save" the most defensible of these "appearances." See Nussbaum, *The Fragility of Goodness*, pp. 240–51.

6. Noddings, p. 14.

7. Ibid., p. 16.

8. Ibid., p. 23.

9. Ibid., p. 14. Noddings indicates on p. 84 that this interest in the ethical self is grounded, not so much in the value I place on my own excellence, but in "the value I place on the relatedness of caring." As we shall see in the following chapter, there is some ambiguity here. Cf. Noddings pp. 50–51.

10. Ibid., pp. 49–50.

11. Ibid., pp. 80, 82, 84.

12. Sometimes Noddings refers to what we have labeled the "I must$_2$," as the "I ought" or the "moral I must," but sometimes she refers to both the "I must$_1$," and the "I must$_2$," simply as the "I must," causing some confusion (see Noddings pp. 49–50).

13. Noddings seems deliberately to avoid logical argumentation on the grounds that it is characteristically "masculine." She claims that her view "would be badly distorted if it were presented in . . . the 'language of the father.'" My view is that Noddings's analysis cannot be understood or evaluated (at least not by me) apart from the use of logic. Far from being the prerogative of those with a "masculine spirit," logic is something that both men and women can and (I think) should make use of in order to insure the conceptual clarity, consistency, and soundness of their positions. See Noddings pp. 1–2. Noddings makes numerous appeals to logic herself. See p. 69.

14. Noddings, pp. 49, 83.

15. This crucial premise seems to be implicit on pp. 83–84 and 38–39.

16. Ibid., p. 84. Noddings assumes that there will always be a latent "I must$_1$," available for awakening (p. 84), but she does not indicate *how* a person can awaken a latent "I must$_1$," and thus care well for someone whom she does not naturally and spontaneously find "engrossing." She makes reference in a footnote to some authors who *have* dealt with the issue of "summonability," namely,

Lawrence R. Blum, *Friendship, Altruism, and Morality* (London: Routledge & Kegan Paul, 1980); Henry Sidgwick, *The Methods of Ethics* (Indianapolis: Hackett, 1981); and Philip Mercer, *Sympathy and Ethics* (Oxford: Clarendon Press, 1962).

17. Ibid., p. 25.
18. Ibid., p. 16.
19. Ibid., p. 31.
20. Ibid., p. 33.
21. Ibid., p. 32.
22. Ibid., pp. 34–35.
23. Ibid., p. 34.
24. Ibid., p. 16.
25. Ibid., p. 33.
26. Ibid., p. 19.
27. Ibid., p. 16.
28. Ibid.
29. Ibid., p. 14.
30. Ibid., p. 24.
31. Ibid., p. 30.
32. Ibid., p. 31.
33. Ibid., p. 63.
34. I urge the reader to keep in mind that this chapter addresses only one aspect of compassion. To read this chapter in isolation from those that follow could only result in a serious misunderstanding of my purposes.
35. My treatment of pain and emotion is influenced by Roger Trigg, *Pain and Emotion* (Oxford: Clarendon Press, 1970). Trigg says that a desire to be rid of something is part of the concept of distress (p. 8), but he does not go on to distinguish, as I do in what follows, between the different desires that are ingredient in "wanting to be rid of something."
36. This is the aspect of pain on which Thomas Aquinas focuses in the *Summa Theologica*. See, e.g., I–II 35.4.
37. All of these pain components are mentioned by Trigg.
38. Elaine Scarry, *The Body in Pain: The Making and Unmaking of the World* (Oxford: Oxford University Press, 1985), p. 5.
39. Ibid., p. 30.
40. Scarry has in mind especially (but not exclusively) the pain that is experienced in torture. I imagine that, at least in its ebb and flow, if not in its very immediacy, this sort of pain, too, is partly constituted by loathing and longing. It, too, has *some* passional content (e.g. terror). I want to avoid here the mind-body bifurcation or dualism that can be implied by speaking of physical pain *qua* simply physical.

41. Scarry, p. 4.

42. Trigg, p. 19.

43. My discussion of the different senses of "sameness" that pertain to the sharing of pain is influenced by Stanley Cavell, *Must We Mean What We Say? A Book of Essays* (New York: Scribner, 1969), chapter 9.

44. If Scarry is even partly right about the way in which physical pain resists objectification by means of language (and I think that she is), then physical pain is notoriously difficult to describe, which means that it is probably impossible to determine for sure if our physical pain is descriptively the same as another's. It is not impossible, however, to imagine that our pain is descriptively the same or, at least, descriptively very much alike. Such imaginings, tested and reformed through attentive interaction with the person in pain, are central to the experience of compassion.

45. One way to explore the notion of shared body might be in terms of Theravada Buddhist teachings of *anatman* (not-self) and related teachings of the five *skandhas* (heaps, aggregates, or groups of grasping). Imaginative reflection upon these teachings can yield a powerful sense of the virtual nonexistence of physical boundaries between separate selves. This is not to say, however, that these teachings are consistent with the larger conception of compassion toward which we are aiming in this project.

46. See Cavell's example of "First" and "Second," in "Knowing and Acknowledging" in *Must We Mean What We Say? A Book of Essays*, pp. 251–53.

9. COMPASSION AND CHOICE (1)

1. Keep in mind the many respects in which this helpful representation comes up short. See chapter 1, especially pp. 7–11.

2. Noddings, p. 14.

3. Ibid., p. 16.

4. Ibid., pp. 14, 80, 82.

5. Ibid., p. 80.

6. Ibid., p. 104.

7. Ibid., pp. 49–51.

8. Ibid., p. 5.

9. Ibid., p. 50.

10. Ibid., pp. 49, 80–81. Cf. p. 84, where Noddings says that what I aim at is "to increase my own virtue as one-caring."

11. Ibid., p. 50.

12. Ibid., p. 75.

13. Ibid., p. 5.

14. Ibid., pp. 83, 84.

15. Ibid., p. 95.

16. Aristotle, *Nicomachean Ethics* 1098b23.

17. Character excellence is not sufficient for *eudaimonia*, in Aristotle's view, but it is necessary. See *NE* 1099a29–35.

18. *NE* 1094b7–12.

19. Noddings, p. 24.

20. Ibid.

21. Ibid., p. 67.

22. The distinction between a thin and a thick or full theory of the good is rather commonplace in contemporary moral philosophy, but I encountered it first in John Rawls, *A Theory of Justice* (Cambridge, Mass.: The Belknap Press of Harvard University Press, 1971), p. 396.

23. Noddings says that the "active virtue" of caring requires both "natural caring" and "ethical caring," which means that "ethical caring" is not, in itself, sufficient for virtuous caring. "Ethical caring" must move us, not only to act morally, but also to "fetch . . . out of recalcitrant slumber" the "natural caring" that fails to arise spontaneously (pp. 79–81, 84).

24. Ibid., p. 112.

25. The reader should feel free to identify more with the "I" than with the "you."

26. There is a puzzle here in that, inasmuch as I experience myself to be located closer to the you-pole, the you-pole seems to me to *be* the me-pole, i.e., the place where I experience myself to be. Evidently, I discern shifts in self-location relative to my "other selves" only through the passage of time. For example, I might be immediately caught up in another's terror of death (i.e., her frustrated desire to fend off or to escape it), but when other desires arise and begin to make their entrance into my awareness—desires that I associate (on the basis of memory) as being most characteristic of "me," then I realize that what just happened to me was this: I experienced as my own a configuration of desire that I would not have experienced (at least, not in that way), but for the fact that someone else experienced certain desires to be at the center of his self-awareness. At the time, those desires *became* my desires (i.e., my desires were constituted partly the "same" as the other's), but now I am aware of myself as being defined by a separate and different set of desires that have a much more distant relation to the desires of the other.

27. I introduce a different model of the self, but to similar ends, in "Toward an Ethic of Shared Selfhood" in *The Annual of the Society of Christian Ethics* (1991), ed. D. M. Yeager, pp. 249–57.

28. Recall from the previous chapter some of the ways in which this "sameness" is limited.

29. John P. Reeder, Jr., presses this question in his paper, "Extensive Benevolence" (unpublished), which includes a marvelous interpretation and analysis of several attempts since Hume to determine the nature of extensive benevolence and its role in the moral life.

30. From a Christian ethical point of view, I want to empower you by inviting you to participate with me in the Power of Being itself, which is the unfathomable source of all "saving" power.

31. Noddings, p. 1.

32. Ibid.

33. Ibid., p. 2. Noddings says that calling her view of ethics a "feminine" one "does not imply that all women will accept it or that men will reject it; indeed, there is no reason why men should not embrace it. . . . It may indeed be the case that such an approach is more typical of women than of men, but this is an empirical question I shall not attempt to answer" (p. 2). I think, however, that Noddings *has* answered this empirical question to her own satisfaction, and that she assumes throughout *Caring* that her "feminine ethic" is one with which women, in particular, will resonate. See pp. 8, 36, 40, 42, 96.

34. Ibid., pp. 2–3.

35. Ibid., p. 42.

36. Ibid., p. 37.

37. Ibid., pp. 35, 25.

38. Ibid., pp. 26, 35–36.

39. Ibid., p. 36.

40. Ibid., p. 26.

41. Noddings's use of terms like "feminine" and "masculine" is, in my judgment untenable. There may, indeed, be important differences in the ways that women and men in the United States tend to be oriented vis-à-vis others in the exercise of their moral agencies, but identifying and describing these differences accurately and fairly is a complex and delicate matter. Many members of our communities do not fit (and do not care to fit) socially contrived categories of gender identity. Identifying and describing differences in the moral orientations of women and men is also a dangerous matter. Feminist ethicists must be careful lest we inadvertently perpetuate caricatures and overgeneralizations that serve, in effect, to dominate the self-understandings of women (and women-identified men).

42. Ibid., pp. 35, 31.

43. Ibid., pp. 26, 31.

44. Ibid., p. 25.

45. Ibid., p. 36.

46. Ibid.

47. Ibid.

48. Ibid., p. 35.

49. Ibid., p. 36. Noddings does make reference to the notion of "subjective thinking," but she does not define it. She appears to associate it with the "feeling mode," rather than associating it with the bridging of the "feeling" and "thinking" modes (p. 26).

50. Ibid., p. 25. A phrase like "judgment (in the impersonal, logical sense)" implies that there is such a thing as "judgment (in the personal, non-logical sense)," but it is not clear what the latter amounts to, and Noddings gives no indication. The implicit suggestion that the "personal" and the "logical" are fundamentally incompatible is, in any case, incredible to women who are deeply intuitive and, at the same time, deeply analytical.

51. Noddings says, for example, that "clearly, rationality (in its objective form) does not of necessity mark either the initial impulse or the action that is undertaken. If I care enough, I may do something wild and desperate in behalf of the other—something that has only the tiniest probability of success, and that only in my own subjective view" (p. 36).

52. Ibid., p. 26. In question here is what Noddings means by "objectivity."

53. That is so say, our best passion is passion that observes the mean. The mean of compassion, in particular, will be explored in the next chapter.

54. Ibid., p. 36.

55. Ibid., p. 34.

56. Noddings says explicitly that the moves made between separate modes of consciousness are "lateral moves—that is, moves which are neither up nor down," evidently to avoid the charge of "dualistic thinking" (*Caring*, p. 36). But throughout her book, the "approach of the mother" is construed as being fundamentally different from the "approach of the father," "feminine" is construed as being "other" than "masculine," "feeling" is construed as functioning over and against "thinking," and the related polarities of passivity vs. activity, concrete vs. abstract, nonrational (or irrational) vs. rational continue to crop up (see, e.g., pp. 7–8). It is not enough to argue for the elevation of "feminine" qualities to a position of equality (or even superiority) relative to "masculine" qualities. Simply in presupposing the categories, we reinforce oppressive gender stereotypes and the socio-political-economic conditions that will continue to be legitimated with reference to them. The categories themselves must be deconstructed and stripped of their power to predetermine the identities of "men" and "women."

10. COMPASSION AND CHOICE (2)

1. Noddings, p. 83.

2. Ibid., pp. 51, 83.

3. Ibid., p. 35.
4. Ibid., p. 81.
5. Ibid., pp. 17–18.
6. Ibid., p. 81.
7. Ibid., p. 84, my emphasis.
8. Lawrence Blum, *Friendship, Altruism, and Morality* (London: Routledge & Kegan Paul, 1980), p. 197.
9. Immanuel Kant, *The Doctrine of Virtue*, trans. Mary Gregor (New York: Harper & Row, 1964); Henry Sidgwick, *The Methods of Ethics*, 7th ed. (Chicago: University of Chicago Press, 1962).
10. Blum, p. 195.
11. Ibid., p. 197.
12. Ibid., pp. 186–87.
13. Philip Mercer, *Sympathy and Ethics* (Oxford: Clarendon Press, 1972).
14. Blum, p. 200.
15. Anthony Kenny, *Action, Emotion, and Will* (London: Routledge & Kegan Paul, 1963); Stuart Hampshire, *Freedom of the Individual* (New York: Harper & Row, 1965).
16. Blum, p. 202.
17. Ibid., p. 203.
18. Ibid., p. 204.
19. Ibid., p. 187.
20. If I do not have a second-order desire to become complacent in other persons' painful wantings, then the issue of how I might *choose* to become complacent here and now will not even arise for me, i.e., there is no point in asking *how* such a choice could be made. Thus, what I have to say here is likely to be compelling only to those who are already somewhat disposed toward being compassionate, but would like to become better disposed. We have come up against a classic problem in virtue theory and a pressing question for contemporary ethics and moral education: how can a disposition toward compassion (virtue) be elicited in those who are not already to some extent compassionate (virtuous)?
21. The term "reflective equilibrium" is used by John Rawls to refer to a cognitive state. *A Theory of Justice*, p. 20.
22. I suspect that Aristotle is right when he claims that the virtues are inseparable from each other, i.e., that we cannot acquire one virtue in its fullness without also acquiring the others. *NE* 1144b33–1145a2.
23. Aristotle, *NE* 1106b20.
24. Noddings, p. 13.
25. Ibid., p. 48.
26. Ibid., p 80.

27. Ibid., pp. 82, 105, 132.

28. Ibid., pp. 23–24. Noddings says that we wish to please the cared-for "for his sake and not for the promise of his grateful response to our generosity," but she also says that we wish to please the cared-for for the sake of the "joy" that we feel when our caring is "completed" by the other. The apparent conflict between these claims is not recognized. I would argue that the "completion" Noddings has in mind is a "grateful response to our generosity," and that, insofar as we seek the "completion" of our caring, we wish to please the other partly for our own sake.

29. Ibid., pp. 64, 67.

30. Ibid., p. 95.

31. Ibid., p. 85.

32. Ibid., pp. 83, 100–101; the concern for "community" is mostly implicit in *Caring.*

33. Ibid., pp. 6, 101.

34. Ibid., p. 101. See also p. 85.

35. Ibid., p. 99.

36. Ibid., p. 100.

37. Ibid., p. 99.

38. Ibid.

39. Ibid., p. 100.

40. Ibid., pp. 84, 33.

41. I disagree with Noddings when she says that "I may use my reasoning powers to figure out what to do once I have committed myself to doing something. But clearly, rationality (in its objective form) does not of necessity mark either the initial impulse or the action that is undertaken. If I care enough, I may do something wild and desperate in behalf of the other—something that has only the tiniest probability of success, and that only in my own subjective view" (p. 36). Setting aside the many problems associated with the way in which "rationality" is construed by Noddings, I would argue to the contrary that, if I care enough, my desire to benefit the other will sway me to be thoughtful as well as passionate on behalf of the other.

42. Noddings, p. 46.

43. Ibid., p. 47.

44. Ibid., p. 86.

45. Ibid.

46. Ibid.

47. Ibid., p. 87.

48. Ibid.

49. Ibid., p. 86.

50. Ibid., pp. 47, 67.

51. Ibid., p. 47.

52. Consider Søren Kierkegaard's discussion of the duty to help others "to stand alone—by another's help" in *Works of Love*, trans. Howard and Edna Hong (New York: Harper & Row, 1962), pp. 255–60. Kierkegaard's religious ethical argument could also be cast in secular philosophical terms. Rather than keeping one's help "hidden behind a dash" in order to promote the other's sense of dependence upon God (and thus to discourage a sense of dependence on oneself), one could remain "hidden behind a dash" in order to promote the other's moral autonomy.

53. A practically wise person will keep in view the broader social consequences of anonymous caring, including the possibility that some of this caring (e.g., the continued caring of certain women for notoriously uncaring men) may sustain unjust social practices. See Sarah Lucia Hoagland, "Some Thoughts about 'Caring'" in *Feminist Ethics*, ed. Claudia Card (Lawrence, Ks.: The University Press of Kansas, 1991), pp. 259–61. In my view, the problem isn't so much with continuing to care for users or abusers (although there is a moral choice to be made here regarding how to spend our limited moral resources); the problem is with misunderstanding what it is to "care" for them. One fails to care for an individual (and also for oneself and for other members of the community) when one enables an individual's self-centeredness and abusiveness.

54. Noddings, p. 86.

55. Ibid., p. 79.

56. Again, caring for others includes caring that they flourish (where it is understood that they will flourish only to the extent that they love and seek the good). Caring for someone who is vicious, then, includes caring that his or her viciousness be undermined. To tolerate exploitation, oppression, and violence in the name of care is, in fact, not to care for anyone, but rather to exhibit moral cowardice and to assist someone in his or her own self-destruction as well as the destruction of others. This is not to say that "victims" are personally responsible for "saving" their "abusers," but that victims and abusers alike (and most of us qualify as both) are responsible for being caring persons to the best of their ability and for exhibiting that care toward particular persons in a way that is consistent with the realization of a variety of other goods, each of which is worthy of coordinated choice (e.g., the upbuilding of self-respect, self-confidence, self-enjoyment, and relationships in which mutuality is forthcoming).

57. Notably, we are sometimes in a better position to assist strangers than we are to assist our friends, by virtue of the fact that we have not developed a particularly strong bond of affection toward the former and are thus better able to take (appropriate) risks in order to benefit him/her. Consider, e.g., the case of a heart surgeon whose husband is in need of heart surgery.

58. What if the reader cannot identify with this "we"? There is no way that I can argue for one vision of the good over another apart from the dynamics of

actual conversation. All I can do within the framework of this project is to present a possibility that is attractive enough to sway at least some readers into a serious consideration of its promises/limitations. I could, of course, complement this eudaimonistic argument with deontological or utilitarian arguments, but each of these, too, has its limits.

11. COMPASSION AND THE CHRISTIAN LIFE

1. Donald P. McNeill, Douglas A. Morrison, and Henri J. M. Nouwen, *Compassion: A Reflection on the Christian Life.*
2. I use the term "elevated" with caution, as I do not wish to imply that friendship with God elevates Christians above others in moral value, nor do I wish to suggest that moral elevation is cause for anything but proper self-love, humility, gratitude, and loving service. I do think that the imagery can be useful insofar as it suggests (as if from a mountaintop) a widening of vision, a broadening of perspective, a heightening of passional sensitivity, and a sense of moral freedom, all of which remain grounded in liberating praxis.
3. When I refer to God's "befriended," I refer to all beings to whom God has extended the offer of friendship (which includes every human being)—even those who have not (yet) taken up God's offer.
4. McNeill, Morrison, and Nouwen, pp. 21, 50, 67.
5. Ibid., p. 21.
6. Ibid., p. 15. The authors say that they "cannot emphasize enough that when Jesus calls God his Father, he speaks about a love that includes and transcends all the love we know. It is the love of a father, but also of a mother, brother, sister, friend, and lover" (p. 37). Hence, I believe that I do not distort the authors' good intentions by correcting (nearly a generation after the first publication of *Compassion*) for the unfortunate use of exclusively male God-language.
7. Ibid., p. 14.
8. Ibid., p. 25.
9. Ibid., pp. 64, 63.
10. Ibid., pp. 19–20.
11. Ibid., p. 20. Many feminist and liberation theologians and ethicists will want to take issue with the authors' insistence that we ought not to establish our personal identities primarily on the basis of our differences vis-à-vis others. Oppressed and marginalized people have been taught that it is precisely their differentness from the "norm" that makes them bad, dirty, misfit, and unrecognizable. It is excellent, I think, that we who are "other" than "generic man" have raised our consciousnesses to such an extent that we can proudly proclaim cer-

tain aspects of our differentness to be good. At the same time, however, we ought to take care lest we overemphasize our differentness to the point that we seem to have nothing in common with our oppressors. The refusal to recognize a fellow human being as being *like* us in the dignity of his/her humanness is always morally unacceptable.

12. The authors maintain that Jesus is "the sinless son of God," but they also maintain that "In and through Jesus Christ we know that God is . . . a God who has experienced our brokenness, who has become sin for us (2 Co 5:21)" (Ibid., p. 17). The precise sense in which Jesus is *like* us in our sinfulness is not explicated.

13. Ibid., p. 18.

14. Ibid., p. 91.

15. Ibid., pp. 20–21.

16. Ibid., pp. 64, 108.

17. Ibid., p. 110.

18. Ibid., p. 4.

19. Ibid., p. 15.

20. I am thinking of Søren Kierkegaard's brilliant discussion of despair in *The Sickness Unto Death* (Princeton: Princeton University Press, 1954).

21. Although God's offer of friendship is itself unconditional, there are obviously conditions for what *counts* as a friendship-constituting response to this offer.

22. I argue that a *lack* of "complacency" in self, other, and God is a root cause of much moral evil in "Wickedness," *The Annual of the Society of Christian Ethics* (1992), ed. Beckley.

23. An appropriate perspective is that which observes the mean. We discussed the mean of compassion's complacency in the previous chapter, and we shall discuss it further in what follows.

24. This is one sense, then, in which Christ can remain sinless and yet become "sin for us": he can in perfect obedience (i.e. without sin) undergo complacency relative to the sinful desires of other human beings (i.e., suffer these desires as partly "his own" by virtue of his oneness with us), yet with the clear recognition that these desires are sinful (i.e., inconsistent with the desires that are "his own" by virtue of his oneness with the first person of the Trinity).

25. McNeill, Morrison, and Nouwen, p. 90.

26. Ibid., pp. 63–64.

27. Ibid., p. 64. Recall our discussion in chapter 10 of the access that persons have to compassion's complacency, especially pp. 174–83.

28. Ibid., p. 71.

29. Ibid., p. 73.

30. Ibid., pp. 98, 72.
31. Ibid., p. 93.
32. Ibid., p. 105.
33. Ibid., pp. 106–7.
34. Ibid., p. 110.
35. Ibid., p. 109.
36. Ibid., pp. 53–55.
37. Ibid., p. 55.
38. Ibid., p. 56.
39. Ibid., pp. 56, 51.
40. Ibid., p. 57.

41. I do not wish to suggest that *Christian* community is a privileged locus for the cultivation of compassion; I simply wish to explore some ethical implications of Christian faith.

42. The Bible is a central text for Christians who wish to wrestle with the meaning of compassion. The stories of The Good Samaritan (Luke 10) and The Prodigal Son (Luke 15), for example, and many of the sayings of Jesus in the gospels have had an enormous impact on my own thinking about compassion. But I cannot bring the Bible into the argument of this book in an explicit way. I believe that even the simplest of biblical interpretations has to be defended in terms of an explicit hermeneutic, which itself has to be defended. I cannot undertake such an effort here.

43. As Darrell Fasching argues, it may be even more important to focus on the search for further questions, given the way in which we tend to "idolize" partial answers. See *Narrative Theology After Auschwitz: From Alienation to Ethics* (Minneapolis: Fortress Press, 1992).

44. For an extensive analysis of Christian community as a "school of virtue," see Stanley Hauerwas, *A Community of Character: Toward a Constructive Christian Social Ethic* (Notre Dame, Ind.: University of Notre Dame Press, 1981).

45. McNeill, Morrison, and Nouwen, p. 31.
46. Ibid., p. 32.
47. Ibid., p. 80.
48. Ibid., p. 81.
49. Ibid., p. 124.
50. Ibid., p. 81.
51. Ibid., p. 36.
52. Ibid., p. 32.
53. Ibid., p. 36.
54. Ibid., p. 81.

55. I assume, as I believe Thomas would, that there is a natural (i.e. rational) human desire to be compassionate. I assume that this desire has become cor-

rupted by sin, but that it has not been utterly destroyed. See *Summa Theologica* I–II 85.2.

56. I cannot discuss here the many problems associated, in general, with using scripture to exhort contemporary believers to assume particular moral postures. A brief introduction to modern discussions on this issue is provided by Lisa Sowle Cahill, *Between the Sexes: Foundations for a Christian Ethics of Sexuality* (Philadelphia: Fortress Press, 1985), chap. 2.

57. McNeill, Morrison, and Nouwen, p. 109.

58. For a detailed discussion of the relationship between the Christian love command and the moral demand of impartiality (with respect to the interests of self and others), see Gene Outka, "Universal Love and Impartiality" in *The Love Commandments: Essays in Christian Ethics and Moral Philosophy*, Edmund N. Santurri and William Werpehowski, eds.

59. I'm thinking especially of the many works by Elizabeth Schussler Fiorenza, Carter Heyward, Beverly Harrison, Rosemary Ruether and other feminist religious thinkers.

60. For a fine analysis of the way in which Christian faith can condition the formation of moral character, see James Gustafson, *Can Ethics Be Christian?* (Chicago: The University of Chicago Press, 1975). See also Donald Evans, *Struggle and Fulfillment: The Inner Dynamics of Religion and Morality* (Philadelphia: Fortress Press, 1979); Craig Dykstra, *Vision and Character: A Christian Educator's Alternative to Kohlberg* (Glen Rock, N.J.: Paulist Press, 1981); Robert C. Roberts, *Spirituality and Human Emotion* (Grand Rapids, Mich.: William B. Eerdmans Publishing Company, 1982); Don E. Saliers, *The Soul in Paraphrase: Prayer and the Religious Affections* (New York: The Seabury Press, 1980); and assorted essays by Stanley Hauerwas.

61. McNeill, Morrison, and Nouwen, p. 32.

62. Ibid., p. 39.

63. Ibid., pp. 31–32.

64. Ibid., p. 42.

65. Ibid., pp. 40, 81; my emphasis.

66. Ibid., pp. 39, 93.

67. Warren Thomas Reich argues convincingly that alleviating pain will often require helping persons in pain to construct narratives in order to make sense out of seemingly senseless situations. See "Speaking of Suffering: A Moral Account of Compassion," *Soundings* LXXII/1, Sp. 1989, pp. 83–108. My point is that compassionate Christians will co-construct narratives in light of their convictions about and passions for what is ultimate (although they may never speak to certain others explicitly about "God").

68. McNeill, Morrison, and Nouwen, p. 109.

69. Ibid., p. 111.

70. This is my phrase, not the authors'.

71. McNeill, Morrison, and Nouwen, pp. 57–58.

72. Ibid., p. 58.

73. Ibid., p. 57.

74. Ibid.

75. Many of us educate our affections in this way by learning, at the request of our friends, to feel a love of friendship for the friends of our friends, even when our natural impulses resist this befriending. We seek to befriend the friends of our friends in the interest of pleasing our friends and deepening our friendships with them.

76. I am thinking of Søren Kierkegaard's discussion of Christian love in *Works of Love*, trans. Howard and Edna Hong (New York: Harper & Row, 1962), even though Kierkegaard argues that love of the self for its "other I" has no part in authentic Christian love.

Bibliography

Ackrill, J. L. "Aristotle on Action." In *Essays on Aristotle's Ethics,* ed. Amelie Oksenberg Rorty. Berkeley: University of California Press, 1980a, 93–101.

———. "Aristotle on *Eudaimonia.*" In *Essays on Aristotle's Ethics,* ed. Amelie Oksenberg Rorty. Berkeley: University of California Press, 1980b, 15–33.

Andolson, Barbara Hilkert, Christine E. Gudorf, Mary D. Pellauer, eds. *Women's Consciousness, Women's Conscience: A Reader in Feminist Ethics.* San Francisco: Harper & Row, 1985.

Annas, Julia. *The Morality of Happiness.* New York: Oxford University Press, 1993.

Aristotle. *De Anima (On the Soul).* Trans. J. A. Smith. In *The Basic Works of Aristotle,* ed. Richard McKeon. New York: Random House, 1941.

———. *De Generatione Animalium (On the Generation of Animals).* Trans. Arthur Platt. In *The Basic Works of Aristotle,* ed. Richard McKeon. New York: Random House, 1941.

———. *De Motu Animalium.* Trans. and ed. Martha Craven Nussbaum. In *Aristotle's De Motu Animalium.* Princeton: Princeton University Press, 1978.

———. *Ethica Nicomachea (Nicomachean Ethics).* Trans. W. D. Ross. In *The Basic Works of Aristotle,* ed. Richard McKeon. New York: Random House, 1941.

———. *Eudemian Ethics: Books I, II, and VIII.* Trans. Michael Woods. Oxford: Clarendon Press, 1982.

———. *Nicomachean Ethics.* Trans. Terence Irwin. Indianapolis: Hackett Publishing Company, Inc., 1985.

———. *Politica (Politics).* Trans. Benjamin Jowett. In *The Basic Works of Aristotle,* ed. Richard McKeon. New York: Random House, 1941.

———. *Rhetorica (Rhetoric).* Trans. W. Rhys Roberts. In *The Basic Works of Aristotle,* ed. Richard McKeon. New York: Random House, 1941.

Baier, Annette. "Master Passions." In *Explaining Emotions,* ed. Amelie Oksenberg Rorty. Berkeley: University of California Press, 1980, 403–24.

———. *Postures of the Mind: Essays on Mind and Morals.* Minneapolis: University of Minnesota Press, 1985.

Baker, Richard R. *The Thomistic Theory of the Passions and their Influence Upon the Will.* Dissertation: University of Notre Dame, 1941.

Binyon, Millard Pierce. *The Virtues: A Methodological Study in Thomistic Ethics.* Chicago: University of Chicago Press, 1948.

Blum, Lawrence. "Compassion." In *Explaining Emotion,* ed. Amelie Oksenberg Rorty. Berkeley: University of California Press, 1980, 507–17.

———. *Friendship, Altruism and Morality.* London: Routledge & Kegan Paul, 1980.

Bond, Leo M. "A Comparison Between Human and Divine Friendship." *The Thomist* 3/1 January 1941: 54–94.

Brink, David O. "Rational Egoism, Self, and Others." In *Identity, Character, and Morality: Essays in Moral Psychology,* ed. Owen Flanagan and Amelie Oksenberg Rorty. Cambridge, Mass.: MIT Press, 1990, 339–78.

Burnyeat, M. F. "Aristotle on Learning to Be Good." In *Essays on Aristotle's Ethics,* ed. Amelie Oksenberg Rorty. Berkeley: University of California Press, 1980, 69–92.

Cahill, Lisa Sowle. *Between the Sexes: Foundations for a Christian Ethics of Sexuality.* Philadelphia: Fortress Press, 1985.

Castiello, Jaime. "The Psychology of Habit in St. Thomas Aquinas." *The Modern Schoolman* 14/1 (November 1936): 8–12.

Cates, Diana Fritz. "Taking Women's Experience Seriously: Thomas Aquinas and Audre Lorde on Anger." *Aquinas and Empowerment: Classical Ethics for Ordinary Lives.* Washington, D.C.: Georgetown University Press, 1996, 47–88.

———. "Toward and Ethic of Shared Selfhood." *The Annual of the Society of Christian Ethics,* ed. Diane Yeager. Washington, D.C.: Georgetown University Press, 1991, 249–57.

———."Wickedness." *The Annual of the Society of Christian Ethics,* ed. Harlan Beckley. Washington D.C.: Georgetown University Press, 1992, 251–62.

Cavell, Stanley. *Must We Mean What We Say? A Book of Essays.* New York: Scribner, 1969.

Charles, David. *Aristotle's Philosophy of Action.* Ithaca, N.Y.: Cornell University Press, 1984.

Chenu, M. -D. *Toward Understanding Saint Thomas.* Trans. A. -M. Landry and D. Hughes. Chicago: Henry Regnery Company, 1964.

Cooper, John M. "Aristotle on Friendship." In *Essays on Aristotle's Ethics,* ed. Amelie Oksenberg Rorty. Berkeley: University of California Press, 1980, 301–40.

————. *Reason and Human Good in Aristotle*. Cambridge, Mass.: Harvard University Press, 1977.

Crowe, Frederick E. "Complacency and Concern in the Thought of St. Thomas." *Theological Studies* 20/1, 2, 3 (1959): 1–39, 98–230, 343–95.

Dahl, Norman O. *Practical Reason, Aristotle, and Weakness of the Will*. Minneapolis: University of Minnesota Press, 1984.

de Finance, J., S.J. "Etre et Subjectivité." *Doctor Communis* II. May-Aug. 1948: 240–58.

de Sousa, Ronald. *The Rationality of Emotion*. Cambridge, Mass.: MIT Press, 1987.

Dent, N. J. H. *The Moral Psychology of the Virtues*. New York: Cambridge University Press, 1984.

Diggs, Bernard James. *Love and Being: An Investigation into the Metaphysics of St. Thomas Aquinas*. New York: S. F. Vanni, 1947.

Dykstra, Craig R. *Vision and Character: A Christian Educator's Alternative to Kohlberg*. Glen Rock, N.J.: Paulist Press, 1981.

Edwards, Steven Anthony. *Interior Acts: Teleology, Justice, and Friendship in the Religious Ethics of Thomas Aquinas*. Lanham, Md.: University Press of America, Inc., 1986.

Engberg-Pedersen, Troels. *Aristotle's Theory of Moral Insight*. Oxford: Clarendon Press, 1983.

Evans, Donald. *Struggle and Fulfillment: The Inner Dynamics of Religion and Morality*. Philadelphia: Fortress Press, 1979.

Farley, Wendy. *Tragic Vision and Divine Compassion: A Contemporary Theodicy*. Louisville: Westminster/John Knox Press, 1990.

Fasching, Darrell. *Narrative Theology After Auschwitz: From Alienation to Ethics*. Minneapolis: Fortress Press, 1992.

Fiering, Norman. "Irresistible Compassion: An Aspect of Eighteenth Century Sympathy and Humanitarianism." *Journal of the History of Ideas* 37 (1975): 195–218.

Fortenbaugh, W. W. *Aristotle on Emotion: A Contribution to Philosophical Psychology, Rhetoric, Poetics, Politics and Ethics*. London: Gerald Duckworth & Company Limited, 1975.

Fox, Matthew. *A Spirituality Named Compassion and the Healing of the Global Village, Humpty Dumpty and Us*. San Francisco: Harper & Row, 1979.

Garrigou-Lagrange, Reginald. *Grace: Commentary on the Summa Theologica of St. Thomas, IaIIae, q. 109–14*. Trans. The Dominican Nuns of Corpus Christi Monastery. St. Louis, Mo.: B. Herder Book Co., 1952.

Gilbey, Thomas. *Poetic Experience: An Introduction to Thomist Aesthetic*. New York: Sheed & Ward, Inc., 1934.

Gilleman, Gerard. *The Primacy of Charity in Moral Theology*. Trans. William F. Ryan and Andre Vachon. Westminster, Md.: The Newman Press, 1961.

Gilligan, Carol. *In a Different Voice: Psychological Theory and Women's Development.* Cambridge, Mass.: Harvard University Press, 1982.

Gilson, Etienne. *The Christian Philosophy of St. Thomas Aquinas.* Trans. L. K. Shook. New York: Random House, 1966.

———. *Wisdom and Love in Saint Thomas Aquinas.* Milwaukee: Marquette University Press, 1951.

Gordon, Robert. "Emotions and Knowledge." *Journal of Philosophy* 66 (July 1969): 408–13.

Gratsch, Edward J. *Aquinas' Summa: An Introduction and Interpretation.* New York: Alba House, 1985.

Griffin, A. K. *Aristotle's Psychology of Conduct.* London: Williams & Norgate Ltd., 1931.

Gudorf, Christine E. "Parenting, Mutual Love, and Sacrifice." In *Women's Consciousness, Women's Conscience: A Reader in Feminist Ethics,* ed.Barbara Hilkert Andolson, Christine E. Gudorf, and Mary D. Pellauer. San Francisco: Harper & Row, 1985, 175–91.

Gustafson, James M. *Can Ethics Be Christian?* Chicago: The University of Chicago Press, 1975.

———. "Moral Discernment in the Christian Life." In *Norm and Context in Christian Ethics,* ed. Gene Outka and Paul Ramsey. New York: Charles Scribner's Sons, 1968.

Hadewijch. "Vision 7." In *Hadewijch: The Complete Works.* Trans. Mother Columba Hart, O.S.B. New York: Paulist Press, 1980.

Harak, G. Simon, S.J., ed. *Aquinas and Empowerment: Classical Ethics and Ordinary Lives.* Washington, D.C.: Georgetown University Press, 1996.

———. *Virtuous Passions: The Formation of Christian Character.* New York/ Mahwah: Paulist Press, 1993.

Hardie, W. F. R. *Aristotle's Ethical Theory.* Oxford: Clarendon Press, 1980.

Hauerwas, Stanley. *Character and the Christian Life: A Study in Theological Ethics.* San Antonio: Trinity University Press, 1985.

———. *A Community of Character: Toward a Constructive Christian Social Ethic.* Notre Dame, Ind.: University of Notre Dame Press, 1981.

———. *Vision and Virtue: Essays in Christian Ethical Reflection.* Notre Dame, Ind.: University of Notre Dame Press, 1986.

Hauerwas, Stanley, with Richard Bondi and David B. Burrell. *Truthfulness and Tragedy: Further Investigations into Christian Ethics.* Notre Dame, Ind.: University of Notre Dame Press, 1977.

Hepburn, R. W. "The Arts and the Education of Feelings and Emotion." In *Education and the Development of Reason,* ed. Dearden, Kirst, and Peters. London: Routledge and Kegan Paul, 1972.

———. "Vision and Choice in Morality (1)." In *Christian Ethics and Contemporary Philosophy,* ed. Ian Ramsey. New York: Macmillan, 1966.

Hinze, Christine Firer. "Power in Christian Ethics: Resources and Frontiers for Scholarly Exploration." *The Annual of the Society of Christian Ethics,* ed. Harlan Beckley. Washington, D.C.: Georgetown University Press, 1992, 277–90.

Hoagland, Sarah Lucia. "Some Thoughts about 'Caring.'" In *Feminist Ethics,* ed. Claudia Card. Lawrence, Ks.: University Press of Kansas, 1991, 246–63.

Hudson, Stephen. "Character Traits and Desires." *Ethics* 90 (1980): 539–49.

Hughes, M. A. "Our Concern with Others." In *Philosophy and Personal Relations: An Anglo-French Study,* ed. Alan Montefiore. Montreal: McGill-Queen's University Press, 1973.

Hunt, Mary E. *Fierce Tenderness: A Feminist Theology of Friendship.* New York: Crossroad, 1992.

Hutchinson, D. S. *The Virtues of Aristotle.* London: Routledge & Kegan Paul, 1986.

Irwin, T. H. "The Metaphysical and Psychological Basis of Aristotle's Ethics." In *Essays on Aristotle's Ethics,* ed. Amelie Oksenberg Rorty. Berkeley: University of California Press, 1980, 35–53.

———. "Reason and Responsibility in Aristotle." In *Essays on Aristotle's Ethics,* ed. Amelie Oksenberg Rorty. Berkeley: University of California Press, 1980, 117–55.

Johann, Robert O. *Building the Human.* New York: Herder and Herder, 1968.

———. *The Meaning of Love: An Essay Towards a Metaphysics of Intersubjectivity.* Glen Rock, N.J.: Paulist Press, 1966.

———. "A Meditation on Friendship." *The Modern Schoolman* 25/2 (1948): 126–31.

Jones, L. Gregory. "The Theological Transformation of Aristotelian Friendship in the Thought of St. Thomas Aquinas." *The New Scholasticism* 61/4 (1987): 373–99.

Keller, Catherine. "Feminism and the Ethic of Inseparability." In *Women's Consciousness, Women's Conscience: A Reader in Feminist Ethics,* ed. Barbara Hilkert Andolson, Christine E. Gudorf, and Mary D. Pellauer. San Francisco: Harper & Row, 1985, 251–63.

———. *From a Broken Web: Separation, Sexism, and Self.* Boston: Beacon Press, 1986.

Kenny, Anthony. "Intellect and Imagination in Aquinas." *Aquinas: A Collection of Critical Essays,* ed. Anthony Kenny. New York: Doubleday & Company, Inc., 1969, 273–96.

Kirkpatrick, Frank. *Community: A Trinity of Models.* Washington, D.C.: Georgetown University Press, 1986.

Kittay, Eva Feder, and Diana T. Meyers, eds. *Women and Moral Theory.* Totowa, N.Y.: Rowman & Littlefield, 1987.

Klubertanz, George P. *Habits and Virtues.* New York: Appleton-Century-Crofts, 1965.

Kosman, L. A. "Being Properly Affected: Virtues and Feelings in Aristotle's Ethics." In *Essays on Aristotle's Ethics,* ed. Amelie Oksenberg Rorty. Berkeley: University of California Press, 1980, 103–16.

Levin, David Michael. *The Body's Recollection of Being: Phenomenological Psychology and the Deconstruction of Nihilism.* London: Routeledge & Kegan Paul, 1985.

Lewis, Steven. "The Remains of One Man's Day." *Commonweal* 16 (1995): 31.

Madinier, M. *Conscience et Amour: Essai sur le "nous."* Paris: Alcan, 1938.

McFague, Sallie. *The Body of God: An Ecological Theology.* Minneapolis: Augsburg Fortress, 1993.

———. *Models of God: Theology for an Ecological, Nuclear Age.* Philadelphia: Fortress Press, 1987.

McGinnis, Raymond R. *The Wisdom of Love.* Rome: Officium Libri Catholici, 1951.

MacMurray, John. *Persons in Relation.* New York: Harper and Brothers, 1961.

McNeill, Donald P., Douglas A. Morrison, and Henri J. M. Nouwen. *Compassion: A Reflection on the Christian Life.* New York: Doubleday & Company, Inc., 1983.

McWilliams, Warren. *The Passion of God: Divine Suffering in Contemporary Protestant Theology.* Macon, Ga.: Mercer University Press, 1985.

Mandelbaum, Maurice. *The Pheonomenology of Moral Experience.* Glencoe, Ill.: Free Press, 1955.

May, W. E. "Knowledge, Connatural." *New Catholic Encyclopedia.* Vol. 8. New York: McGraw-Hill, 1967, 228–29.

Meilander, Gilbert C. *Friendship: A Study in Theological Ethics.* Notre Dame, Ind.: University of Notre Dame Press, 1981.

Mercer, Philip. *Sympathy and Ethics.* Oxford: Clarendon Press, 1972.

Milhaven, John Giles. "Ethics and Another Knowing of Good and Evil." *The Annual of the Society of Christian Ethics,* ed. Diane Yeager. Washington, D.C.: Georgetown University Press, 1991, 237–48.

———. *Good Anger.* Kansas City, Mo.: Sheed & Ward, 1989.

———. *Hadewijch and Her Sisters: Other Ways of Loving and Knowing.* Albany, N.Y.: State University of New York Press, 1993.

———. "Thomas Aquinas on Sexual Pleasure." *Journal of Religious Ethics* 5/2 (1977): 157–81.

Milo, Ronald Dmitri. *Aristotle on Practical Knowledge and Weakness of Will.* Paris: Mouton & Co., 1966.

Morrison, Toni. *Sula.* New York: New American Library, 1973.

Murdoch, Iris. *The Sea, The Sea.* Harmondsworth, Middlesex, England: Penguin Books, Ltd., 1983.

———. *The Sovereignty of Good.* London: Ark Paperbacks, 1985.

———. "Vision and Choice in Morality (2)." In *Christian Ethics and Contemporary Philosophy,* ed. Ian Ramsey. New York: Macmillan, 1966.

The New Oxford Annotated Bible with the Apocrypha, Revised Standard Version. Ed. Herbert G. May and Bruce M. Metzger. New York: Oxford University Press, 1977.

Niebuhr, H. Richard. *The Responsible Self.* New York: Harper & Row, 1963.

Noddings, Nel. *Caring: A Feminine Approach to Ethics and Moral Education.* Berkeley: University of California Press, 1984.

Nussbaum, Martha C. "Finely Aware and Richly Responsible: Moral Attention and the Moral Task of Literature." *Journal of Philosophy* 82 (Oct. 1985): 516–29.

———. *The Fragility of Goodness: Luck and Ethics in Greek Tragedy and Philosophy.* Cambridge: Cambridge University Press, 1986.

———. *Aristotle's De Motu Animalium.* Princeton: Princeton University Press, 1978.

———. "The Discernment of Perception: An Aristotelian Conception of Private and Public Rationality." In vol. 1 of *Proceedings of the Boston Area Colloquium in Ancient Philosophy,* ed. John J. Cleary. Landam, Md.: University Press of America, 1986, 151–201.

———. "Shame, Separateness, and Political Unity: Aristotle's Criticism of Plato." In *Essays on Aristotle's Ethics,* ed. Amelie Oksenberg Rorty. Berkeley: University of California Press, 1980, 395–435.

Nygren, Anders. *Agape and Eros: The Christian Idea of Love.* Trans. Philip S. Watson. Chicago: The University of Chicago Press, 1982.

O'Connor, William R. *The Eternal Quest: The Teaching of St. Thomas Aquinas on the Natural Desire for God.* New York: Longmans, Green and Co., 1947.

Ogletree, Thomas W. *Hospitality to the Stranger: Dimensions of Moral Understanding.* Philadelphia: Fortress Press, 1985.

O'Mahony, James. *The Desire of God in the Philosophy of St. Thomas Aquinas.* London: Longmans, Green and Co. Ltd., 1929.

Outka, Gene. *Agape: An Ethical Analysis.* New Haven: Yale University Press, 1972.

———. "Character, Vision, and Narrative." *Religious Studies Review* 6 (April 1980): 110–18.

———. "Universal Love and Impartiality." In *The Love Commandments: Essays in Christian Ethics and Moral Philosophy,* ed. Edmund N. Santurri and William Werpehowski. Washington, D.C.: Georgetown University Press, 1992, 1–103.

Pears, David. "Courage as a Mean." In *Essays on Aristotle's Ethics,* ed. Amelie Oksenberg Rorty. Berkeley: University of California Press, 1980, 171–87.

Peters, R. S. *Reason and Compassion.* London: Routledge and Kegan Paul, 1973.

Pieper, Josef. *The Four Cardinal Virtues.* New York: Harcourt, Brace & World, Inc., 1967.

——. *Reality and the Good.* Trans. Stella Lange. Chicago: Henry Regnery Company, 1967.

Porter, Jean. "Desire for God: Ground of the Moral Life in Aquinas." *Theological Studies* 47 (1986): 48–68.

——. *The Recovery of Virtue: The Relevance of Aquinas for Christian Ethics.* Louisville: Westminster/John Knox Press, 1990.

——. "The Subversion of Virtue: Acquired and Infused Virtues in the *Summa theologiae.*" In *The Annual of the Society of Christian Ethics,* ed. Harlan Beckley. Washington, D.C.: Georgetown University Press, 1992, 19–41.

Price, A. W. *Love and Friendship in Plato and Aristotle.* Oxford: Clarendon Press, 1989.

Raymond, Janice G. *A Passion for Friends: Toward a Philosophy of Female Affection.* Boston: Beacon Press, 1986.

Reeder, John P., Jr. "Analogues to Justice." In *The Love Commandments: Essays in Christian Ethics and Moral Philosophy,* ed. Edmund N. Santurri and William Werpehowski. Washington, D.C.: Georgetown University Press, 1992, 281–307.

——. "Extensive Benevolence." Unpublished.

Reich, Warren Thomas. "Speaking of Suffering: A Moral Account of Compassion." *Soundings* LXXII/1 Spring 1989: 83–108.

Roberts, Robert. *Spirituality and Human Emotion.* Grand Rapids, Mi.: William B. Eerdmans Publishing Company, 1982.

Rorty, Amelie Oksenberg, ed. *Essays on Aristotle's Ethics.* Berkeley: University of California Press, 1980.

——. ed. *Explaining Emotions.* Berkeley: University of California Press, 1980.

——. "The Place of Contemplation in Aristotle's *Nicomachean Ethics.*" In *Essays on Aristotle's Ethics,* ed. Amelie Oksenberg Rorty. Berkeley: University of California Press, 1980, 377–94.

Rush, Anne Kent. *Getting Clear: Body Work for Women.* New York: Random House, 1972.

Ryle, Gilbert. *The Concept of Mind.* London: Hutchinson, 1949.

Saliers, Don. *The Soul in Paraphrase: Prayer and Religious Affections.* New York: Doubleday-Anchor, 1980.

Scarry, Elaine. *The Body in Pain: The Making and Unmaking of the World.* New York: Oxford University Press, 1985.

Scheman, Naomi. "On Sympathy." *The Monist* 62 (1979): 320–29.

Schopenhauer, Arthur. *On the Basis of Morality.* Trans. E. F. J. Payne. Indianapolis: Bobbs-Merrill, 1965.

Sherman, Nancy. *Aristotle's Theory of Moral Education.* Dissertation: Harvard University, 1982.

———. *The Fabric of Character: Aristotle's Theory of Virtue.* Oxford: Clarendon Press, 1989.

Singer, Irving. *The Nature of Love, 1: Plato to Luther.* 2nd ed. Chicago: University of Chicago Press, 1984.

Slote, Michael. *Goods and Virtues.* Oxford: Clarendon Press, 1983.

Smith, Ruth L. "Feminism and the Moral Subject." *Women's Consciousness, Women's Conscience,* ed. Barbara Hilkert Andolson, Christine E. Gudorf, Mary D. Pellauer. San Francisco: Harper & Row, 1985, 235–50.

Solomon, Robert C. "Emotions and Choice." *Explaining Emotion,* ed. Amelie Oksenberg Rorty. Berkeley: University of California Press, 1980, 251–81.

Sorabji, Richard. "Aristotle on the Role of Intellect in Virtue." In *Essays on Aristotle's Ethics,* ed. Amelie Oksenberg Rorty. Berkeley: University of California Press, 1980. 201–19.

Stocker, Michael. "Values and Purposes: The Limits of Teleology and the Ends of Friendship." *Journal of Philosophy* 78 (1981): 747–65.

Telfer, Elizabeth. "Friendship." *Proceedings of the Aristotelian Society: Containing the Papers Read Before the Society During the Ninety Second Session* 1970–71, 223–41.

Thomas Aquinas, St. *The Disputed Questions on Truth,* vol. III. Trans. Robert W. Schmidt. Chicago: Henry Regnery Company, 1954.

———. *St. Thomas Aquinas on Aristotle's Love and Friendship: Ethics—Books VIII–IX.* Trans. Pierre Conway. Providence, R.I.: The Providence College Press, 1951.

———. *Summa Theologica.* Trans. Fathers of the English Dominican Province. Westminster, Md.: Christian Classics, 1981.

Thomae Aquinatis, S., *Summa Theologiae.* Taurini, Romae: Marietti, 1950.

Urmson, J. O. "Aristotle's Doctrine of the Mean." In *Essays on Aristotle's Ethics,* ed. Amelie Oksenberg Rorty. Berkeley: University of California Press, 1980, 157–70.

Wadell, Paul J. *Friends of God: Virtues and Gifts in Aquinas.* New York: Peter Lang, 1991.

———. *Friendship and the Moral Life.* Notre Dame, Ind.: University of Notre Dame Press, 1989.

Wallace, James D. *Virtues and Vices.* Ithaca, N.Y.: Cornell University Press, 1978.

Wiggins, David. "Deliberation and Practical Reason." In *Essays on Aristotle's Ethics,* ed. Amelie Oksenberg Rorty. Berkeley: University of California Press, 1980, 221–40.

———. "Weakness of Will, Commensurability, and the Objects of Deliberation and Desire." In *Essays on Aristotle's Ethics,* ed. Amelie Oksenberg Rorty. Berkeley: University of California Press, 1980, 241–65.

Williams, Bernard, and J. J. C. Smart. *Utilitarianism: For and Against.* Cambridge: Cambridge University Press, 1973.

Wiseman, Mary. "Empathetic Identification." *American Philosophical Quarterly* 15 (1978): 107–13.

Yuasa, Yasuo. *The Body: Toward an Eastern Mind-Body Theory.* Trans. Nagatomo Shigenori and Thomas P. Kasulis. New York: State University of New York Press, 1987.

Index